PRAISE FOR *WHATEVER HAPPENED TO TRADITION*

'This is a rich and reflective book, based on wide reading and personal experience.'

Literary Review

'*Whatever Happened to Tradition?* is stuffed with marvellous vignettes … the reader is left feeling grateful for the abundance of knowledge and the ebullient conviction with which it is shared.'

Allison Pearson, *The Telegraph*

'This book is brilliant. It's really radical in a way that all the other stuff that says it's radical is not. It really gives you an idea that there is something else outside this airless bubble of the self we are stuck in today. I find that kind of inspiring.'

Adam Curtis, documentary filmmaker

'He persuasively presents tradition as rooting us in the world and in society, and as subtly adaptable.'

Jane O'Grady, *the Daily Telegraph*

'Roger Scruton's death deprived public discourse of its most intelligent and cogent defender of tradition, but Tim Stanley's *Whatever Happened to Tradition?* steps bravely into the breach.'

The Church Times

'Tim Stanley suggests in his engaging way that fidelity to the past determines future happiness – for our civilisation, not just our souls.'

Christopher Howse, *The Spectator*

'Informative and even inspiring.'

Rod Dreher, author of *The Benedict Option*

WHATEVER HAPPENED TO TRADITION?

History, Belonging and the Future of the West

TIM STANLEY

BLOOMSBURY CONTINUUM
LONDON · OXFORD · NEW YORK · NEW DELHI · SYDNEY

BLOOMSBURY CONTINUUM
Bloomsbury Publishing Plc
50 Bedford Square, London, WC1B 3DP, UK
29 Earlsfort Terrace, Dublin 2, Ireland

BLOOMSBURY, BLOOMSBURY CONTINUUM and the Diana logo are trademarks
of Bloomsbury Publishing Plc

First published in Great Britain 2021
Paperback 2022

A catalogue record for this book is available from the British Library

Library of Congress Cataloguing-in-Publication data has been applied for

ISBN: PB: 978-1-3994-0487-7; eBook: 978-1-4729-7413-6;
ePDF: 978-1-4729-7414-3

2 4 6 8 10 9 7 5 3 1

Typeset by Deanta Global Publishing Services, Chennai, India
Printed and bound in Great Britain by CPI Group (UK) Ltd, Croydon CR0 4YY

To find out more about our authors and books visit www.bloomsbury.com
and sign up for our newsletters

Contents

FIGURE 1 Notre Dame burns on 15 April 2019.

Introduction

This book is an exploration of the philosophy and history of tradition, its uses and abuses, its beauty and necessity. Tradition is not just a pretty thing, much less dead or to be curated – it is the past brought to life, guiding us through the present, offering a roadmap to the future. Here in the West we've been at war with our traditions for decades, if not centuries, in the mistaken belief that emancipating ourselves from our history would set us free. We have obsessively deconstructed our past, customs, rituals and beliefs, all at a terrible cost. They say you only miss something when it's gone. That's even truer when it's taken rather than given away. In 2019, a mysterious calamity, most likely an accident, engulfed a powerful symbol of European religious and artistic tradition, causing many of us to stop and reflect upon the values and direction of our troubled society.

Around 6.30 p.m. on 15 April, a fire broke out in the attic of Notre Dame Cathedral, Paris. It ran along the roof and up the 300-foot spire; within an hour, this magnificent church, over eight hundred years old, was an inferno. President Emmanuel Macron, speaking on behalf of the French people, said, 'Notre Dame is our history, our literature, our collective imagination ... Her story is our story, and she is burning.'[1]

Other responses captured the twenty-first century in all its *fin-de-siècle* loopiness. There were far-right conspiracy theories ('did the Muslims do it?'), accusations of racism ('the widespread coverage and expressions of pain,' wrote one columnist, 'are an example of white supremacy') and the inevitable dash to rebuild its damaged parts in the contemporary style, 'spiritual' yet inclusive. Among the silliest proposals were a crystal spire, a zoo, a swimming pool, a torch shining into the clouds and a giant gold flame nailed to the roof that looked like the contents of King Midas' handkerchief.[2] Sanity prevailed. The French Senate voted to rebuild Notre Dame to look exactly as it had before, a deference to history, a rare acknowledgement that, when it comes to comparing old and new architecture at least, things ain't what they used to be.[3]

Modern culture encourages us to examine our ancestors with scepticism, even contempt: 'They were superstitious, ignorant and dead by forty.' But when we look backwards, we occasionally find that some things used to be done better. A lot better. So much so that when the achievements of the past are injured or destroyed, it hurts. No work of architecture finished in the last hundred years is more beautiful than Notre Dame, nor as delicate yet robustly designed (the reason why the fire didn't bring the entire structure down is that its medieval architects built it to resist exactly this scenario). And as Notre Dame burned, Parisians did something few of us would do for an airport terminal or a Trump hotel: they got on their knees and they prayed. Journalists weaving their way through citizens reciting the rosary appeared confused, unable to find the words to describe an outpouring of faith that, like the cathedral itself, belonged to another age. A headline by the Associated Press read: 'Tourist mecca Notre Dame also revered as a place of worship.'[4]

A cathedral is much more than a building. It's a sacred space where the divine blesses the ordinary. All human life happens here: babies are baptized, lovers marry, the grieving say goodbye. Given the thousands of bodies that pass through them every day, cathedrals could be as noisy as a railway station – yet visitors fall silent. We do it out of respect for others, of course, but we also feel an instinctive respect for the space itself, for its extraordinary claims to victory over sin and death, expressed in its architecture and relics. Notre Dame housed what is claimed to be the crown of thorns, placed on the head of Jesus before his crucifixion, and the tunic of King Louis IX, a saint. Put those objects in a museum and they bring the past closer to us. Put them in a temple and they bring the past alive. Then is now; now is then; standing before the altar of God, we find ourselves in communion with the infinite.

Notre Dame represents a unity of faith and art, purpose and design, making it the very pinnacle of the Christian tradition – and that, I believe, is why Parisians were so deeply upset when the spire crashed through its ceiling. Consciously or subconsciously, they looked around themselves and admitted that nothing this wonderful is being constructed today – for the simple reason that so few of us now believe in the things that its architects used wood and stone to articulate. If Notre Dame was the product of a certain way of life, and if that life is gone, can we ever build another Notre Dame? Once tradition is destroyed, can tradition be restored?

I

The answer is yes. It's been done before.

Traditions do not pop out of the oven fully formed and stay the same forever: they adapt and evolve. Work began on Notre Dame in 1163. The original plan was for a heavy roof that required heavy stone walls to support it, which limited the size of the windows. But in the two hundred years it took to complete the structure, architecture changed dramatically. The Gothic innovation of using rib vaults in the ceiling reduced the pressure laid on the walls, allowing for more windows, and the invention of flying buttresses transferred the weight of the ceiling to the exterior of the building, leaving the interior free of supports. This opened up the space and allowed it to breathe. In the eighteenth century, tastes changed again, arguably for the worst: the rood screen was torn down and most of the stained glass was replaced by clear windows.[5]

Then came the French Revolution. The dreamers of 1789 saw Notre Dame as a symbol of royal and clerical excess: they smashed the heads off statues and pillaged the lead roof to make bullets. Even the bronze bells were melted down for cannons. But human nature abhors a vacuum, and having cleared out one religion, the revolutionaries felt they needed another to take its place – so Notre

Dame was transformed into a temple of reason. Historian Simon Schama describes the pantomime:

> In the interior a gimcrack Greco–Roman structure had been erected beneath the Gothic vaulting. A mountain made of painted linen and papier-mâché was built at the end of the nave where Liberty (played by a singer from the Opéra), dressed in white, wearing the Phrygian bonnet and holding a pike, bowed to the flame of Reason and seated herself on a bank of flowers and plants.[6]

Napoleon seized power in 1799 and returned Notre Dame to the Catholic Church in 1801–2, now a shadow of its former self. At the dawn of the nineteenth century, birds nested in the galleries, flying in and out through broken windows. What was done to Notre Dame, wrote the novelist Victor Hugo, had happened to churches across France, 'mutilated' not only by their critics but by their own clergy, desperate to keep pace with fashion: 'The priest whitewashes them, the archdeacon scrapes them down; then the populace arrives and demolishes them.'[7]

These lines appear in the preface to *The Hunchback of Notre-Dame*, published in 1831. Hugo was part of the European Romantic movement that venerated the Gothic era and aspired to revive its spirit through art and literature, and his description of Quasimodo and Esmerelda frolicking through a fantasy version of medieval Paris moved Parisians to rebuild their cathedral. In 1844, the task was handed to a precocious architect named Eugène Viollet-le-Duc, whose commitment to Gothic went beyond a few repairs. He wanted to 'unveil and reveal the essence and original character' of the building: he not only fixed the west façade and headless statues but added new gargoyles, chimeras and the famous spire, surrounded by statues of the twelve apostles. In other words, many of the features that we now regard as synonymous with Notre Dame are only around a century and a half in construction – and were created by an atheist.[8] This doesn't make these additions a fraud; it certainly doesn't compromise tradition. As Victor Hugo wrote in

The Hunchback of Notre-Dame: 'Great edifices, like great mountains, are the work of centuries' – they develop slowly, layer upon layer, the names of each architect lost in time, until what is complete (and in truth still growing) belongs to the people. What lies beneath these many fashions is something unchangeable: the skeleton of belief. 'It is art which has changed its skin. The very constitution of the Christian church is not attacked by it. There is always the same internal woodwork, the same logical arrangement of parts.' Traditions develop but at the heart of them is contained the original truth they were built to express.

The story of Notre Dame is a common one. The eighteenth and nineteenth centuries saw a series of political and economic revolutions that turned the world upside down, from Paris to Washington, from Kyoto to Moscow. Some people looked forward to a brighter, industrialized future with confidence. Others looked backwards. They restored flagging traditions, revived dead ones and even invented a few of their own that they pretended were very old. Today we are nervous about nostalgia – our culture associates it with prejudice and right-wing fantasy – but it nourishes our very human need for roots and belonging, and it provides respite from modernity's propensity for change and aggressive individualism. To make yourself part of a tradition requires some submission of ego. That doesn't mean it isn't creative – Viollet-le-Duc's magnificent stone grotesques suggest otherwise – but it embeds us in a historical community and acknowledges a mind and a purpose beyond our own.

II

I have split this study of tradition into two parts. Part I opens with an attempt to define the term, followed by an exploration of how the West launched a war on tradition and why it made us unhappy. The primary villain in my story is liberalism, the political inheritance of the Enlightenment, which has created a state of permanent rebellion against the past. But I'm also very critical of the ability, or desire, of our conservative establishment to reverse that trend. Conservative elites believe their job is to preserve the status quo; if the status quo is liberal then that is what they will defend. The novelist Evelyn Waugh once complained that he couldn't vote for the British Conservative Party because 'they have never put the clock back a single second'. This has started to change. Brexit and Donald Trump were part of a new populism, a post-liberal conservatism, that says 'things used to be good, then we made mistakes, so can we go back to the way things were?' Establishment conservatives allege that this radical spirit is revolutionary, a dangerous break from tradition. I disagree, and to prove my point I will show how earlier generations of conservatives also utilized nostalgia to deal with change.[9]

Part II explores the ways in which traditional forms of living can help us navigate such a frighteningly mutable world. We'll look at tradition as the basis of identity, order, liberty, fairness and faith – and how other cultures do it, from Aboriginal Australia to Japan, from Chinese childhood ritual to the funeral rites of Indonesia. These chapters are vaguely structured around the human lifespan, from birth to adulthood to death; tradition lends us both a structure to live by but also a language with which to articulate what we're going through. I shall conclude by considering the efforts to revive tradition today, which contain some bad, some good.

This book is not a defence of snobbery, elitism or pickling things in aspic; progress is integral to tradition. Nor is it a chauvinist defence of the Western perspective. On the contrary, if I achieve one thing I hope it is to encourage conservative readers to widen their horizons, to look beyond the Enlightenment, beyond Britain and America, which are far too wedded to the Enlightenment, and even to read beyond conservatism itself, to take a second look at Marx and postmodernism, which contain critiques of modernity that are accurate and useful. I am also conscious that tradition is frequently hijacked by cynical or unpleasant people who imagine their culture is uniquely brilliant and has developed hermetically sealed from all others. In reality, cultures converse and overlap.

Take the obvious reach of Islamic architecture into the West, such as the Gothic's use of a pointed arch. The fusion of East and West can be so strong that, in 2014, a member of the right-wing United Kingdom Independence Party (Ukip) demanded to know why the BBC was filming from a London mosque (as if such a thing were objectionable) when, it turned out, the BBC was standing outside Westminster's Catholic cathedral.[10] The error made the Ukip member look silly, but it was forgivable. Westminster Cathedral, completed in 1903, was designed not to be confused with the Anglican abbey down the road, which is Gothic and resembles a mini-Notre Dame; the cathedral was modelled instead on the churches of Venice and Byzantine Constantinople, and it contains elements reminiscent of a mosque, such as a domed roof and tower.[11] Today it stands just around the corner from where I work as a journalist at the *Daily Telegraph*, and on a slow news day I'll pop in for Mass. It's like stepping into another country, another century. The golden mosaics, almost alien in countenance, shimmer by candlelight; confessors whisper in the gloom. It's a reminder that Catholicism might be officially accepted in Britain, after hundreds of years of persecution, but it remains *different*.

Where am I coming from as a guide to tradition? I started my career as a historian, specializing in the United States, before becoming a reporter; I am English and I am a Catholic – a convert, in fact – and I was a Marxist into my twenties, but now work for a squarely conservative newspaper. My politics sounds like it has the consistency of an Eton mess: some would call me a High Tory, others a Christian socialist. The line between the two is thinner than you think. I am living proof that you can wind up somewhere very different from where you started and juggle more than one tradition at a time, and among my generation, born in the latter part of the twentieth century, I suspect this is quite common. We grew up in the aftermath of one of the most destructive periods of the West's war on tradition – the swinging sixties. Liberated from the prison of the past, went the theory, the children of tomorrow would be free to define themselves as they wish and to pursue happiness on their own terms. What we inherited was a consensus of economic and social liberalism that translated into soulless consumerism, and, while some flourished, many felt alienated and unfulfilled. For a long time, I was one of the lost. My embrace of religion, plugging me into a ready-made community and giving me something to live for other than myself, lifted me out of the doldrums. Lots of us have done it: I know people raised atheist who have become Orthodox Jews, Mormons, Buddhists or otherwise dedicated themselves to maintaining cultural traditions that were dead before they were born.* One of my friends quit the rat race to raise chickens in Somerset; another, the child of left-wing psychiatrists, now manages a shrine in Birmingham. A third, who teaches philosophy at Oxford, trumped us all: he learnt classical Japanese and joined the Coptic Church. His fellow parishioners are mostly Egyptian or Eritrean.

You could say we have applied the consumerist spirit to tradition. We were invited to invent our own identities and we did – but we didn't choose freedom as the sixties generation defined it but returned instead to the very conservative ideals and habits the baby boomers went out of their way to reject. My purpose here is not to win you around to my particular politics or religion – though I will explore conservative and Christian themes in some depth because I am familiar with them and they provide ample evidence for my argument – but to stress the ways in which tradition can be useful to those looking for ballast, which I think a lot of us are. If the individual in the modern world is cut adrift on a stormy sea, tradition is the bit of driftwood floating past that one can cling on to for safety. As it goes for the individual, so it goes for society. The problems we face together today – cultural conflict, grotesque inequality, environmental crisis – are nothing new. If the answers seem further from our grasp than ever, and I fear our present liberal order is out of ideas, that's partly because by cutting out the past we have deprived ourselves of valuable experience.

When you look back, there are surprises to be found: in this book we will encounter nineteenth-century socialists who took church and high culture very seriously, as well as conservatives who sided

---

* I quote the butler in the film *A New Leaf* by Elaine May (1971).

with the poor against greed or ecological decay. The common thread was fidelity to history. Rather than tear things up, as a revolutionary or a violent reactionary might do, they refined and improved; they answered the vandalism of modernity with a commitment to beauty and community, and they spoke of natural rights balanced by the responsibilities we have to each other as fellow human beings. Here is a very different model of human development, and it offers hope. Today, the frequent cry of conservatives – though plenty on the left say it, too – is that this epoch is the worst on record, that we are doomed. But this can't be true, if only because human beings have said the same thing many times before, and the fact that we have so often appeared to be 'lost' only to rediscover and fix ourselves, usually by drawing upon our enormous reserves of historical and spiritual wealth, proves that it can be done again.

Traditions, like temples, can be rebuilt, stronger, more beautiful than before.

III

A photograph emerged from Notre Dame that caught the world's attention. It showed that in the blackened interior, amidst the charred remains, the altar had survived almost intact and that above it still hung a giant gold cross. The cross appeared to glow.

The boring explanation was that this part of the church was protected by a stone roof and the material that the cross was made out of could resist intense heat – but many observers used the word 'miracle', elevating the scene to the order of universal significance. The cross represented resurrection, a theme common to traditions the world over. By working in the present to preserve the best of the past, we hope to pass something on to the future, something bigger than ourselves but which also contains a little piece of what each individual has contributed to it. As Gustav Mahler is supposed to have said, tradition 'is not the worship of ashes but the preservation of fire'.

Part One

FIGURE 2 Yazidis play instruments at the temple of Lalish, Iraq, on 9 October 2019.

1

Defining Tradition

Tradition is everywhere. Music has a tradition, as does politics, the military, literature, art – and you. Your life will be shaped by traditions whether you're aware of them or not, from the laws that govern your country to that ominous doorbell on Halloween. Even when we defy tradition, we acknowledge our debt to it (the rebel has to rebel against something) and when we say that a thing is new, we are comparing it with the old. Tradition is a sticky web. The more we kick against it, the more we realize it's all around us – defining who we are.

So, what is it? The consensus is that a 'tradition' is something that is handed down from one generation to the next, that when we say something is 'traditional' – a style of architecture or a manner of dress – we're saying that its origins lie in the past and that an effort is being made to keep it going.[1] The German philosopher Josef Pieper argues that when a tradition is handed down, the generation that briefly takes charge of it does their best not to tinker with it, so that they can pass on as much of what they received as possible. This faithfulness to the design, says Pieper, is what gives a tradition its authenticity and integrity. It's akin to the process of memory. When I try to remember what my late grandmother looked like – her hair, her handbag, her woolly hat – I don't make stuff up and add it to the recollection, because that would turn it into a personal fantasy. Those who are most passionate about tradition often see it as a way of getting as close as possible to origins of things, to their primary state and purpose. It's a search for the 'Truth' with a capital T.[2]

In practice, however, almost all traditions evolve and can wind up looking quite different from how they began. There is innovation, adaptation, rebellion and synthesis. Traditions collide and shape each other; they die and are resurrected. The real genius of tradition, says the American sociologist Edward Shils, is its ability to undergo change while remaining recognizably itself thanks to its historic roots and its loyalty to certain core principles.[3] For example, the Queen of England no longer has the power she once had: she's not going to declare war on France nor cut off your head. But she's still recognizably a queen. The principle of monarchy remains intact, even though she governs a democratic country.

A true tradition has durability and depth. It's more than a custom or a ritual; these are only the outward manifestations of the tradition to which they belong. The Queen wears a crown (a custom) and is publicly crowned in a coronation (a ritual), but these things are not definitional. When the Queen removes her crown to eat her breakfast, she doesn't cease to be queen while she enjoys her scrambled eggs. Custom and ritual symbolize a tradition, they help us to 'read' that tradition and to take part in it, but our instinct tells us that the tradition behind them is something much more substantive.[4]

There are three characteristics to an authentic tradition. First, it ties the individual to the collective. When you or I submit to a tradition, we acknowledge that we are part of something bigger and that we are defined by history.[5] Second, traditions impose an order on the way we behave by teaching us 'social knowledge', the invisible architecture of human behaviour, the customs and rituals that have been hammered out down the centuries to determine how we live. These can be grand concepts such as common law or sexual morality; they can also be small, everyday things that we do unconsciously and that 'exist through repeated exercise', to quote Roger Scruton, such as shaking hands.[6] It's a simple sign of greeting, yet surprisingly complex because it can communicate affection, dominance, desire or the pulling of rank. The codes can be taught, but often they are unconsciously transmitted by the culture we were raised in, and people from outside that culture might find them strange. In this way, knowledge of a tradition sets borders of identity. Within the group, there is understanding; beyond it, there is mystery.[7]

Third, traditions affect how a human being experiences the phenomenon of time. In the modern world, we are encouraged to forget the past and live for the moment because tomorrow might never come. The writer Tom Wolfe summed it up with the catchphrase of Clairol hair dye: 'If I've only one life, let me live it as a blonde!'[8] Western man experiences time in purely linear terms: history is one thing after another, and when the day is done, that's that and we have to move on. This is not only bad for retaining historical knowledge, which might be why our society keeps making the same mistakes, but it also results in a tragic poverty of imagination that helps explain the decline of art, faith and the family, all of which rely upon a willingness to transcend the immediate. Traditional societies, by contrast, exist in the present but with one foot in the past, and they memorialize that past with the intention of passing it on to future generations so that they can benefit from it, too. In short, observing the eternal order of tradition renders the individual part of society – not just now but always and forever. It binds us to those who have been and those who are yet to come.

So, the practice of tradition is, at its simplest, the art of passing things on. But what's the point of it? I believe that tradition is not just beautiful but practical – that it is necessary for human happiness and, *in extremis*, a tool for survival.

I

In 2019 I accompanied a priest on a tour of northern Iraq. Using his local contacts, we blagged our way past the roadblocks and drove to Mosul, which was occupied by the Islamic State from 2014 to 2017. The old part of the city, once home to a thriving Christian community, had been bombed back to the Stone Age. Incredibly, some people were still living in the ruins and commerce was beginning to return. Iraqi men are wonderfully vain; there was a barber shop on every corner.

The priest had visited Mosul shortly after its liberation: he said he walked into an abandoned nunnery and found a noose hanging from the ceiling. The Islamic State gave the Christian population three choices; they could flee, stay and convert, or die, and deserted churches were repurposed as prisons and torture chambers. In one of them I saw evidence from the bullet holes in the walls, that the building had been used as a shooting range. This desire not only to claim Christian temples but to defile them, to transform them into something so unholy that Christians would probably never return, betrayed the Islamic State's astute understanding of the relationship between culture and identity. The goal of the caliphate wasn't just to conquer or convert, but to eradicate every alternative to their form of Islam. To do that, you don't just kill people, you have to annihilate their culture as well. One group that suffered terribly were the Yazidis.

After Mosul we took a drive to Lalish, a holy city in a small valley in Kurdistan. From outward appearances, you would struggle to tell a Yazidi from a Muslim or a Christian because they look and dress much the same, but Lalish is home to a very distinct culture. The first thing one notices are the beautiful sculptures on the walls, rare in this part of the Islamic world, including a long black snake that points the way through a door into a series of chambers that descend into the ground (the entrance to the inner temple can be seen in Figure 3). The path is lit by cotton doused in oil and the pillars are wrapped with coloured rags that the pilgrim ties a knot in for luck. In the penultimate chamber sits a monolith with a stone on top (the monolith is apparently unnecessary: the stone is suspended magically mid-air, but some Yazidis of little faith built a wall to support it just in case). Here I performed a trial of skill and luck. The pilgrim is given a cloth, they must close their eyes, make a wish and throw the cloth at the stone. You have three goes; if you hit it, your wish is granted. I did it in one (at time of publication, I have yet to win the lottery).

Lalish, according to Gerard Russell, author of *Heirs to Forgotten Kingdoms*, is the centre of the Earth, where creation began, and somewhere here is a holy spring called Zemzem. The name is akin to the spring at Mecca, revered by Muslims; the believer is baptized in it, not unlike a Christian. Yazidism, thousands of years old, has

FIGURE 3 A Yazidi enters the exterior door to the temple at Lalish, 15 February 2000.

emerged from a cultural melting pot of ideas and customs, some of them adopted, one suspects, in a conscious attempt to 'blend in'. There's more than just survival at work, however. If Yazidi customs do not directly state what they mean, or even disguise it, this is because they are not an evangelical faith. They are a mystery religion. Their traditions are oral rather than written down, passed on from parent to child, and while it might be difficult for us to understand – with our modern taste for transparency and sharing – the Yazidis do not want to be understood.[9]

Think of it this way: Islam and Christianity are like great waves that wish to sweep over the Earth and convert mankind. Yazidism is more like a deep well, its truths invisible from the surface and only reachable with a lifetime's exploration. What do we know? We know that they don't eat lettuce and won't wear blue. They believe Abraham was the first prophet and Muhammad the last, but that the natural elements are more important than any man, which is why the Yazidis won't eat fish because they swim in water and, by logical deduction, must be sacred. God himself is unknowable. You can't have a personal relationship with him like many Christians have with Jesus, but he does have intermediaries, including the sun and a bird-like angel called Melek Taoos who comes down once a year in a festival marked by the painting of eggs (rather like Easter). In the beginning, say the Yazidis, the world was colourless; Melek Taoos laid his peacock feathers upon it, and suddenly it was blue and green.

Unfortunately, other faiths find elements of Yazidism too familiar, particularly Melek Taoos who is associated in several traditions with the angel who rebelled against God so that he could reign in Hell. If you ask them about it, the Yazidis will strongly deny that they worship Satan. In fact, it's best not to ask: the 'S' word is taboo. In the nineteenth century, the Yazidis wrote to their Ottoman rulers to explain that if the word is ever used in their presence, they must kill the person who spoke it and then kill themselves for having heard it. Russell argues that they don't believe in a devil at all. In one poetic version of Yazidi myth, the rebellious angel spent several thousand years in exile and regretted his sin so much that he 'extinguished the fires of hell with his tears'. God forgave him and he was restored to favour.[10]

But the lie of diabolism has stuck. When the Islamic State swept into northern Iraq and Syria, they ranked the Yazidis as lower than Christians and Jews. Islam is an intensely literate tradition. It takes the view that even if Christians and Jews are missing the bigger picture, aspects of their beliefs are found in the Koran, so they are at least 'people of the book'. The Yazidis, partly because of the mysterious nature of their faith, were classed as Satanists and polytheists, and the Islamic State declared that it had found evidence from the Koran that polytheists can be kept as slaves. They butchered Yazidi communities and destroyed their temples; the women were kidnapped and sold in markets, into a life of drudgery, physical abuse and rape. Even when the Islamic State was defeated and its soldiers ran into the desert, they took their Yazidi slaves with them. Thousands are still missing.[11]

In 2020, a group of liberated Yazidi girls visited London as part of a cultural tour and I had the privilege of meeting them. For the first time, I really came face-to-face with what the Islamic State had done. The girls were so young. The youngest had been enslaved at 11, her brother at 9. They would laugh one minute, cry the next, classic symptoms of post-traumatic stress disorder, and there was a wall of pain between us. An English guest asked one girl if she had any ambitions: 'Do you want to be a doctor when you grow up?' It was the sort of thing you might ask at a school prize day. The answer came back via a translator: 'She says she wants to see her mother again.'

The girls performed for us. Two men played instruments and sang, and the girls, holding hands in a semi-circle, danced around them. They seemed transported and transformed, as if they were back in Iraq. As if the Islamic State had never happened.

II

Music is essential to the Yazidis. They believe that after Adam was created in the Garden of Eden, he only gained a soul the first time he played an instrument.[12] I also had the honour in London to meet Michael Bochmann, the virtuoso violinist who had helped organize this tour, and Bochmann explained that the girls were singing about their traditions: when to sow seeds, when to harvest, how to be a Yazidi. Yazidi society is divided into various castes, and only one caste, the *qwals*, is permitted to play religious music. This knowledge is inherited through the male line of the family. Today, thanks to the Islamic State, the *qwals* are an endangered species: there are only 16 of them left. Bochmann told me that when they first settled in the refugee camps, the Yazidis ceased singing and dancing for fear of being identified and persecuted. In other words, this is a culture that is defined by its music, a music that contains their collective memories and beliefs – their social knowledge – and should anyone suppress that music then their culture would disappear, taking an entire people with it. Bochmann was part of a project to record and transcribe the Yazidi music, to rescue it from the grave. Before this, he said, he had seen his musical career as being largely about expressing himself. With this project, he felt part of something, part of a collective endeavour.[13]

When I heard what Bochmann said, I instantly thought of Ralph Vaughan Williams, the composer and socialist who, in 1934, wrote a superb book on the theory of folk music. Folk, argued Vaughan Williams, is the origin of everything we listen to today. He rejected the modern cult of genius, the idea that history and culture are created by one-off individuals who pluck ideas out of their head. The beginnings of music, he said, lie in oral poetry, which was an attempt by early man to articulate his emotions and to bring 'the word' to life. Because this poetry was spoken rather than written, there was no ownership or copyright; it belonged to the community that had inspired it, passed down from one generation to the next, rewritten along the way. Even if an artist could claim authorship of a poem or a song, it would only achieve popularity if it articulated people's experiences, in a language they could understand. From this, Vaughan Williams concluded that art is an intrinsically collective enterprise, that a true artist engages with tradition – whether they defer to it or break with it – and surrenders some part of their ego to the wider community. Good music tells us something about the composer *and* the audience they wrote for.[14]

Vaughan Williams gave the example of the seventeenth-century genius Johann Sebastian Bach. I play beginner's church organ (badly) and one of the appeals of this most mathematical of composers is the feeling of universality and timelessness that flows from his music; its beauty, when played accurately, transcends the moment.

And yet, as Vaughan Williams pointed out, J. S. Bach was the product of a very specific time and place. He was 'no more than one of a fraternity of town organists and "town pipers" whose business it was to provide the necessary music for the great occasions in church and city. He never left his native country, seldom even his own city of Leipzig … it was the tradition of his own country which inspired him' – namely German organ music and the popular hymns of his day. Bach was part of a family business from a long line of musical ancestors, and the craft did not die with him 'for he had several sons who would have shone brightly in the musical firmament if they had not been partly eclipsed by their great father'. He 'was only able to produce his fugues, his Passions, his cantatas because there had preceded him generations of smaller composers, specimens of the despised class of "local musicians" who had no other ambition than to provide worthily and with dignity the music required of them: craftsmen, perhaps rather than conscious artists'. In this sense, there is no difference between J. S. Bach – a venerated German composer – and the anonymous Yazidi *qwal*, both products of their birthplace, both keeping tradition alive.[15] Music, insisted Vaughan Williams, is neither a commodity nor a luxury. It is 'the expression of the soul of a nation, and by a nation … I mean any community of people who are spiritually bound together by language, environment, history and common ideals and, above all, a continuity with the past.'[16]

Vaughan Williams defined music as a 'spiritual necessity'. For the Yazidis it is clearly a thing of 'spirit' but also a 'necessity' because keeping their rituals and customs going reminds them of who they are and how to be themselves. No matter how few Yazidis might now be left, so long as there is belief and practice, their culture endures.

III
At this point, I might be accused of cheating. I'm trying to define tradition and I've chosen the most benign example possible, the Yazidis. But what about the Islamic State? Aren't they defenders of

tradition? And isn't slavery a tradition, too? Mankind has been doing it since the dawn of time. Isn't there a risk that in defending tradition in principle, I open the door to the return of ideas and practices that belong on the scrapheap of history?

Tradition can certainly be oppressive. The word might be purely descriptive ('This is what we do'), but it can also be prescriptive ('This is what we should do.') Some readers might feel that even Yazidi society, with its castes and patriarchal leadership is out of the Ark. Many of us have benefited from the social changes that took place in the West in the last century and Evelyn Waugh's idea of 'turning back the clock' sounds like an invitation to exclude and discriminate. But I am not arguing here that all traditions are equal in moral worth. That would be intellectually dishonest and a betrayal of my own, Christian tradition, which is steeped in debate and self-criticism. There are traditions of oppression, but also traditions of liberation, and contrasts are frequently found within the same tradition.

The Catholic Church, for example, has both tolerated slavery and condemned it. When the Spanish conquered the New World in the sixteenth century, they stole people's lands and enslaved them, a practice that some clerics deemed permissible, because the slaves were judged 'irrational' and therefore incapable of governing themselves, and merciful because it might bring them to Christ. Theological authority was thrown behind brutality and theft. But the violence committed in the New World became so transparently unjust, and the trade so patently hypocritical, that the same theological tradition that had been interpreted to justify slavery was soon invoked to condemn it. In 1537, Pope Paul III issued an encyclical in which he forbade the enslavement of the people indigenous to the Americas, along with anyone else 'discovered' by Europeans in the future. The Spanish crown followed suit in 1542.

Is the fact that influential Catholics changed their minds about slavery evidence of contradiction? Does this not undermine their claim to authenticity and integrity? No. When confronted with new facts, Catholics interrogated their own traditions and returned to first principles. Jesus died for the salvation of anyone who was willing to put their faith in him; fair-minded Europeans who met the indigenous peoples could tell they were rational; hence they had natural rights, including a right to property, and all the intelligence necessary to come to Christ by conviction rather than compulsion. By learning to love the indigenous peoples, Catholics did not reject their traditions but applied them in a more compassionate and accurate manner. Tragically, they failed to do so in the case of African slavery, being of the near-unanimous view that Africans were insufficiently intelligent. When indigenous labour dried up in the New World, Africans were shipped in to fill the gap.[17]

It would take several centuries for the principle of human dignity to become truly universal, but this slow struggle to reconcile ideals and practice can be placed into the Christian narrative of progress. It's a misunderstood word. In the modern world, our standard metrics of progress are things like living longer thanks to medical advances getting richer or Apple releasing an update. But one can also have progress that is natural (growing up, getting taller), moral or spiritual, and the purpose of many religious traditions is to progress towards a greater knowledge of God. In the Christian worldview, mankind once knew God intimately, in the Garden of Eden, and in that blessed state human beings were without sin. But when Adam and Eve broke God's law by eating from the tree of knowledge, they were cast out of the Garden – naked and separated from their creator. The whole of human history, and arguably the point of life itself, is to repair that damaged relationship, and thus many Christians perceive themselves as being on a journey towards becoming a better person – much as society can progress towards becoming more just. Conservative Christians complain that the modern world has lost its way, but in some senses Western society today is far more Christian in its ethics than it was five hundred years ago when the Spanish conquered the Americas. We no longer keep slaves, for a start. In those areas where the West has obviously and mercifully progressed, it has done so largely in accord with the teachings of Christ.

How true was the Islamic State to Islam? The Yazidis I interviewed in Iraq were unanimous: it was 100 per cent Muslim and everything it did found its justification in the Koran, which was why they thought the 2003 invasion had been such a stupendously bad idea. Saddam Hussein was a dictator, but he was relatively secular. The Yazidis did not want to live in a democracy in a majority-Muslim country: 'Democracy,' one of them told me, 'is like giving a gun to a child.'

This was difficult to hear. In the West, the message is constantly hammered home that Islam is a religion of peace and that terrorists misrepresent it or even misunderstand it. In 2014, it was revealed at the trial of two British jihadis that, before they travelled to Syria to join the Islamic State, they had first bought a book off Amazon called *Islam for Dummies*. But these were just foot soldiers: the leaders of the Islamic State were theologically literate students of history. The plan was to emulate the heroic seventh century, when the Prophet Muhammad liberated Mecca, along with Islam's early expansion from Persia to Spain, and they imagined that if they fitted all the pieces in the right order, it would fulfil a prophecy that would trigger the apocalypse. That yearning to get back to the beginning, in order to bring about the end, justified reviving the religious laws and recreating the social conditions of the Prophet's Arabia, including conquest and slavery.[18]

But much of what the Islamic State did bucked the longer, more complicated trends in Islamic history, and much of what they revived was drawn from a shallow pool of Muslim experience. The Islamic State said there was no place for representations of the living world in art, and yet the Islamic Mughal empire in South Asia produced some of the most stunning paintings of people and animals in history. They said there could be no dialogue with other religions, and yet the Sufis evangelized others by accommodating their customs and practices. They said there was no role for women in public leadership, and yet

Muslim-dominated societies, from Indonesia to Pakistan, have elected female heads of state.[*][19]

The Islamic State was not an example of religious traditionalism, which involves a sophisticated reading of the past and an openness to progress, but of fundamentalism, and like all fundamentalists, in trying to recreate the purest form of their faith possible, they missed out the fundamentals. I have travelled throughout the Muslim world and I do not recognize the Islamic State's impoverished form of Islam. Where was Islam's thirst for justice, its veneration of women, its inner peace or aesthetic grace? Islam's understanding of beauty is subtly different from the West's, which accounts for some of the misunderstanding between our civilizations. Islamic art, generally speaking, doesn't reproduce the physical characteristics of its subjects but tries instead to communicate what they represent through calligraphy or geometry; the purpose of Islamic aesthetics is to help us get closer to Allah. If you read the Koran in English, it makes very little sense, but that's because it is best recited, or 'sung', in Arabic, not unlike the use of Latin in church or Hebrew in a synagogue. These universal languages cut across cultures to speak to a brotherhood of believers, which makes them very practical – but they also attract the fascination of those who cannot understand them because, like standing on the boundary of a dark forest, it is their very mystery that draws us in.[20] Mystery begets wonder. When I am lying in bed at night and I hear an owl hoot at the moon, I have no idea what he is saying, but it is beautiful and haunting, and precisely because I

---

[*] One of them, Benazir Bhutto of Pakistan, was assassinated in 2007. Precisely by whom and why is unclear. If you wish, you could see her killing as an indictment of Islamic culture – if so, you're going to have to explain how that same culture gave her such power and prominence that she became a target for murder. As Shahla Haeri points out, she probably wasn't killed 'because she was a woman politician; there are in fact quite a few of them in Pakistan', but because 'she had become a *powerful woman*, a formidable and popular political leader without parallel. It was this serious challenge to the "establishment", the male elite, and its traditional monopoly of power and privilege that had to be met at all costs; even at the cost of annihilating her. Religion was used to give a thin veneer of justification.' Shahla Haeri, *The Unforgettable Queens of Islam: Succession, Authority, Gender* (New York: Cambridge University Press, 2020), pp. 181–2.

cannot decode his song my mind is free to enjoy the sound. My ego is lost. I become part of the audience in his midnight realm.[21]

Fundamentalism is devoid of enigma. The Islamic State was all 'kiss, kiss, bang, bang'. One recruitment photograph disseminated on Twitter showed a group of women, clothed head to toe in black niqabs, posing casually on a white BMW. The tagline was 'chillin' in the caliphate, lovin' life'.[22]

The Islamic State's shameless appeal to money, violence and sexual slavery was vastly removed from the historical and ethical context of the seventh-century Islam it was trying to reincarnate. Slavery was a fact of life in contemporary Arabia. It would've been revolutionary to try to eliminate it. But Muhammad and his successors encouraged kindness, praised manumission and taught that the believing slave is superior to the free pagan, all of which raised the status of the Arabian slave to that of a human being with quasi-legal rights. The trend was towards gradual emancipation. The Islamic State, by contrast, not only resurrected slavery but operated their trade with ruthless commercial efficiency: it maximized profits, it distributed girls as rewards for loyalty. It drew up a code for owners that, for all its complexity, permitted anything except rape during pregnancy (to avoid this likelihood, they forced the women to use birth control), so the rules of this regime really did not limit the individual jihadi but gave him licence to do whatever he wanted.[24] The soul of Islam, along with its sublime quality of mercy, was missing; custom and ritual were enforced to assert dominance and power. During my visit to Iraq, I interviewed people who had lived in Mosul during the occupation, and they described the Islamic State's attempt to create a medieval theme park in what had been a very cosmopolitan city. Non-religious music was banned. So were alcohol, cigarettes and jeans. Beards had to be grown. If the religious police discovered a woman wearing rings, they would bite her fingers. Women had to dress head to toe in the niqab. One of my interviewees recalled that Mosulites who were unfamiliar with this custom kept tripping on the garment and falling over in the street. Attendance at executions was mandatory. This instilled terror; it was also meant to suggest that thuggery was part and parcel of living in a genuinely Islamic society, that modernity – with its short skirts and cigarettes – had been a blip. This was what Iraq used to be like, said the Islamic State; this is what it will become again.[25]

It's a familiar story. The Nazis were revolutionaries as well: they wanted to do away with liberal democracy and put a vast new state apparatus in its place. But they appealed to conservatives by suggesting that their programme wasn't novel so much as it was radically traditional, that they wanted to scrape away the recent innovations of German democracy to return the nation to its glorious past. In his book *How Societies Remember*, Paul Connerton illustrates how the Nazis manufactured legitimacy by rewriting the calendar, filling it with events that appeared ancient when they were actually brand new. Every year, Hitler delivered a eulogy for the Nazis who had died in the Munich Putsch; the show was choreographed to feel like a war memorial service for mythical heroes. At their annual Hitler Youth gathering, boys swore an oath to the Führer that was similar to the Christian confirmation service. And the May Day festival was turned into a celebration of work and agriculture, replete with pagan imagery.[26] In a village in Bavaria, Joseph Ratzinger, the future Pope Benedict XVI, watched as one of his teachers, a committed Nazi, launched a bizarre festival of the sun intended to eclipse the Catholic obsession with sin and redemption with some Nordic heathen fun. The teacher put up a maypole, a classic symbol of fertility. Ratzinger suspected that the young men who danced around the pole were less interested in the neo-paganism than the sausages that the teacher hung from it, yet he understood the seriousness of what was happening.[27] Encouraging the entire community to join in was essential; the Nazis wanted to intimidate the individual, but also to involve them, to compromise them and to foster the idea that everything the Nazis did was an authentic articulation of Germanness. By participating in Nazism, the average German might conclude that they were just being themselves.

As Connerton argues, our experience of the present is strongly informed by our knowledge of the past, by what we consider 'normal' – therefore, 'images of the past commonly serve to legitimate a present social order'. This is why, when considering tradition, we have to be incredibly careful to sort historical fact from fiction, to understand the past as it really was and not rewrite it to suit our prejudices or needs. We must exercise discernment and conscience.[28]

IV

The good news is that the invented rituals of dictatorships never match the legitimacy of real traditions; once the dictator is gone, they generally disappear. This implies that there is an almost Darwinian quality to tradition, that the most attractive and useful – the fittest – survive, and that while fundamentalism is rigid and sterile, tradition outlasts it precisely because it demonstrates adaptation and growth.[29] Tradition is the full tree grown to maturity. Fundamentalism is worship of the dead stump. One cannot have a fruitful conversation with a fundamentalist because fundamentalism is defined by its purity and thus cannot engage with outsiders for fear of compromise. By contrast, authentic tradition enjoys the self-confidence that comes from old age, and most of the major religions are happy to chat.

While in Iraq, I was granted an audience with the then Baba Sheik, the spiritual leader of the Yazidis, a venerable old man with a long, white beard (he died shortly before publication). We ate watermelon in his house and talked about God. I was keen to know what we had in common: baptism, yes, guardian angels, life after death and, of course, a pope. The Yazidi pope had met my pope, and he had a photograph of them together on his wall. Traditions can be eccentric and parochial, yet from the particular we draw universal themes.

Historical encounter is one explanation for the similarities between religions; another is that traditions have developed to serve human needs, and, given that those needs are universal, it is inevitable that religions have a lot in common. Because most of us have children, we have invented rites of initiation; because we all die, we tell ourselves stories about what happens afterwards and why. This could be interpreted cynically: it sounds less like God created man than man created God, to make sense of his own existence. Most religious traditions, however, present a supernatural explanation for our commonality. The eighteenth-century philosopher Joseph de Maistre observed that the theme of heroic self-sacrifice is not unique to Jesus Christ but found also in the pagan cultures of Rome and Greece.[30] From this he deduced that there existed a template religion before Christ, a set of religious archetypes of which Jesus was the most perfect example. According to Christian teaching, we are all born with an instinct to worship and with the capacity to be a good person. This is the Christian understanding of conscience: not something we invent for ourselves but a gift from God planted in each of us at our birth. Over the course of our lives, we are invited to cultivate the seed. Because every single human being – regardless of time or place – is born with that conscience, bits and pieces of the Christian ideal can be found in cultures that don't follow Jesus or haven't even heard of him. Sometimes non-Christians behave in a way that appears more Christian than so-called Christians do.[31]

Other traditions have a variant of this view. I was told by a temple guide in India that I might think I'm a Catholic but I am in fact an imperfect Hindu, because Hinduism was around before Christianity, so Christianity is its descendant. These conversations can easily descend into a contest of claims – 'we were here first!' – but when believers meet, the fact that they have faith in something greater than themselves at least gives them a basis for dialogue. My conversation with Baba Sheik and his family brought home to me that though tensions between religions exist and are a source of violence, there is an equally important tension between belief and unbelief, between the traditional way of life – which venerates society, family and history – and the vacuum of modernity.

Iraq's religious minorities believe their voice has been lost in that vacuum. Yazidis and Christians have been ruthlessly persecuted – the number of Christians has dropped from around 1.5 million under Saddam Hussein to below 120,000 today – and yet the West seems reluctant to speak out, the media doesn't much report on it and the public probably doesn't care.[32] The United Kingdom has taken refugees from the Middle East, it's true, but not as many as voters think – and far too few Christians among those that we have. This has fed a perception among Iraqis that stupid British liberals are kinder to Muslim fanatics than they are to their victims. A joke among Iraqi Christians goes, 'Why won't Britain take me? Because I'm not Islamic State!'

The culprit, argues Baba Sheik's family, is the West's loss of identity. The Sheik's sons travel; they have been to Europe. From what they've seen, they are convinced that within a few years there will be more mosques in Britain than in Iraq, and it's not a judgement on the Muslims – one cannot help but admire their commitment – but on lazy Christians who can't be bothered to drag themselves out of bed on a Sunday morning for church. 'You don't have children,' one of Baba's sons said. 'You abort your babies. You are homosexuals. Your churches are empty.' He was saying that because we do not know who we are or what we stand for, we don't know how to defend our own civilization, let alone the Yazidi or Christian communities of the Middle East.

The average Westerner might reply, 'Hang on, we might not be like you, but that doesn't mean we are being untrue to ourselves – because we are different. The modern West is built upon a tradition of religious pluralism, sexual freedom and female emancipation. If we look like an open society that's because we want to be an open society. We are children of the Enlightenment.'

On the other hand, there is this inconvenient truth that Christians now amount to the most persecuted religious group in the world and yet Britain, despite centuries of Christian heritage, has been slow to act. This is partly for grubby reasons – we don't want to upset our trade partners in China or Saudi Arabia – but also, exactly as the Yazidis suspect, because we are at war with our own history.[33] Christianity was once the religion of slave holders and colonial missionaries. Many Westerners can't even begin to think of it as persecuted – and if they do stand up for it, they're terrified of being accused of slandering Muslims, even though this fear contradicts the official belief (and mine) that the Islamic State does not represent Islam. Rather than acknowledge a particular responsibility to defend Christians, the West has hidden behind a general principle of human rights; the end result is that it shuts its door on those who are in some instances the most in need. I left Iraq feeling impotent and ashamed.[34]

It would be stupid to say that I was envious of the Yazidis. They were living in a conflict zone; I was able to go home to peace and the rule of law. But, I wondered, if all that broke down, would the average Westerner have the same tools to hand that the Yazidi has to cope with trauma? I fear not. Across the West there is a dearth of purpose and spirit: we can't agree on who we are or what we're about, or even if these big existential questions matter. Many of us are happy to find definition in our job, our family or hobbies – but there's also a lot of anger out there, paranoia, depression and decay. It does not feel as if we are in control of our destiny. Things just happen to us, the same things, over and over again. Nothing seems to be learned.

How did the West lose this critical sense of self? The answer, curiously, is that rejecting tradition, turning our back on history, is part and parcel of the Western tradition. Where we are now is not a diversion. It has been our direction of travel for centuries.

FIGURE 4 President Donald Trump hugs the flag of the United States of America at National Harbor, Maryland on 29 February 2020.

2

The West's War on Tradition

By many standards, the twenty-first-century West is a wonderful place to live, which is why so many people want to come here. In his book *Enlightenment Now*, the eminent psychologist Steven Pinker counts our blessings:

> ... newborns who will live more than eight decades, markets overflowing with food, clean water that appears with the flick of a finger and waste that disappears with another, pills that erase a painful infection, sons who are not sent off to war, daughters who can walk the streets in safety, critics of the powerful who are not jailed or shot, the world's knowledge and culture available in a shirt pocket.

So how does he account for our present despair and political turmoil, for the niggling sense that our best years are behind us? In Pinker's view, the problem is that human beings can't let themselves be happy. We're programmed to feel dissatisfied, to always want more, and our reason is in constant conflict with our basest fears and desires. If only we could appreciate what we've got – and heaven knows, we're much safer and richer than the Yazidis – then we would see that, first, we should be more grateful and, second, the things we enjoy are not 'cosmic birth rights' but the product of a very distinct way of thinking.[1] Pinker wants us to pay more attention to the Enlightenment, a revolution in thought that occurred in the seventeenth and eighteenth centuries that gave birth to liberalism, the pre-eminent tradition in the West, a philosophy of freedom that has pushed science and liberty to new frontiers of human accomplishment.*

Pinker speaks for many of our elites: Bill Gates called *Enlightenment Now* 'my new favourite book' and his previous #1 was also by Pinker. But the conviction that liberalism is the father of our prosperity is being challenged by thinkers on left and right who argue that, on the contrary, it is a cause of much of our misfortune.[2] Liberalism is a tradition, but it is also a tradition that is anti-tradition – so it undermines itself.[3] Sceptical of religion, wary of anything inherited, it tears up everybody's roots, including its own, which is why our society doesn't have some of the coherence and certainties that other cultures enjoy – the qualities human beings need to navigate economic and social change. And because liberalism promotes freedom almost at the expense of responsibility, it destroys the very basis for a successful liberal society.† Human beings can only exercise liberty if they are disciplined and self-giving: liberalism encourages us to put our own appetites first.[4] The more freedom liberalism promises, the bigger the state has to grow to meet those expectations, and the more the state has to do to clean up the consequences of our actions. You'd imagine that a society committed to liberty would have a tiny bureaucracy, yet the twenty-first-century liberal state employs an army of public

---

* The Enlightenment and liberalism, let alone Professor Pinker, do not have a monopoly on definitions of freedom – and twentieth-century liberalism has found itself pulled in different directions by varying preferences for positive or negative liberty, i.e. freedom from restraint vs freedom to act upon one's free will. Jean-Paul Sartre, who would probably hate this book, argues that we have no control over the circumstances into which we are born, but once we become self-aware, we have to start making choices about how to respond to them: we are all free, in effect, but it's a burden, not a thrill.

† 'We have made an idol of progress,' wrote Roger Scruton, 'but progress is simply another name for human dreams, human ambitions, human fantasies. By worshipping progress we bow before an altar on which our own sins are exhibited.' Put another way, the liberal conception of freedom, decoupled from traditional morality, becomes about the right to do whatever human beings want, which could very easily be oppressive or self-destructive. Roger Scruton, *Gentle Regrets: Thoughts from a Life* (London: Bloomsbury Continuum, 2006), p. 237.

servants to tax us, teach us, heal us, protect us and keep an eye on what we're thinking and saying.[5] During the coronavirus pandemic, it felt at times as if the government had attempted to outlaw death.

To understand why the West is such an existential mess, we need to go back to the Enlightenment, to the birth of this anti-tradition tradition. What we discover is that liberalism laid several traps for itself, into which liberals have now stumbled.[6] We also find a glaring, rather worrying contradiction – that liberalism, despite being a philosophy of freedom, can also be surprisingly oppressive, that it offers not just licence but also a rigid model of thinking and being, its own sense of the right or wrong way to live. Anyone who deviates from its norms faces social sanction. Liberalism says, 'you can think whatever you want to think, within the boundaries of what is reasonable', which sounds generous, but it is constantly moving and shrinking those boundaries to exclude any serious alternative to a status quo that elites love because it's what makes them elites.

I

Before the Enlightenment, the medieval consensus put God at the centre of all things and defined human beings by their relationship to him and to each other. This was the basis for the feudal order – everyone knew their place – and the purpose of studying nature was to understand better the mind that created it. We dwelt 'not in a cold, meaningless universe but in a cosmos, in which everything has meaning because it participated in the life of the Creator'. C. S. Lewis wrote that contemplating this cosmos was 'like looking at a great building' – think of Notre Dame – 'overwhelming in its greatness but satisfying in its harmony'.[7]

This breathtaking vision of reality was challenged by a series of natural disasters and religious wars that forced Europeans to confront the mystery of suffering. If God loves us, why does he put us through the mill? In 1755, there was a terrible earthquake off the coast of Portugal. Lisbon was shaken to ruins, drowned by a tsunami and then incinerated by fires. The death toll was between twenty and thirty thousand. The medieval model said that God was in control of everything, so this had to be a divine punishment and the logical response was penance and prayer. But what was it a punishment for? Lisbon was a deeply religious city. The earthquake happened on a holy holiday and many of the people killed were at Mass (around 86 per cent of the city's churches, monasteries and convents were destroyed). François-Marie Arouet, the French writer better known as Voltaire, asked, if this had been a sanction for guilt, then why did God kill innocent children, and why level Lisbon rather than Paris or London, which were synonymous with vice? 'A hundred thousand ants, our neighbours, suddenly crushed on our ant hill and half of them probably perishing in inexpressible anguish amidst the debris from which they could not be extricated' – what kind of cosmic order was this? Perhaps what happened to Portugal was not a supernatural event but a natural phenomenon, in which case surely it made more sense to investigate the causes of the disaster and rebuild stronger and safer, rather than fall pitiably to one's knees?[8]

You could always do both. In the revolution of ideas that followed Lisbon, it's important to stress that not every Enlightenment thinker was critical of faith or convinced of the superiority of reason – and most Christians today, entirely at ease with science, would argue that a natural disaster is not a chastisement but a test of our abilities and compassion.[9] Nevertheless, the emergence of the scientific method and the study of natural phenomena as just that – natural, not divine – went hand-in-glove with a new sensibility that ordered the universe around man rather than around God. If we can understand what makes the Earth move, can we also understand what makes man tick? Enlightenment thinkers studied human beings much the same way one might study the flowers or the birds, seeking to strip away all artifice, all the myths and conventions laid down by centuries of Christian civilization, to find the real us, the 'noble savage' hidden underneath. They wanted to empower human beings through a better understanding of themselves and the world around them.

It followed that many Enlightenment thinkers were critical of tradition. Tradition, they argued, holds back progress; it is superstitious and unscientific; it ties us to other people, to places and to conventions of thought that we haven't chosen for ourselves after weighing up all the options, but have had imposed upon us as an inheritance. You are an individual, said the new philosophers. You should be free to work out who you are and what you believe through rational inquiry, and your life should be governed by the supreme quality of reason.[10] 'Reason is non-negotiable', writes Pinker. 'As soon as you show up to discuss the question of what we should live for ... as long as you insist that your answers, whatever they are, are reasonable or justified or true and that therefore other people should believe them too, then you have committed yourself to reason, and to holding your beliefs accountable to objective standards.'[11] The Enlightenment encouraged us to question as much as possible, on the basis that the more questions we ask – the more forensic we can be – the better the answers we're likely to get.

Not that the Enlightenment preached anarchy. On the contrary, if reason is at war with prejudice and passion, then we're going to need to keep these negative emotions in check and we'll require strong institutions to do it. At the same time as the Enlightenment discredited medieval foundations, such as the Church or absolutist monarchy, it built new ones of its own, such as parliaments or universities, with the goal of guaranteeing good government, peace and freedom.[12] If you want a latter-day example of an Enlightenment institution, one could pick the European Union: it provides mutual rules, resolves disputes and defends the right of individuals to cross borders and trade freely, all on a continent that was once divided by war and dictatorship.

The argument over how we should best govern ourselves gave birth to a new political tradition: liberalism. The meaning of the word 'liberal' has a complex history. The historian Helena Rosenblatt points out that when the Romans contemplated 'liberalitas', they defined it as generosity of spirit, which was essential to the functioning of a happy society; the concept was Christianized and politicized and turned into a theory of education – if we want our children to grow up into good citizens, went the argument, then we must teach them virtue – and liberalism in its early forms was the very opposite of self-obsessed individualism.[13] As the power of churches and kings waned during the Enlightenment, so liberal ideas could now be tested in the writing of constitutions, and that was when liberalism both established its dominance and fractured into competing schools of thought. Some liberals wanted to drive religion out of the public sphere; others saw it as essential to morality and freedom. Some were pro-democracy; others believed that if you give the mob the vote, they would turn on the minority. And while some took it for granted that a liberal state would be as small as possible, others argued that it must grow in order to guarantee and expand freedom. Defining liberalism could be as tricky as nailing a jelly to a wall, but this very confusion was a sign of success because it shows how Enlightenment values came to permeate left and right. The strongest traditions are always capable of adaptation while remaining loyal to their first principles, and running through the history of liberalism we find a disposition towards freedom, equality, the individual, the scientific method and that constant emphasis upon growth through reason.[14]

Contrast provided clarity. In the twentieth century, liberalism was challenged by two vastly different alternatives: fascism and communism. Some, such as the philosopher John Gray, argue that these were in fact by-products of the Enlightenment; most liberals disagree.[15] In the judgement of Pinker what distinguished, say, communism from liberalism is that communism was unreasonable and anti-individual – and it didn't work. Fascism was defeated in war; communism, which led to dictatorship and famine, simply couldn't compete with the ingenuity of Western capitalism and it collapsed under the strain. By 1989, when the Berlin Wall came down, it looked as if the Enlightenment had indeed been vindicated in the laboratory of history. In the summer of that year, the political scientist Francis Fukuyama wrote a courageous essay in which he suggested that history was effectively at an end. Stuff would continue to happen, granted, but with communism on the way out, the grand battle of ideas was over and governments around the world would now converge on liberalism. Not because liberalism had imposed itself violently, as other systems tried to do, but because it was enormously appealing on both a material and an emotional level. Capitalism, as in free markets governed by strong institutions, had delivered a degree of economic improvement that no other system could match. Consumerism meant choice and choice meant freedom, and liberalism was far better than any of the alternatives at recognizing the rights and desires of the individual. Most ideologies force us to submit to a higher power: God, the nation or 'the people'. Liberalism encourages pluralism, inquiry and self-definition, and while dictators insist that we subscribe to a one-size-fits-all version of the truth, liberalism gives us a range of options to choose from. It flatters us, it makes us feel special. What's not to like?

II

Fukuyama spoke too soon. It's true that the Soviet Union collapsed in 1991, but Russia's experience of liberal capitalism was horrible – gangsterism and theft – and it quickly returned to authoritarianism under Vladimir Putin. China embraced capitalism without bothering with democracy. The Middle East burned with fundamentalism. In his defence, Fukuyama foresaw all of this. 'The end of history,' he wrote, 'will be a very sad time.' The Cold War had been frightening but also exciting: the conflict between abstract ideas will now be replaced by the deadening consensus of rationality, of government by expertise and troubleshooting. 'There will be neither art nor philosophy, just the perpetual caretaking of the museum of human history.' The global elite would move in one direction – towards closer cooperation through trans-national institutions, like the EU – but beneath the radar, pockets of the population will feel left behind and angry. There will be ethnic wars, he said, and terrorism. The two major alternatives to liberalism will be nationalism and religion. 'The revival of religion,' which, in 1989, was already happening in both the Middle East and in American politics, 'attests to a broad unhappiness with the impersonality and spiritual vacuity of liberal consumerist societies.'[16]

If tradition is defined by three qualities – it connects the individual to their society, passes on social knowledge and transcends time and place – liberalism often does the complete opposite. It prioritizes the individual: institutions that place restrictions on individual liberty, such as church or marriage, have been cut down to size, and our sense of belonging has been weakened, leading to atomization. Man is increasingly psychological in nature – inward looking, narcissistic – a characteristic exacerbated by liberalism's emphasis upon questions rather than answers, on the rejection of inherited assumptions in favour of self-exploration and debate.[17] Certainties that once provided stability are eroded; unity feels near-impossible. Is there a god? Are male and female physical realities or conceptual labels? Is objectivity a credible concept, or is the world experienced differently if you are white, black, male, female, straight or gay? 'Walk in your truth,' the kids like to say. In the summer of 2020, there was an illuminating debate about whether or not one could state with confidence that $2 + 2 = 4$: the collapse of certainty in microcosm. Kareem Carr, a biostatistician at Harvard, argued that it can sometimes equal five, because numbers are abstractions of real things, and those things might function differently in life from how they appear on paper. If I put a rooster and a hen together, said Carr, and come back a year later, the numbers might look like this: $1 + 1 = 3$. If I put a hen and a fox together and come back five minutes later, it's likely to look like this: $1 + 1 = 1$.[18] Carr's theory was intriguing, even cute, but if we cannot agree in principle on what $2 + 2$ equals then we cannot confidently do mathematics, and it probably becomes a lot easier to commit tax fraud or give the wrong change.* Abstractions and categories are useful. It doesn't always help to overthink them. If

---

* As Douglas Adams joked, for an encore man shall prove that black equals white and get himself killed on the next zebra crossing.

we cannot talk with clarity about right and wrong – if we throw our social knowledge out of the window and try to operate without a common moral language – then it's going to be hard to run a coherent society.*

Finally, liberalism is the enemy of transcendence, not only because it favours science over tradition and rationality over spirit, but because individualism, particularly the consumerist kind encouraged by capitalism, compels us to live for the moment. As the social critic Christopher Lasch warned, 'We are fast losing the sense of historical continuity, the sense of belonging to a succession of generations originating in the past and stretching into the future.' In a liberal culture, said Lasch, the past is presented as an embarrassment, an irrelevance or a joke, never invoked as authority and never anything we can learn from. Dwelling upon it is dismissed as nostalgia.[19] All of this sets liberalism against the human passions like faith and patriotism, but also, eventually, against reason itself. If the individual is self-obsessed, what becomes of the qualities that a liberal culture relies upon to thrive, such as communication, affection, self-discipline and, as the Romans conceived of it, generosity of spirit? If there is no common language, what happens when the liberal culture hosts people who are illiberal and refuse to fit in? How does a society that is opposed to moral judgement condemn or police ideas that seek to destroy it? And if there is no sense of debt to the past, it is easy to imagine society forgetting Pinker's history lesson and reaching the conclusion that we are where we are – with our wonderful democracy and liberties – by accident or luck, that the Enlightenment was unimportant and 'things have just

---

* A classic example: looting. There is a distinction, say some, between outright theft and looting as an expression of political rage. Vicky Osterweil, author of *In Defense of Looting: A Riotous History of Uncivil Action*, argues that ownership of things is 'innately, structurally white supremacist' and stealing those things an 'experience of pleasure, joy, and freedom'. Riots 'rip, tear, burn, and destroy to give birth to a new world', a 'queer birth' that is also 'femme as fuck'. Argued from the right perspective and articulated in the correct language, immorality can easily be cast as reasonable, justified and sexy. Graeme Wood, 'The Pinnacle of Looting Apologia', *The Atlantic*, 2 September 2020. https://www.theatlantic.com/ideas/archive/2020/09/there-no-defense-looting/615925/, last accessed 19 October 2020.

happened to us'. There is a school of thought that says the West isn't very special at all, that it might even be racist to claim that it is.

The contradictions of liberalism are most dramatically exposed in politics, the sphere of existence to which liberalism probably devotes the most attention. If you see life as a debating society, if you are forever knocking down institutions and rebuilding them, politics inevitably becomes the chief arena for trying to fix society and ourselves. At the same time as investing a near-religious degree of emotion in politics, liberalism has also attempted to apply a version of the scientific method to it, to tear out those prejudices and passions and address all problems with pure reason. In theory, liberalism is beyond the ideological zeal of left or right: it simply does what is rational and what works.[20] Therefore, politics becomes a matter of technique, which is one reason why, since 1989, mainstream politicians have increasingly said the same things, harmonizing towards a near-global consensus on the best way to manage a society. Conservatives, most already economically liberal, have become more socially liberal; the left, most already socially liberal, have become more economically liberal.[21] It almost seems as if politicians not only think a similar way but look and sound similar, too, which would make sense because every tradition has its own fashion and language, and our elites tend to be drawn from a small number of universities that literally teach them how to do politics, as if the sensible governance of a nation could be condensed into a textbook and replicated from San Francisco to Timbuktu.

This emphasis upon technique might be more compelling if the elites didn't keep cocking things up – but they do, again and again (and again). The Iraq War was a horror show; the deregulation of banking a colossal error of judgement. The smart thing would be to learn from one's mistakes and change tack; liberals, in many instances, have doubled down. Republican and Democrat administrations poured troops into the Middle East; the cost of the financial crisis was placed onto the shoulders of the poor. Liberalism is supposed to operate upon conclusions drawn from rational inquiry, but the fact that Western elites have tried to solve the problems associated with liberalism with yet more liberalism – a popular definition of madness – implies that this is not pure reason at work but a tradition that has developed a hard, very ideological edge. It can even deform into an enemy of freedom.

In its desire to protect us the liberal state has metastasized, going so far as to wage a war on prejudice itself – an admirable but difficult goal for it means policing not just bad actions but bad thoughts and bad speech, and it has required new laws and bureaucracies to do the job. To uphold one set of freedoms, the modern state ends up eroding others.[22] One of the biggest assaults has been upon freedom of speech, which is painfully ironic because, to repeat, liberalism holds that progress advances through dialogue – yet we can't even begin to have a discussion unless we are free to speak our minds. Liberalism's emphasis upon reason is partly to blame. Recall Steven Pinker's insistence that 'reason is non-negotiable', that what matters is that we appeal to reason and allow our arguments to be judged by objective standards. Fair enough – but who gets to define what 'reason' is and who defines the 'objective standards' by which we are judged? What sounds like a recipe for free speech can easily become a recipe for managing speech, because it fosters the idea that you can say whatever you like so long as someone in power judges that what you are saying is reasonable. Pinker, for example, does not believe reasonableness can extend to religious belief: 'To take something on faith means to believe in it without good reason, so by definition faith in the existence of supernatural entities clashes with reason.'[23] He adds 'opposing reason is, by definition, unreasonable'.[24] Pinker is a defender of free speech, for sure, but the implication of this view is that religious belief has nothing of worth to contribute, and he's not many steps away from saying it is unhealthy, delusional and a threat to freedom as we presently define it.

Imagine an office worker is invited to a same-sex wedding and he politely says no. Imagine if he said that while he was delighted to be asked, he is a Christian, he believes marriage can only be between a man and a woman, and though he wishes the couple all the happiness in the world, he cannot take part. If he isn't sacked, he'll be ostracized. 'Rightly so', some would say, because to think that two people can't get married because of a couple of passages in the Bible – 'in this day and age!' – might be construed as unreasonable, a blind prejudice that deserves to be called out. But it's worth noting that, only a few years ago, Hillary Clinton and Barack Obama were also against same-sex marriage, and both used Judeo-Christian language when talking about it.[25] In my lifetime, the speed and certainty with which gay rights have gone from an aspiration to something tolerated, to something protected and, finally, promoted, is remarkable – tracking the development of the liberal state from one that not only tolerates but sanctions and not only permits but enables. Some have felt left behind by the dizzying pace of change, and you might ask 'who cares?' – but the fact that an opinion that was widely held ten years ago can be considered totally unacceptable today ought to give us pause for thought. Societies change their mind. The consensus evolves. The definition of reason is not as self-evident as Pinker implies, which is why many religious conservatives live in a state of neurotic anxiety. They are waiting for the day that they are redefined as not only unreasonable but intolerant – and thus intolerable.

III

If that happens, it won't necessarily be the state that shuts them down. Social pressure might do the job, or even self-censorship. Many of us have internalized liberal values to the point that we might think certain things but we'd never say them, and it requires an enormous psychic effort to keep up the front.[26] A handful of conservative thinkers have compared this to life behind the former Iron Curtain, suggesting that liberalism and communism have more in common than we'd like to admit. The communist system was broken but the state wouldn't acknowledge it and the people weren't allowed to say it. The public became partners in a grand theatre of the absurd in which everyone asserted that communism was normal and working well, that 2 + 2 = the five-year plan.[27]

This comparison between liberalism and communism is a stretch: we do not confine the politically incorrect to a gulag or the mental hospital. The subtler, more effective point is that, like other traditions, the word 'liberalism' can be both a description of what we generally believe – and most of us in the West are wedded to it whether we realize it or not – and a prescription for what we should believe. If liberalism is righteous here, in America or Western Europe, isn't it righteous everywhere? If so, it should be exported – and by this leap of logic, even a tradition of liberty can become a form of colonialism.

In *The Light that Failed*, Ivan Krastev and Stephen Holmes examine why, when communism collapsed, so many countries in Eastern Europe first embraced liberal democracy and then rejected it. In the last two decades, a number of regimes have come to power in the East that eschew liberal norms, elevating the Church, resisting Muslim immigration, even meddling with the press and judiciary. Krastev and Holmes theorize that this is because communism and liberalism made similar mistakes. What Easterners really wanted during the Cold War was the freedom to be themselves, to speak their own languages, run their own businesses, go to church and govern their country as they saw fit. Communism tore up those traditions and tried to eliminate the historical memory of a different way of life. When the Berlin Wall fell, there was instant, thrilling liberation – but with communism gone and hardly any memory of the world before it left, what regime of reality would the East embrace? There was only one on the table. 'No-alternative Soviet communism,' write Krastev and Holmes, was suddenly replaced by 'no-alternative Western liberalism.' The intention of the anti-communist revolution was to reassert the nation state, but instead Easterners were invited to privatize their economies and embrace Western-style modernity, producing a new spiritual malaise that was interpreted in some quarters as 'an invitation to cultural suicide'.[28] This situation was psychologically unsustainable: 'The imitation of moral ideals ... makes you resemble the one you admire but simultaneously makes you less like yourself at a time when your own uniqueness and keeping faith with your group are at the heart of your struggle for dignity and recognition.' Membership of the EU rubbed salt into the wound. The EU set policies and rules from the centre and expected Easterners to enact them while pretending to make decisions for themselves; when Western Europeans visited Romania or Slovakia and encountered corruption or conservatism, they accused the Easterners of only going through the motions of democracy. This was deeply patronizing.[29]

Especially as it became clear that the West didn't actually know what it was doing. The financial crisis of 2007–8 exposed Westerners as immoral and incompetent. The migrant crisis of 2015–16, in some eyes, made them look suicidal. When over a million people from the Middle East, including Syrians and Iraqis, sought asylum in Europe, Germany decided to throw open its doors – an act of Christian charity, no doubt, but to Easterners it smacked of moral imperialism. The migrants were walking through *their* countries and Germany had no right, they felt, to legitimize trespass. Historic roles were reversed. The West, once a beacon of hope, now appeared to have gone mad, and politicians in the East – once under the yolk of atheistic communism – now cast themselves as the last defenders of European civilization, especially given that these asylum seekers were overwhelmingly Muslim. Some Christians regarded what was happening across the continent as an invasion by other means.

They needn't have worried. There was no Islamic 'conquest'; on the contrary, most of the Muslims who passed through Eastern Europe kept going until they reached Germany, France or Scandinavia, where hopefully they will, in time, integrate. The East has a demographic crisis, but it's not overcrowding. It is depopulation. As is so often the case with populism, outsiders, be they migrants or EU officials, are blamed for problems that begin at home, and the shrillest protests ring with hypocrisy. The anti-immigrant East is shrinking for one embarrassing reason: a large part of its population has done exactly what Syrians or Iraqis have done and migrated to the West, in search of a better life.[30]

Nevertheless, Fukuyama has been vindicated by populism, by the return to politics of the themes of religious conservatism in the

Islamic world and national sovereignty in the West, most famously in the twin revolutions of 2016, Brexit and the election of Donald Trump. These revolts at the ballot box – completely rejecting expert opinion, even when it might have been correct – are an alarm bell. They tell us that despite all the good things going for us, many citizens are desperately unhappy.[31] Not all of them: it's important to stress that populists can be surprisingly unpopular, that they usually squeeze into office on a plurality and the 'silent majority' they claim to speak for is, more often than not, a vocal minority.[32] Whatever the true balance of power, the population seems uncomfortably divided between the winners and losers of the liberal era, between those on board with its precepts and those who feel they have been compelled to accept rapid, sometimes traumatic change without their consent.

The journalist David Goodhart characterizes this conflict as the Anywheres vs the Somewheres. The Anywheres 'value autonomy and self-realisation before stability, community and tradition' – they appreciate free movement and free trade. The Somewheres are more likely to be materially threatened by mass migration or the loss of manufacturing jobs to developing nations, and they resent the condescending elites who tell them globalization is in their best interest. The Somewheres are pulled towards populism by nostalgia. 'Make America Great Again', Trump's 2016 slogan, implied that America used to be great, something went wrong, so let's turn the clock back. 'Take Back Control', the chief promise of the official Brexit campaign, suggested that control did once exist – over Britain's laws and borders – that it was stolen, and now must be returned, via the restoration of parliamentary sovereignty. These are not, at face value, extreme demands. They are almost sentimental. Goodhart believes that the Somewheres are neither racist nor homophobic, that they simply regret 'the passing of a structured and tradition bound world', of the decline of family or patriotism, along with shrinking union membership and job insecurity. One might even say they are nostalgic for an earlier version of liberalism – before it eroded those very things that make liberalism work, such as a sense of continuity or social knowledge. Such is the triumph of liberalism as the Western tradition that even when we kick against it, it's hard to imagine an alternative.[33]

'Why would you want to?!' comes the challenge. For those who voted against Brexit or Trump, the very idea that one would consciously slow or stop progress was offensive: the world had been moving in the right direction, so why throw it into reverse? Some prominent conservatives argued that this was itself a very unconservative thing to do. After years of painstaking integration into the EU, Brexit yanked Britain out – probably at the cost of jobs and the UK's international reputation. As for Trump, almost everything he did seemed to challenge conservative orthodoxy. Republicans had pushed free trade for decades; he launched a trade war with China. They promoted family values; he had the ethics of a libidinous chimp. They believed in limited government; he spoke like a tyrant and had scant regard for constitutional norms. Populism was revolution and whenever there's a revolution, surely it's incumbent upon conservatives to defend the institutions under attack? It seemed doubly ridiculous that Donald Trump, a self-described billionaire, could present himself as a champion of the people.[34]

But populist conservatives generally do see themselves as outsiders. They revere old institutions but believe they've been locked out of them, that they've been captured by a committee of self-appointed liberal experts operating on ideological cruise control, using the institutions to undermine the very principles they were established to promote. In other words, populism is far from revolutionary, it is counter-revolutionary, and one could argue that it articulates the core differences between liberalism and conservatism that date all the way back to the eighteenth century.

Roger Scruton, Britain's most significant conservative philosopher of the late twentieth century, argued that liberalism and conservatism started out as products of the Enlightenment, as kissing cousins who shared a fondness for liberty – but they diverged over the question of 'settlement'. Liberals, said Scruton, saw man as an autonomous individual best left to himself. Conservatives believed we come into the world bearing obligations, that the individual is shaped by society and that freedom is best served by 'obedience' to tradition. 'The conservative response to the liberal enlightenment has been to insist on the contingent and attached nature of the human individual.'[35] If we want to enjoy freedom, paradoxically, there must be limits on freedom: 'Only where customs and traditions exist will the sovereignty of the individual lead to a true political order rather than to anarchy; only in a community of non-contractual obligations will society have the stability and moral order to make secular government possible.' Scruton concludes: 'Liberalism makes sense only in the social context that conservatism defends. But liberals and conservatives are temperamentally quite distinct. Liberals naturally rebel, conservatives naturally obey.'[36]

The true nature of conservatism, its deference to tradition, was hidden by the Cold War: conservatives allied with liberals against the mutual threat of communism and put aside some of their natural commitments. In the 1920s, for instance, the US Republican Party was isolationist and protected industry with tariffs. It changed its position in the 1950s partly to help its allies build up their economies and hold socialism at bay; when the Cold War ended, a dormant tradition of Republican nationalism reawakened, culminating in the nomination of Donald Trump in 2016.[37] With communism gone, conservatives have slowly rediscovered, or placed new emphasis upon, their profound disagreements with liberalism, and it's no coincidence that some of the most politically salient issues of today touch upon the question of settlement – of religious or national identity, the importance of borders or self-government. We are debating the fundamental questions raised by the Enlightenment.

Many conservatives are now in despair at the state of the world. There are riots, the culture is debased, freedoms we took for granted are tested and our economic and political systems are pushed to breaking point as the centre erodes. And yet none of this is really new. Change is a constant in history. If we look at conservative responses to liberalism and industrialization in the tumultuous nineteenth century, we find that they tried to reduce the psychological strain of novelty by anchoring their societies in a sense of tradition – even if they had to invent a few traditions to do it. The lesson is that there is a more comfortable way forward by looking backwards – and outwards, beyond Europe, to societies that sometimes do a better job than we do of remembering who they are and where they've come from.

FIGURE 5 Prince Edward (later King Edward VIII) wears both traditional Japanese clothing and a bowler hat during his 1922 tour of Japan.

3

The Invention of Tradition

Modernity can be a liberation. It can also be traumatic. Ancient landscapes are transformed; old gods die. Social knowledge is lost. A way of life that has defined people for centuries is swept away, and while modernity can come from within – as an authentic desire for progress – it is often experienced as a conquest from without. Take the politely enforced globalization of Japan.

Before the 1850s, Japan was an isolated feudal society. On paper it had an emperor, but the emperor was just a figurehead; power was in the hands of the shoguns, a caste of military dictators who, in the words of historian Christopher Harding, 'achieved stability at the cost of flexibility, with the codification of everyday life stretching even into which foods and fabrics people of differing social status might enjoy; fine silks for samurai, down through the plainer kind for townspeople ... finishing at rough cotton for lowly peasants'.[1] In this tightly regulated culture, contact with Europeans presented a challenge. The Portuguese arrived in 1542 and hunted duck with guns; the Japanese were so impressed that they built their own firearms and, by the seventeenth century, 'had more and better guns than any other country in the world'. Catholic missionaries, on the other hand, imported something the shoguns definitely did not want. By 1600, there were around 300,000 Christians in Japan, and they committed the sin of revering a foreigner, the Pope. The elite decided to purge this treason. Thousands of believers were tortured or executed – crucified or dangled in excrement or forced into boiling hot springs. The shogunate now placed Japan in quarantine, ordering that no foreigner might enter and most Japanese couldn't leave. An exception was made for Protestant Dutch traders who, being less interested in evangelism than in profit, weren't classed as a threat – but even they were confined to a tiny island in Nagasaki harbour, and any foreigner who was shipwrecked and had the misfortune to wash up on the shores of Japan would either be murdered on the spot or thrown into prison.

The system worked so long as the Pacific was relatively free of traffic, but that changed with the California gold rush. Suddenly the ocean was teeming with ships and the United States government wanted its sailors to be given a guarantee of protection. In 1853, President Millard Fillmore wrote a letter to the Emperor of Japan encouraging him to open his country to trade and offer safe passage to Americans. Fillmore's language was obliging, but this was an offer the shogunate couldn't refuse; it was delivered by four ships – two steam-powered and gun-bearing, more powerful than anything the Japanese had – that sailed into Edo Bay on 8 July.[2] Thousands of samurai lined the beach and up a hill; an intimidating sight in a different age, but nothing compared to the well-drilled marines who marched in sharp formation and presented the President's letter in a display of alarming technical superiority. The Japanese were told they had a year to think things over. After that, the marines would be back for an answer. As the American ships sailed away, 'hulls coated in pitch, and two spewing smoke from their funnels', the Japanese dubbed them 'the black ships – omens of dark days ahead'.[3]

The shoguns had made a mistake. They thought they could protect the country from the virus of foreign influence via quarantine; on the contrary, by isolating themselves from new technology and new ideas, they had weakened their immune system and lay open to invasion. They could refuse the American demands but that might mean military engagement, which they probably wouldn't win – so the only serious option was to adapt to modernity in order that no foreigner could make demands like these again. To save their way of life they had to change their way of life, though there was a risk that if they changed too much, too fast, they might as well have been occupied by the Americans.

The Japanese elite attempted to chart a middle way. They would modernize but in a manner that seemed to complement, even enhance, Japanese tradition. By doing this, they echoed a similar effort taking place in Europe – almost a global conservative project to navigate, or even effect, great change while giving the impression that nothing had changed at all.

I

The job of the conservative, wrote the journalist William F. Buckley in 1955, is to 'stand athwart history, yelling Stop'. It's a magnificent image, appropriate to the shoguns, whom one can imagine standing on the shoreline shouting 'go home!' at the frightening black ships. It's also an image of impotence – intended to conjure up King Canute telling the tide to stop coming in – and it's funny, too. A rich seam of irony runs through conservatism: Donald Trump joked about his hair, Ronald Reagan about his age. The humour is partly a concession of defeat, a recognition that what they stand for is absurd by the standards of the day – that the battle they've thrown themselves into was probably lost a long time ago.[4]

For example, when have conservatives ever been happy with universities? In *The Coddling of the American Mind*, a wildly popular book among right-wingers, published in 2018, Greg Lukianoff and Jonathan Haidt argue that the contemporary university is the victim of left-wing fashion, of anxiety and depression, paranoid parenting, vastly expanded definitions of injustice and the bureaucracy of health and safety. It's a serious flaw of Lukianoff and Haidt's thesis that in a book 352 pages long, the cost of going to an American college is only mentioned once, on page 199 (attendance at Berkeley for Californians in 1968 was $300 a year; today, before financial aid, it's about $40,000) – but even if what they say is true, a conservative with a good memory would know that it's hardly new.[5] The book's title is a reference to *The Closing of the American Mind* by Allan Bloom, who argued that the university was in trouble in 1987.[6] When Ronald Reagan ran for governor of California, he claimed that Berkeley had been hijacked by left-wing extremists – in 1966.[7] In 1951, Buckley published a widely read account of his time as a student at Yale, which he said was staffed by 'atheists' and 'collectivists' (later he declared 'I would rather be governed by the first 2000 people in the Manhattan phone book than the entire faculty of Harvard.').[8] And in the 1930s, the German theologian Dietrich Bonhoeffer attended a seminary in New York and found it obsessed with politics and theologically shallow. 'They preach about virtually everything,' he said. 'Only one thing is not addressed … the gospel of Jesus Christ.'[9]

Every generation has its jeremiads and dystopias, and they all say the same sort of thing: not enough breeding, too much sex for pleasure, masculine women and effeminate men, the death of the West and the threat from the East.* As for the nineteenth century, that was the very worst time to be alive. Max Simon Nordau, a Hungarian–French physician, concluded, based upon studies of his

---

* A particular pleasure of mine is spotting complaints from the past that could be made today. For example, John Henry Newman on newspapers: 'The subject-matter of thought and belief has so increased upon us, that a far higher mental formation is required than was necessary in times past, and higher than we have actually reached. The whole world is brought to our doors every morning, and our judgement is required upon social concerns, books, persons, parties, creeds, national acts, political principles and measures. We have to form our opinion, make our profession, take our side on a hundred matters on which we have but little right to speak at all.' He could be describing rolling news and social media, much as Leo Tolstoy seemed to do in 1882: 'We were all then convinced that it was necessary for us to speak, write and print as quickly as possible and as much as possible, and that it was all wanted for the good of humanity. And thousands of us, contradicting and abusing one another, all printed and wrote – teaching others. And without remarking that we knew nothing, and that to the simplest of life's questions: What is good and what is evil? We did not know how to reply, we all not listening to one another, talked at the same time, sometimes backing and praising one another in order to be backed and praised in turn, sometimes getting angry with one another – just as in a lunatic asylum.' John Henry Newman, *An Essay in Aid of a Grammar of Assent* (Frankfurt: Outlook, 2018), p. 141; Leo Tolstoy, *A Confession* (Mineola: Dover, 2005), p. 8.

patients, that the world had gone mad and was intent on suicide – in 1892. He found his contemporaries to be decadent and feckless, 'striving in vain to snatch one more pleasure of sense' before an end that couldn't come a moment too soon.[10]

Nordau was a compelling pessimist, one of the best. He predicted the rise of fascism based upon the popularity of Wagner among right-wing Germans: small lunatics are attracted to big lunatics, he said, like filings to a magnet.[11] The society he read about in his newspaper was, again, eerily familiar; a culture so greedy, he wrote, that a king would sell his claim to the throne in exchange for a waiver of his gambling debts, and so obsessed with celebrity that a policeman removed the skin of a famous murderer and had it made into souvenirs for his friends and family. Nordau recalled with particular disgust the story of 'an American [who] weds his bride in a gas-factory, then gets with her into a balloon held in readiness, and enters on a honeymoon in the clouds'. He might read like a curmudgeon, but Nordau was liberal and he was Jewish. His great jeremiad, *Degeneration*, was written by a man who felt he had a personal stake in the death of 'traditional discipline' and the 'end of an established order, which for thousands of years has satisfied logic, fettered depravity, and in every art matured something of beauty'.[12]

Let's not dismiss the possibility that Nordau was also onto something, that what happened to European society in the eighteenth and nineteenth centuries had indeed been traumatic, with consequences that echo into our own era. The most tangible change was industrialization. Europeans had migrated away from the countryside, where they had lived a fixed existence dominated by church and ritual, in search of work in the towns and cities. The factory was now the primary economic unit, sucking up the time and energies of its workers in appalling conditions that belied the new era's promise of wealth and freedom. There was always the army, navy or colonization as an alternative career – but that first rush of globalization mixed adventure with disease and violence, and the old world that men returned to, if they ever came back, was transformed beyond recognition. 'In 1840 there were in Europe

3,000 kilometres of railway,' wrote Nordau, 'in 1891 there were 218,000 kilometres.' In 1840, the English sent 277 million letters; by 1881, they sent well over a billion. This broadened people's horizons – Nordau noted that the contemporary yokel knew far more about the world than a prime minister did a century ago – and altered their understanding of the nation, even of time itself, as local time zones were merged into one and the world ticked along to the schedule of the railway timetable. In Nordau's opinion, people simply couldn't cope with this pace of change. He cited a spike in murder, suicide and insanity as proof that progress had taken us by surprise, that mankind's character hadn't evolved fast enough to deal with the crowded conditions and sensory overload. In his patients he diagnosed 'fatigue and exhaustion … the effects of contemporary civilization, of the vertigo and whirl of our frenzied life, the vastly increased number of sense impressions and organic reactions, and therefore of perceptions, judgments and motor impulses, which at present are forced into a given unity of time.'[13]

Nordau felt that his adopted home of France was particularly ill-equipped to handle industrialization because it had weakened its immune system with an earlier period of revolution and war.[14] The revolution of 1789, which culminated in the declaration of a republic in 1792 and the execution of King Louis XVI the following year, touched every aspect of life. The state took control of schools and charity; titles were abolished; feudalism swept away. Ancient localities disappeared and were replaced by equally sized *départements*. The seven-day week became ten days; the months were renamed; the calendar began with the establishment of the republic, Year One in the history of the world. France even underwent a mini reformation. Monasteries were suppressed and priests and bishops had to take an oath to the new order. Resistance could end at the guillotine.[15]

If conservatives are at heart social critics – literally reacting to events – then it's logical that an era of great change would produce an equal and opposite reaction, and we can indeed trace the origins of modern conservatism to the 1790s. Two brilliant thinkers stood out: Edmund Burke, a member of the British parliament, and Joseph de Maistre, a philosopher from Savoy.[16] In *Reflections on the Revolution in France*, Burke wrote that among the French revolutionaries 'humanity and compassion are ridiculed as the fruits of superstition and ignorance. Tenderness to individuals is considered as treason to the public. Liberty is always to be estimated perfect, as ownership is made insecure.' With biting irony, he concluded that 'Amidst assassination, massacre, and confiscation,' the revolutionaries were 'forming plans for the good order of future society.'[17]

The incredible thing is that Burke wasn't in France for the revolution and he published these words in November 1790 when things were going relatively well. He even predicted the return of pseudo-monarchy nine years later, under Napoleon.[18] What gave him such uncanny insight into the future? The answer was a sophisticated evaluation of the past. The revolutionaries believed you could remake the human character through the application of philosophy; Burke and de Maistre argued that human character was timeless, so it was human character that would shape the revolution, not the other way around.[19]

If you wipe away an established order, they warned, you might destroy some injustices – and both men conceded that King Louis' *Ancien Régime* was imperfect – but you also eliminate centuries of accrued rights and freedoms. Moreover, the injustices of the old system were not the unique preserve of a bad king or a corrupt Church but were commonplace sins of greed and vanity, so they would quickly establish themselves in a revolutionary regime – all the more so because the restraining influences of authority and religion have been disestablished. While you are 'terrifying yourselves with ghosts and apparitions' of dead tyrants, Burke wrote, France will be 'the haunt of robbers.'[20]

The Enlightenment conceit that society and state are contracts that the individual can enter and exit at will might sound superficially liberating, but it eroded respect for society and state and made it all too easy to overthrow both. The conceit was also inaccurate.

One did not choose to be born French or English, Protestant or Catholic, yet these things define who we are and we cannot walk away from them.[21] If society and state are a form of contract, concluded Burke, it is not chosen but inherited: 'It is a partnership not only between those who are living, but between those who are living, those who are dead, and those who are to be born.' Burke compared this arrangement to a family, and if the constitution is the father of the nation, and the king is the living embodiment of that constitution, then it would have made more sense if the French had tried (metaphorically speaking) to mend and heal their father than to slice off his head.[22] This is important: Burke defined tradition by the principles of 'conservation' – i.e. trying to keep as much of society the same as possible – and 'transition' – i.e. passing on what one has inherited.[23] But if we are to see the constitution as a natural, almost biological thing, we must accept the possibility of decay and so, precisely for the sake of keeping that tradition alive, it must occasionally be updated and improved, much as giving one's father a heart by-pass fixes him without changing who he is.

Some scholars have identified a divergence between Burke and de Maistre and between British and continental schools of conservatism. Burke was happy to compromise with modernity to keep the best of the old order alive; de Maistre's prose was disturbingly violent and his faith in human nature microscopic.[24] 'The nation owes more to the sovereign than the sovereign to the nation,' he said, and the moment a king is compelled to justify his authority, the spell is broken and his authority is lost. De Maistre extended the same principle of infallibility to the Pope, so it's easy to see why he was later written off as a kinky Catholic proto-fascist.[25] But I think it's significant that the example he chose to use of why a pope deserves unquestionable authority was the Church's condemnation of slavery – only a supreme spiritual power, he said, could force human beings to do the right thing against their economic self-interest – and even as de Maistre ridiculed reason, he frequently deployed reason to make his point (never have so many books been written to argue that writing books is a waste of time).[26] Burke and de Maistre had to justify things that previously had never required justification. Both used a novel version of the scientific method to do it. The Enlightenment put great store by proving things with empirical evidence, yet when it came to building a new society, the revolutionaries paid little attention to practical experience, to the very trial and error principles one finds in the laboratory. Burke and de Maistre saw the past as a place of experiment and learning, and regarded history as a superior compass to intellectual abstraction. De Maistre, needless to say, distrusted universities. Too many scientists, he said.[27]

If conservatives are 'borne back ceaselessly into the past', it's because they are convinced their ancestors were on to something, and that we'll miss it when it's gone, and surveying the nineteenth century one might well conclude that the promise of liberty was indeed a con, that it meant the freedom for the rich to get rich and the poor to slave away in factories or on plantations. The psychological reaction to industrialization and revolution, wrote Nordau, was a mix of nervous breakdown and nostalgia. The desperate fear that what was lost couldn't be recovered, that humanity was essentially doomed, was reflected in Matthew Arnold's famous poem 'Dover Beach' (1867), in which he imagined the 'sea of faith' going out like the tide:

now I only hear/ Its melancholy, long, withdrawing roar,/ Retreating, to the breath/ Of the night-wind, down the vast edges drear/ And naked shingles of the world.

Arnold played up to that conservative self-image of being 'beautiful losers', morally right but outgunned by the times.[28] Yet, as the American historian Russell Kirk observed, this wasn't actually true. Faced with a choice between Burke or de Maistre, many conservative movements of the nineteenth century chose evolution over resistance: they 'knew that change ... is natural, inevitable and beneficial', wrote Kirk. Presumably, God either wants it or permits it, hence 'the statesman should not struggle vainly to dam the whole stream of alternation, because then he would be opposing Providence; instead, his duty is to reconcile innovation and prescriptive truth, to lead the waters of novelty into the canals of custom.'[29]

Successful conservative parties adopted elements of social reform because they recognized that they had to iron out the iniquities of empire and industrialization if they were going to stay in power. They occasionally pursued reforms far more efficiently than did radical politicians who, by pushing for too much too soon, discredited themselves and their agenda. This way, many conservatives, though defenders of the inherited order, internalized Enlightenment ideas and became some of their most effective administrators, helping to spread them to the four corners of the Earth – even to East Asia.

II

Trade between Japan and the West developed slowly in the few years following President Fillmore's ultimatum; samurai protested with a wave of terrorist atrocities against Europeans and any Japanese who welcomed them. The shogunate tried to buy time, a tragic miscalculation because the Europeans lost patience and enforced a number of 'unequal treaties' on the nation that piled on the humiliation. Finally the hotheads acknowledged that the only way to beat the West was to imitate it.

When Emperor Meiji ascended to the throne in 1867, aged 15, nobles conspired with his grandfather to seize control of the imperial palace and overthrow the shogunate the following year. It was not a 'revolution'; it was called the Meiji 'restoration', and the framing was important. In principle, the Japanese elite did not create a new order. They restored the ancient powers of the emperor that had been stolen by the shogunate, apparently moving in the opposite direction of Europe, reaffirming the authority of an emperor who was believed to be descended from the sun itself. But the sun is visible; the emperor was not. For 265 years, the imperial family had lived in seclusion at the imperial palace in Kyoto and the emperors had left the palace a grand total of three times. Meiji, on the other hand, was relocated to Edo, Tokyo today, and in the course of his 45-year rule encouraged to take 102 trips around his country.[30] The ruler was simultaneously re-elevated and popularized, which jarred with the traditional Japanese impression of the emperor as unknowable and unseen. 'On one such tour in the 1870s,' writes Christopher Harding, 'residents of Kamakura and Enoshima simply did not believe they were looking at the real emperor.' Crowds could be light; mothers breastfed their babies. Officials argued that the response to a visit from the sun god was so underwhelming that it wasn't worth sweeping the roads for. Children, on the other hand, were now being sent to school at the behest of the new regime and so could be educated in the songs and chants of imperial worship. They were easily dragooned into lining the streets, belting out a new national anthem that had been composed by a British bandmaster.[31]

Behind the fantasy of restoration was the reality of rapid modernization. Society was industrialized; Tokyo gained gas street lighting. Everybody wanted a rabbit for Christmas, imported from Europe and selling for as much as $1,000 per bunny.[32] There were now courts with appointed judges; a new tax system; an ambitious national education programme; exams for the civil service; new military technology and conscription. The constitution of 1889 instituted a parliament: a lower chamber elected by a limited franchise and the upper appointed by the emperor. If it sounds familiar, that's because the details were based on Germany and the process of writing it compared to America. As Japanese cities were flooded with Western clothes, theatre, ballroom dancing and novels, the elite travelled the world looking for examples to follow – and they stole the best. They took their postal service from Britain and copied its navy; their army took inspiration from Germany. The school system was first modelled on France, then America, then Germany. According to Jared Diamond: 'The criminal code was initially reformed on a French model, then changed to a German model; the commercial law code used a German model; and the civil law code used French, British and indigenous Japanese concepts before ending up as German-inspired.' They were looking for a template that worked and would be internationally respected, in the hope that the West would recognize an equal and revise its treaties. Torture was banned and the death penalty limited, because that's what Europe had done.[33]

The Meiji transformation was applauded by the rest of the world. It was also misunderstood, the classic imperialist mistake of confusing imitation with flattery. Some of what might appear to be novel was built on foundations that already existed – parts of Japanese society were already highly literate, for example – and the Japanese sought to avoid the mistakes they found in Europe, particularly the slums and pollution that blighted London.[34] The goal, says Diamond, was not to become a Western country but to adapt Western features to Japanese conditions, retaining as much that was traditional as possible.[35] In some cases there was revival. Traditional theatre, art and poetry were encouraged; the emperor himself was said to have composed 90,000 haiku in his lifetime, and even Japanese peasants could now compete in national poetry competitions hosted by newspapers.[36] In other regards, tradition was recalibrated and politicized, to serve the needs of the state. For hundreds of years Buddhism and Shinto had mixed together; now Shinto shrines were nationalized and absorbed more fully into the cult of the emperor. The consequence for Buddhists, suddenly outsiders in a society to which they had hitherto felt integral, was monstrous: temples and monasteries were closed or looted. Monks and nuns were forced out of religion, into the lowly realms of marriage and meat-eating.[37]

As for conversion to Christianity, that remained controversial. When a group of converts marched up a mountain to dedicate themselves to Jesus in 1875, writes Harding, the mother of one threatened to kill herself and the father of another threatened to behead his son. But the group also dedicated itself to the service of Japan. Christians saw themselves both as converts to a new religion and reverts to ancient Japanese values of discipline and self-sacrifice.

Christians played an essential part, says Harding, in the emergence of the 'bushido' code, the so-called way of the warrior that was presented – partly for foreign consumption – as an authentic expression of the soul of Japan, yet was influenced by American missionaries and the British public school (even St Paul was re-imagined as a Christian samurai).[38] Robert Baden-Powell, the founder of the Scouting movement, was certainly impressed. In 1904, he wrote: '[Britain] is a small country surrounded by nations far stronger in arms who may at any time attempt to crush us. The question is, how can we prevent them?' The answer, he said, was found in Asia: 'How do the Japs get their patriotism? By the upper classes learning, as boys, the chivalry of their forefathers, the Samurai (knights of Japan), and as they grow up putting it into practice and teaching it also to their middle and working classes. And they begin as children.' England and Japan studied each other through a glass darkly, spotting signs of common sense that might actually have been a reflection of themselves. The most popular English-language text in Japanese high schools was *Tom Brown's Schooldays*; its 1912 translation ran to ten editions.[39] And when Inazo Nitobe, a Christian convert, published *Bushido: The Soul of Japan* in English in 1900, he explained the Japanese concept of honour to his audience by comparing it to *Tom Brown*. The samurai was a gentleman.[40]

It is remarkable just how much of what is regarded by outsiders as ancient in Japanese culture, and thus evidence of a country that has successfully developed in isolation from the world, was imported or cobbled together in the modern era: regional identities, religious rituals, the intensely private sphere of the closed-off home, the supposedly warm relationship between workers and bosses, even the katsu curry which, legend has it, was in fact a British dish. The contemporary rules of sumo wrestling were laid down in the early twentieth century.[41] Many of the rituals of imperial court life are innovations, too. When the constitution was promulgated in 1889, the emperor first prayed to the goddess of the sun, the mother of his dynasty, and in his speech he described his ascent 'to the throne of a lineal succession unbroken for ages eternal'. He then took off his ancient robes, put on a modern military uniform, unmistakably European (see Figure 6), and presented the constitution as a gift

FIGURE 6   A portrait of Emperor Meiji (1852–1912).

to the prime minister. The beginnings of democracy were thus choreographed not as a revolution from below, in the style of France, but a donation from above, in the style of Great Britain.[42]

III

Something very similar was taking place in Britain, where the elite, keen to hold its position, made strategic concessions to social and economic change all the while promoting a comfortably archaic vision of what it meant to be British. Clever conservatives – artists and statesmen – didn't just uphold tradition, they packaged and sold it. And the public bought it.

Take royalty. As the historian David Cannadine observed, at the beginning of the nineteenth century royal events could be a relatively private affair because the monarch was seen as the head of a family and of a class rather than the entire nation. Coronations might be chaotic, almost cheap: 'the certainty of power and the assured confidence of success meant there was no need to show off.' In case things ran on too long, peers brought their own sandwiches, hidden in their hats. Some monarchs were clearly loved; others were openly loathed. Upon the death of George IV, who had spent his own coronation making eyes at his mistress, *The Times* wrote: 'there never was an individual less regretted by his fellow creatures than this deceased king. What eye has wept for him?'

Monarchs were controversial because they mattered and they still wielded significant power. As the nineteenth century wore on, however, Britain became more democratic and its politics ridden with class conflict. The British monarchy, like Japan's, had to perform a high-wire act, moving forwards while looking backwards, balancing modernity – and the wealth and innovation it brought – with a hankering for a more reassuring past. The solution was not to play down the magic of the British monarchy but to put it on display. Just as the rest of the population was giving things up, the royalty embraced them, including wigs, gold brocade and grand carriages. Edward VII revived the state opening of parliament as a full-dress ceremonial occasion and read his speech from the throne, something Queen Victoria had refused to do for 40 years. When he died, in 1910, he was laid in state at Westminster, offering 250,000 mourners the chance to venerate his person. The newfound pomp, argued Cannadine, was 'not so much the reopening of the theatre of power as the premiere of the cavalcade of impotence'. The monarchy seemed to become more imperial just as Britain's empire was in danger, and more obsessed with the minutiae of pageantry just as its constitutional role was being reduced to puppetry. In 1913, a radical observed: 'the king does what the people want.' If the people wanted socialism then 'he will be a socialist king'. But *did* they want that? The monarchy calculated that the working class enjoyed ritual, whereas it was the middle class that expected the royals to behave as if they lived in a semi-detached house in Guildford – and in that surprising discovery of the sympathy between aristocrat and worker lay the recipe for a powerful political and cultural alliance.[43]

The nineteenth century was an age of radicalism, but also of Romanticism, of escape into the chivalric novels of Sir Walter Scott, the Gothic Revival architecture of Augustus Pugin or the schools of painting that emphasized nature and psychology, folklore and mysticism – anything that rebelled against drab utilitarianism or the hunt for profit.[44] The industrial revolution had 'divided' man, said the Romantics; it separated him from his birthplace and his family and turned him into an economic unit, an extension of the machine. Now we must restore the 'whole man', reuniting the broken parts.[45] In 1891, Pope Leo XIII issued his encyclical *Rerum Novarum* that tried to carve a path between socialism and capitalism, reconciling ancient Catholic teaching with the new social conditions. In England, the Anglican Oxford Movement, returning to the Early Church for inspiration, stressed the importance of the incarnation of God as man: if God walked among us, if the Church is divine, then they reasoned that this should be reflected in a style of worship that was reverential, beautiful and dripping with incense. Just as St Thomas stuck his finger in Christ's wound to prove for himself that he was real, so many human beings crave a tangible relationship to the divine – to hear it, to smell it. The emerging High Church tradition was medieval in aesthetic, a throwback to the pre-Reformation Church, an attempt to prove that Anglicanism was not the product of a rupture but a development of what came before.

Often despised by their bishops, the movement's priests took up placements where no other clergy would go, including the slums.[46] The line between radicalism, tradition and eccentricity in nineteenth-century Britain wore thin; the country could rival Russia for its holy fools. The Harvest Festival, the annual blessing of agricultural produce, was invented by the Reverend Robert Hawker, vicar of Morwenstow in Cornwall, as a way of persuading the locals, whom he regarded as pagans, to go to church. A biographer describes him as 'a profoundly weird individual' who pursued a side vocation as a mermaid. Night after night, Hawker would sit on a rock in the harbour wearing nothing but a seaweed wig and an oilskin wrapped around his legs, singing a lament. What made him cease this activity is uncertain – a likely story is that a farmer threatened him with a gun if he didn't shut up – but one evening he substituted his usual melody with a rousing rendition of 'God Save the King', 'plopped into the water and swam back home'.[47]

It can be hard to reconcile this folkloric spirit with the century that saw the invention of the steam engine or the expansion of the right to vote, but it all found coherence in the One Nation conservatism of Tory prime minister Benjamin Disraeli. Today, One Nation politics is misconstrued; it has come to mean a conservative who is socially and economically liberal (odd, because it's the opposite) or a conservative who tries to unite the country (which, beyond World Cup finals and royal marriages, is impossible). Disraeli in fact saw Britain as two nations, 'between whom there is no intercourse and no sympathy ... who are formed by a different breeding, are fed by a different food, are ordered by different manners, and are not governed by the same laws'. In short, the rich and the poor – and Disraeli's answer to this near-revolutionary situation was to take the side of the poor by reviving aristocratic government.

He had a curious story to tell. Once upon a time, he said, medieval England was a happy patchwork of classes, bound together by a web of rights and responsibilities that kept the peace and preserved the people's welfare. Then came the Reformation. The Church lost its special place, the poor lost their education and land was given over to the nobles, who used their money and power to bully the crown and put rulers on the throne whom they tried, with mixed success, to control. By the mid-nineteenth century, said Disraeli, England was under the yoke of the bourgeoisie: commercial, avaricious, with no respect for the precious ancient order. Although One Nation conservatism sought to put national community before class conflict, in practice it pitched the worker and the aristocracy against the liberal middle-class: Disraeli won an election victory on this programme, in 1874, and stabilized British society by allying privilege to social reform, including workers' rights, cleaner living conditions, better schools and an expanded franchise. He wasn't a socialist, said his supporters; he was reviving chivalric values that had been lost.[48]

As life improved and incomes rose, consumerism flourished. Consumerism, with its cheapness and novelty, can be the enemy of tradition; it can also strengthen tradition by allowing the masses to buy into it. The rich could build a Gothic folly or restore a crumbling pile – Rudyard Kipling purchased a Jacobean house in Sussex and maintained its authenticity by refusing to own a telephone – and the middle class could always cultivate a garden, as a way of reconnecting with the land.[49] In 1822, George IV, who was not incapable of charm, visited Scotland in a blaze of Highland dress – tethering Scottish identity to the crown and giving a shot in the arm to the tartan industry (the kilt in this instance was far too short, cut above the knees. Rather than risk his modesty, George wore a pair of pink tights.).[50]

Consumerism also gave the working class a stake in tradition that hitherto was beyond their reach.[51] Take tea, which today is core to the identity of both the British and the Japanese. Tea only really took off in England in the mid-eighteenth century; it had been around much longer in Japan and was woven into the country's religious and social ethics. The Japanese tea ceremony, divided into schools of practice and overseen by expert tea masters, was ritualized and aesthetically pure – the very definition of good taste, and, as such, it was monopolized by priests and nobles. Tea was masculine. Ceremonies occurred during war talks; cutlery was handed out as prizes for victory in battle. Because of this close association with Japan's feudal past, the ceremony briefly fell out of fashion at the beginning of the Meiji era, and the government denounced it as an example of everything they were trying to put behind them. As the popular mood swung against the excesses of modernization, however, a petition was drawn up by one of the grand masters of the ceremony to recognize the role of tea in the moral life of the nation. Not only was the tea ceremony added to the curriculum in schools but, in a radical innovation, it was now taught to women. The result: the tea ceremony came roaring back to life in a new form. Rather than an expression of social privilege, it was practised by all; rather than being used to display one's status in public, tea ceremonies were conducted within the home. And by the twentieth century, what had been a male preserve was now associated with women.[52]

The factory owners of England were reluctant to permit workers time off to take tea and the English aristocracy were anxious about the lower orders stealing their rituals, but over time it became embedded as a workplace right, and, by taking tea at home, the working man or woman became a king or queen of their own domain. The debate over the best way to serve it still reinforces boundaries of identity. Do you put the milk in first or last? Sugar or none? Some had high tea, which meant sitting at the table, consuming it with a meal; others had low tea at a low table, typically in a higher-class home. At the beginning of the nineteenth century, it was common to sip from the saucer as well as the cup – by the end of the decade it was verboten. Legend has it that in the 1840s, the Duchess of Bedford, complaining of a 'sinking feeling' between lunch and dinner, asked for tea and a snack to be brought to her boudoir – and invented afternoon tea.[53] Whatever the truth, this new edition to the daily routine offered women of all classes a strictly female time and space in which they could be themselves, shielded from the attentions of men and temptations of alcohol, although opium remained quite legal and some housewives put it in their cups.* This did not happen, one hopes, when Queen Victoria invited the wives and children of officers to take tea with her at Windsor Castle. Her Majesty had a half-Gothic, half-Japanese tea house constructed in her garden in 1869, at the height of an English craze for all things Asian, and middle-class consumers could decorate their kitchens with Japanese teaware.[54] Tradition sailed the sea routes of trade, in both directions.

IV

Nineteenth-century Britain and Japan were nurseries of conservative innovation because they were changing so fast; as one ancient set

---

* 'For most of the nineteenth century,' writes Matthew Sweet, 'there was less concern about the perils of taking cocaine than there was about the negative side-effects of drinking green tea.' Matthew Sweet, *Inventing the Victorians* (London: Faber & Faber, 2002), pp. 100–1.

of identities was eroded – the local and the agricultural – invented traditions helped people to integrate into national identities that happened to suit the interests of the ruling classes. The roots of tradition were lifted from the soil of the village or the sacred space of the church and replanted in the home, where the family became the guardians of rituals and the ethic they imparted. In Japan and Britain, pictures of the royal family appeared in living rooms, an act of social deference, no doubt, but with a hint of social mobility, or at least the meeting of worlds. The portraits of royal families in Figures 7 and 8 are, once again, remarkably similar in appearance, and the Japanese emperor was not just imitating European fashion but also political sensibility. To sell themselves to their subjects, royals on both sides of the world dressed down; at the same time, the viewer might be inspired to dress up, to imitate their betters. Wealth and social standing remained out of reach perhaps, but taste and courtly manners were not.

FIGURE 7 The Meiji Emperor of Japan, standing centre, with his imperial family, May 1900. After Torajiro Kasai.

FIGURE 8 Queen Victoria surrounded by members of the royal family at Osborne House on the Isle of Wight.

The historian Eric Hobsbawm, a perceptive Marxist, would have found this culture of imitation unhealthy. Genuine, authentic traditions didn't need to be constructed or promoted, he argued, because they'd never gone away; they endure because they work, whereas these 'invented traditions' were cynical experiments bound to fail because 'one can never develop or even preserve a living past'.[55]

Roger Scruton disagreed. In *The Meaning of Conservatism* he argued that traditions which are dismissed as recent inventions, such as the revival of Gothic architecture or Disraeli's One Nation politics, took off because they built on something that was already there. And if there appeared to be adaptation, even innovation, this was entirely in keeping with how tradition has historically developed: 'each contributor built on previous achievements, discovering problems and solving them through the steady expansion of the common syntax ... To belong to a tradition is also to make that tradition', in other words it is to be part of an ongoing creative process, and 'it is only in practice that the sum of our traditions can be understood'.

When a community reconstructs tradition, said Scruton, maybe it is doing a little inventing, but 'in all attempts to restore, recreate and assimilate tradition, the feature of continuity remains'.

Scruton is right, but Hobsbawm raises some important objections. He sympathized with the longing that working people felt for community and continuity, but was understandably anxious that invented tradition could be manipulated by the powerful to blind the poor to their real class interests. There is a risk that tradition replaces the psychological trauma of modernization with nostalgia, which produces its own painful contortions and eruptions.

Yes, Britain and Japan avoided the excesses of the century of revolutions that Nordau believed drove the French insane. Japan did modernize with remarkable efficiency, although the process was frequently contested. But the by-products were narcissism, racism and flights of imperial fantasy. The point of the Meiji experiment had been to catch up with the West and overtake it; logic dictated that if it required an overseas empire to make Britain or France strong, then Japan should have one, too. The population had already been trained to see Japan as racially superior and the emperor as a divine being worth dying for; the children had already been brainwashed to chant the national anthem as he rode past in his fairy-tale carriage. 'In the early twentieth century,' writes Andrew Cobbing, 'the power of ritual to reinvent and convey emotive imagery was also used as a political tool in mobilizing support for colonial expansion and war.' Even tea served this purpose. It was used to define who the Japanese were and what they were fighting for, and Cobbing makes an excellent point that the very way in which a tradition is taught or handed down lends itself to indoctrination. The appearance of authenticity – that this is the way it has always been done and any deviation would break the sacred code – makes it much easier to transmit ideas without being challenged or confronted with critical thinking.[56]

As Japan began annexing slabs of territory in East Asia, a relatively new regime was able to convince much of its population that the slaughter and domination of foreigners was something integral to Japanese history, that we do what we do because we have always done it. One might argue that what Japan was actually doing was imitating the Europeans, and a small group of anti-war dissenters argued that colonialism was in fact contrary to native tradition. 'Please bury my country for a while,' said the christian pacifist Yanaihara Tadao in 1937, 'so that her ideals might live.'[57] Nostalgia is a doubled-edged sword. It can endorse mindless patriotism; it can also encourage us to interrogate our history with intelligence and compassion, to draw a narrative from the past that serves a moral purpose – perhaps even a subversive one.

FIGURE 9 A famous, staged photo of a milkman doing his rounds after an air raid in Holborn, London, 1940.

4

The Uses of Nostalgia

When I was a boy, my grandmother would sigh and say, 'Christmas isn't what it used to be.' This wound me up. I liked Christmas and if I was enjoying it, what right did she have to tell me that it wasn't as good as I thought it was? Now I'm older, of course, I entirely see her point. I can't bear the adverts, the music, the self-indulgence or how the holiday has been culturally appropriated by supermarkets to sell rubbish – and it seems to me self-evident that it was far better in the 1980s.[*]

How do we explain this ongoing decline of the festival, that each generation thinks it has got steadily worse? The obvious answer is that nostalgia is just a matter of perspective, that things appeared better when we were young *because* we were young. The old, to us, was new. But it's more complicated than that. When I meditate upon the Christmas of my childhood, I remember things that were around before the year of my birth, in 1982; we watched repeats of

---

[*] Part of the problem with consumer Christmas is its calendar. It seems to start in mid-October and culminates on 25 December; everything after that is a hangover. This is unhealthy. We are invited to get excited by the approaching festival but the saturation of advertising and entertainment, not to speak of the booze and chocolate, poisons us against it – by the time we sit down to Christmas lunch, I'm usually sick of the whole thing. Christian Christmas is much better. The four-week build-up, called Advent, has its own carols and customs; Christmas proper lasts 12 days or even, depending on your tradition, as late as February. While the rest of society hurtles towards the 25th and then collapses in a heap of port and panettone, the well-paced Christian is only just getting started. Self-restraint and joy are much better regulated in the context of a centuries-old tradition.

The Morecambe and Wise Show (1970s) and listened to Bob Hope (1940s), and my father would read to me from *A Christmas Carol*, first published in 1843. Christmas, the way most of us imagine it, was repurposed by the Victorians, and the idea of a visitor who dropped presents off on Christmas Eve was popularized by the Americans.* I suspect that I'm not nostalgic for my own youth but childhood as it was experienced long before I was born, and perhaps my grandmother felt the same way. Gnawing away at each of us is a suspicion that the best days are not only behind us but that we never even knew them.

Pre-modern Christmas could be Bacchic: the agricultural year was over, now was the time for food, drink, cross-dressing and fist fights. 'Men dishonour Christ more in the twelve days of Christmas, than in all the twelve months besides,' said Hugh Latimer, chaplain to King Edward VI, in the mid-1500s. Middle-class Victorians sanitized the festival, domesticated it and added their own brand of nostalgia for Christian and pagan tradition. And how did Scrooge spend his famous Christmas? By touring his memories.[1] Nostalgia, writes Svetlana Boym, rode a 'memory boom' in the nineteenth century, a fascination for photographs and pressed flowers, the commemoration of 'lost youth' and 'lost chances' – but the word simultaneously acquired 'negative connotations', appearing, to the more rationally-minded, 'outmoded and unscientific'.[2]

That tension is still felt in the twenty-first century, where the key objections to nostalgia are, first, that the past was riddled with prejudice and is best left buried and, second, that to look back is melancholic and unhealthy. A concern with the health

---

* Christmas personified – Father Christmas – appears in a play by Ben Jonson in 1616, and belonged to the world of adults, feasting and dancing. The contemporary Santa Claus, a twist on St Nick who hands out presents, probably originates from the Dutch and was imported to America, to be revived by nineteenth-century writers Washington Irving and Clement Clark Moore, who shifted his date of operation to Christmas Eve. The cartoonist Thomas Nash depicted him as a large gnome in 1863; by the 1880s he was well established as a jolly chap in a red suit and hood. It's often claimed that Coca-Cola 'invented' Father Christmas in the 1930s and it's untrue. Ronald Hutton argues that retailers followed where poets, artists and the public had already gone, not the other way around. *The Stations of the Sun: A History of the Ritual Year in Britain* (Oxford: Oxford University Press, 2001), pp. 117–18.

effects of nostalgia dates back centuries. The first record we have of the word being used is in the seventeenth century, and is derived from the Greek 'nostos', meaning 'return home' and 'algia', meaning 'pain'. Already the distinction between mourning for a lost place or a lost time was blurred.[3] In 1688, a Swiss scholar called Johannes Hofer publicized the case of a man who had left Berne to study in Basel and, upon arrival, had developed a terrible fever. Local doctors ordered him home. The moment he began the return journey, his breathing improved, and the closer he got to Berne, the better he felt. By the time he arrived at his front door, he was magically cured. Hofer hypothesized that our bodies are kept going by 'living spirits' flowing through it, and that when a patient is obsessed with home, these spirits become distracted and stop doing their job.[4]

His understanding of the body was primitive but his instincts about psychology were right: when we are unhappy, we're more likely to fall sick. And the more people had to move, and the further they went, the more homesickness and nostalgia were reported. During the French Revolution, a doctor named Jourdan le Cointe argued that the best cure was pain and terror. He cited the experience of the Russian army when it crossed into Germany in 1733: Russian soldiers complained of homesickness, so the generals said that the first person to make a fuss about it would be buried alive. The problem disappeared.[5]

The colonization of the United States is popularly remembered as a story of hardy pioneers who never complained and never looked back; however, as historian Susan J. Matt demonstrates, this was far from true. One in six Puritans who made it to the New World went home again; early colonists noted that while scurvy affected everyone, it affected those suffering from nostalgia more than others.[6] When the War of Independence broke out, the American generals found it hard to motivate soldiers who had never travelled more than a few miles from their farms. 'The sudden change in their manner of living,' observed George Washington, 'brings on sickness in many; impatience in all.' During the American Civil War, doctors diagnosed more than 5,000 soldiers with nostalgia and claimed that 74 had died from it.[7] Just as disease could be resisted with vaccination, controlled exposure, so these emotions were nipped in the bud by sending children away to boarding school, to prepare them for a life of detachment from home. White Americans regarded suppressing one's nostalgia as a matter of national, even racial pride; the agony that Native Americans or Africans expressed at being uprooted was therefore cited as evidence of inferiority. In 1733, the *Boston Gazette* reported the distressing case of a slave at Salem who went to a cemetery, took out a knife 'and cut her Belly so much that her Guts came out'. Many slaves believed that after death they would be reincarnated in Africa. She wanted to go home.[8]

Life in America would not stand still. Migrants arrived by ship; they settled on farms. In the nineteenth century, the railroads took them to cities to work in factories. In the twentieth century, the car dropped them off in the suburbs. At each stage of this incessant journey, writes Matt, Americans mourned the places they had left behind, and, as the pace of travel accelerated, so their alienation took on a new dimension. Trains and cars meant that the one big journey they might have taken in previous centuries now became several, yo-yoing back and forth in the course of a single lifetime, and, while they were away, the place they left behind did not stand still; it, too, was subject to migration and change. The prodigal son returned home to discover that his friends were gone; the cinema was closed; the family stores had been replaced by faceless malls; and his town was full of migrants – like him! Matt concludes that for many Westerners, nostalgia became a mourning not only for a particular place, but that place as it had been at a particular time.[9]

This grief was an implicit rebuke of progress. In the modern world, time and space are supposed to have clear direction: things move forward, people spread outwards. As the nineteenth-century industrial society sped towards the future, regimented by the factory clock, so the great powers advanced across the world. Nostalgia, however, moved in the opposite direction: the mind traced backwards, the individual retreated inwards, to the familiar and the local. According to the spirit of the Enlightenment, the best person was unfettered by personal attachments and the best place was the city, where travellers could meet and share their experiences – hence the village, with its parochial and indecipherable customs, was assumed to be an especially unhealthy environment and anyone who yearned for it was mentally unwell. 'By pathologizing any tenacious attachment to the local,' says Matt, the Enlightenment ethic 'began the process of naturalizing wandering and placelessness as essential and celebrated human behaviour and traits, and marginalizing the homesick as unpolished provincials.'[10] This fitted neatly with Darwinian theories of natural selection. 'Nostalgia,' wrote an American anthropologist in 1906, 'is the first and most effective aid to the natural selection of desirable immigrants. It is only the immigrants who are least capable of assimilation that develop the worst symptoms of home-sickness … The hopeless cases are eliminated – by death, suicide, insanity, or by the less heroic method of returning to their native country.'[11] The American ideal of rugged individualism comes naturally to some, of course, but it was also manufactured and prescribed – and it had to be. Capitalism required workers who were willing to move and never look back, as well as consumers who wouldn't cling to things but would throw out the old and buy plenty of new (the virtue of thrift is now completely forgotten).

Yet nostalgia endures and remains politically salient in the twenty-first century. This is because it is natural and it is universal. It must be interrogated honestly for errors, but the ongoing campaign against it overlooks that warm memory, even of war, can help us make sense of what we've been through, who we are, who we want to be. It helps us carry our identity with us, wherever we go.

I

Trumpism was an exercise in weaponized nostalgia: the best time to have lived, he told the *New York Times*, was America at the turn of the twentieth century and the years immediately after the Second World War, when the nation was powerful and self-confident.[12]

In 2011, I filed my first ever report for the *Daily Telegraph* on a speech Trump gave in Washington DC, a curtain raiser to the ideas he would run on five years later. He raged against China, claiming that under the guise of free trade it was stealing jobs from honest Americans, destroying their inheritance. The speech earned a mixed reception: some conservatives said that they were for free trade, not against it, and didn't cheaper goods make for happier consumers? It doesn't pay to dwell on the past. I advised the *Telegraph*'s readers not to write Trump off, however. He was onto something.

Before 2011 I had written two largely unread biographies of American political leaders: of Ted Kennedy, the left-wing Democrat, and Pat Buchanan, the right-wing Republican. Both men ran for president, both appealed to Cold War nostalgia. Kennedy tried to associate himself with his brother John, to the go-ahead spirit of the sixties; his TV ads referenced the moon landing. Buchanan said, quite openly, that he thought the 1950s were the best time to be alive, in large part because a man could keep a wife, kids, a house and a car on a single wage. Campaigning in New Hampshire in the winter of 1991, Buchanan visited a paper mill on the very day that most of its workers had been sacked. As he walked the line, shaking hands, a broken man looked him in the eye and whispered: 'Save our jobs.' Buchanan became a committed protectionist, arguing that a well-paid job for life wasn't just good for the pocketbook, it was essential for the preservation of everything he loved about America – particularly the self-reliance and dignity of the working class.[13] Since the 1990s, working-class Americans, rural communities and young adults have been afflicted by 'sharp rises in fatalities due to drugs, alcohol or suicides' – deaths of despair similar to those recorded by Max Simon Nordau a century before.[14]

The standard free-market answer to unemployment is that if you lose your job, that's bad luck; if you don't find a new one, that's on you. You've got to get on your bike and look for work, just like those hardy colonists who built America. The psychologist and social theorist Ashis Nandy describes the shaming of economic losers as a 'double-displacement', and it occurs in poor countries as well as the rich. According to Nandy, the 1990s and 2000s witnessed an extraordinary epidemic of suicide in India: around 250,000 people took their own lives. This happened not in a period of recession but of growth; not in the 'undeveloped or backwards regions ... but in places where the success story of Indian agriculture has been written.' Agriculture was 'industrialized' and 'corporatized', and tribal farmers, forced from their ancient lands were turned 'into floating populations of the disinherited and the disposable'. The loss of a job was the first displacement, the loss of cultural status was the second – and the tribal farmer was transformed from the backbone of their society to an embarrassing relic. According to Nandy, Indian psychiatrists found fault with the farmers who resorted to suicide.*

Economic change drives nostalgia; I learned this from my time as an activist in the Labour Party (I ran for parliament in 2005 and worked my socks off to win but the voters, damn them, would not meet me halfway). My comrades often spoke of a better age, before Margaret Thatcher unleashed the free market on Britain in the 1980s. Before that, they said, there was community. You could leave your door unlocked; people looked out for each other, and if they

---

* Ashis Nandy, *Regimes of Narcissism, Regimes of Despair* (New Delhi: Oxford University Press, 2013), pp. ix–xii. In a study of suicide rates among 196 First Nation tribes in British Columbia, Canadian psychologists Michael Chandler and Christopher Lalonde found that increased awareness of 'self-continuity' – self-government, successful legal claims to tribal lands or the presence of cultural centres – correlated with a lower level of suicide. 'Cultures offered a more "mythic" time-frame that could be relied on to lend a certain age to things. Even now, when cultures seemingly wink in and out of existence, they still appear to sometimes work in the service of self-continuity by holding our noses to a grindstone of social responsibilities and cultural promises during our own moments of developmental transition. At least this is possible when they are working well.' Jeremy Larson, 'At the End of White Male History', *Jacobite Magazine*, 18 March 2018. https://jacobitemag.com/2019/03/18/at-the-end-of-white-male-history/, last accessed 18 October 2020.

didn't have much, they still shared what they had. The astonishing thing is that I was most often told this by millennials who had no first-hand experience of the era they wanted to turn the clock back to. To develop Matt's thesis, human beings are nostalgic for the world as they once knew it – that's obvious – but the pace of change in the last few decades has been so fast, so alienating, that many people today are nostalgic for a time *they never even knew*, which helps explain their ignorance of its deficiencies. If we were to restore the social conditions of the 1970s, we'd have to swallow wildcat strikes and inflation, too – and, as for Buchanan, he could never give a satisfactory answer to the problem of segregation. How could the fifties have been better than today, let alone more Christian, when blacks and whites lived separately by law? My grandmother was a single parent in the 1950s. She raised my father in dire poverty; half the family wouldn't even recognize his existence. She wouldn't talk about it and he was very angry about it; Dad remembered Christmas as a time of cold, loneliness and shame. He preferred to talk about the war – endlessly – even though he was far too young to remember it. But I guess it makes sense that a man with such a difficult personal history might latch onto social history instead, to locate his own confusing narrative within the clarity of collective experience. Nostalgia helps us understand ourselves through others, and the results can be surprising – to the outsider, even discomforting.

In her book *Chernobyl Prayer*, Nobel Prize-winner Svetlana Alexievich interviewed men and women who had survived the worst nuclear disaster in history. Most of her subjects remembered it as an unfathomable nightmare, as you'd expect, but some of them also expressed pride in the ability of their country to endure suffering. A soldier involved in the Chernobyl operation told Alexievich:

Every year, on 26 April, we get together, those of us who were there ... We look back on those days. You were a soldier in that war, you were indispensable. All the bad stuff gets forgotten, and that is what stays. What lingers is the fact that they couldn't cope without you. You were essential. Our system, our military, operates pretty much superbly in an emergency. Out there you were finally free and needed. Freedom! At moments like that, the Russian people show how great they are. How special! We'll never be like the Dutch or Germans. And we'll never have good roads or groomed lawns. But we'll always have heroes![15]

It's an indictment of the Soviet Union that the soldier only felt free when restoring order amidst chaos, but note how nostalgia helps us make sense of an atrocity, how it made a pawn feel like an essential part of his nation's history, and how the moment defined, in his mind, what makes Russia Russian – and him a Russian, too.

This is not rational, but then a lot of what makes us tick isn't, which is why Enlightenment liberalism so often finds itself in conflict with human nature. Pete Buttigieg, a candidate for the Democratic presidential nomination in 2016 – and the embodiment of the Enlightenment, almost an encyclopaedia in human form – once said that when a citizen fights for their country 'you do it not because it's a country you live in, but because it's a country you believe in'.[16] In the liberal imagination, then, a nation is a political project, and you fight for it because you agree with it – but most of us just don't think that way. During the Second World War, the art historian Kenneth Clark, employed by the Ministry of Information, was often called upon to ponder 'what we are fighting for'. He found himself at a loss: abstractions like parliament or democracy had no emotional resonance.

But in my mind's eye I had a clear vision of a small English town – halfway between a town and a village … There it all was: the church, the three pubs, the inexplicable bend in the road, the house with the stone gate where the old lady lived. I used to think: 'That is what we are fighting for.'[17]

None of this would mean much to an Arab or an Argentine, but the English love it because we know it and it is ours, and if it is invaded or if it needs our help, we'll do what we can. Buttigieg, himself gay, went on to say that America had become a better place because it had legalized same-sex marriage, in other words, as it had progressed, so it had earned greater respect. But, again, for most of us, respect of country is presumed, just as we instinctively cherish our parents, our home and our memories because they are ours. Without them, we'd be nothing. When I was growing up, a phrase that was drummed into me was 'my country right or wrong, my mother drunk or sober' – the point being that my loyalty to these things was not contingent upon whether or not I approved of them, but the very fact of their existence. The soldier evacuating citizens from Chernobyl, soaked in radiation, had been betrayed by the Soviet state; he had good reasons not to believe in his country. That didn't matter. He loved it.

Note also the conscious selectivity of his memories: 'All the bad stuff gets forgotten, and that is what stays.' People are more than capable of figuring out what was wrong with the past, and by sorting out the good from the bad they can create a narrative of idealism, saying not only 'this is what we did' but 'this is why we did it'. Holding that idealism up to scrutiny is important; rejecting it out of hand can be rather cruel, especially if it's all someone's got. If you are destitute or bedridden, memory is all the more precious because it is free: no one can take it away from you. Yet there is a determination in the twenty-first-century West to deconstruct history, even to discredit it, with the implication that anyone who clings on to it is, at best, stupid, at worst, 'literally Hitler'.

In 2020, at the annual concert held on the Last Night of the Proms in London, the decision was taken to cut the lyrics from two patriotic songs that always appear on the repertoire, 'Land of Hope and Glory' and 'Rule, Britannia!'. To tell the truth, I can't recall when the Proms wasn't controversial: the annual 'is the Proms racist?' debate, held every September, is our cue to start shopping for the War on Christmas. But this censorship was irritatingly petty. The official excuse was that they could not be sung satisfactorily because of the coronavirus, yet other lyrics to other melodies were – the real objection, many suspected, was that these songs were shamelessly patriotic and associated with empire. To avoid singing anything that might offend people who probably never watch the Proms, the Proms insulted the millions who do. Deluged with complaints, the BBC reversed its position, restored the words and the concert went ahead without triggering a spontaneous resurrection of the Third Reich. In a concession to bad taste, the orchestra did perform a new atonal arrangement of 'Jerusalem' by Errollyn Wallen. It sounded like a bomb in a chicken coop.[18]

II

To borrow a horror movie cliché, the scariest thing about the deconstruction of our past is that the call has consistently come from inside the house. Venerable institutions have willingly slandered their own history, stripped out their principles and alienated their core supporters, the effort generally led by men and women who joined said institution with the perverse intention of changing it beyond recognition. Why anyone would become a priest, for example, who doesn't believe in God is completely beyond me – but they exist. As there are bishops who erect helter-skelters in cathedrals; headmasters who are against discipline; curators who can't stand art that looks like the thing it represents; and politicians who do the opposite of what they were elected for.* All is vanity.[19] Tradition rests upon the submission of ego; the wrecker takes over with the intention of remaking the tradition in their own image, and if the faithful hate them for it, that must prove they are doing something right. What they don't seem to understand is that the appeal of many institutions to most of us is that they broadly stay the same. For example, few people think about religion all the time,

---

* Critics will say I am confusing 'wrecking' with, say, 'alternative theories of education'. There have been genuine attempts, for example, to run schools without old-fashioned methods of discipline, such as Risinghill School in London or Summerhill School in Suffolk. Risinghill was closed after five years; Summerhill is, at the very least, controversial. It's indisputable that the trend away from personal and academic standards in England coincided with a decline in educational quality, and governments of both left and right have conceded as much by reintroducing school uniforms, the creation of a national curriculum, the involvement of faith groups etc.

so when they do go to church they seek the novelty of consistency – that it'll either be the same as it was when they were a child or, if they're unfamiliar with it, true to itself. When one Christmas they put on a coat and trudge through the snow to the village church only to find that the pews are gone, the organ is now a keyboard and the priest has replaced the Bible with readings from *The Rubáiyát of Omar Khayyám*, it's unlikely they'll return. The thing that was always supposed to just be there – familiar and reliable – has vanished. The wrecker doesn't mind. For some, it's the goal. They enjoy all the advantages of being in the institution while milking the moral superiority that comes from criticising it, and they fantasize about being the last man standing, the last one to look back upon an empty room and turn out the lights.

There is a confusion in the West between sophistication and wisdom, knowledge and insight, and I encounter it often. Some time ago, a flustered BBC producer rang me up to ask if I'd jump in a taxi and appear on her show to discuss whether or not Australia Day is offensive to Aboriginal Australians. I said no – but, I asked out of curiosity, why did you think of me? 'I'm not Australian and I've never met an Aboriginal person.'

'It's all history, isn't it?' she snapped. 'You're a historian, aren't you?'

Historians have been absorbed into the liberal cult of expertise. It is presumed that we know what we're talking about and can discuss with confidence anything that happened the day before yesterday. We play along because, odd for a profession concerned with dead things, we're desperate to seem relevant.

Why are universities disposed against tradition? The answer is cultural and political, of course: academia has been colonized by a liberal-left cohort that promotes its own and it is uncomfortable, given the groupthink, to express dissent. But economics plays its part, too. Take Britain, where, since the 1980s, higher education has become highly commercialized and universities now compete with each other for students and money. As of 2014, universities have to demonstrate that their research has 'impact', that their work has relevance beyond the university or that it's something the taxpayer might want to engage with.[20] The average historian is now overworked, underpaid and under excruciating pressure to be a teacher, a writer *and* a public intellectual, all of which encourages them to direct their research towards the political concerns of the day, to demonstrate why the Peace of Westphalia or the art of Klimt have relevance to Black Lives Matter. It also fosters a bias towards deconstruction – because so long as one is chipping away at the received narrative, one will always have something to say.

Historical research is a balance of micro- and macro-narratives. It can be compared to the fable of the blind men who lay their hands on an elephant and have to guess what it is. One feels the trunk and calls it a snake; another, feels a leg and calls it a tree. This is the micro-narrative, the study of the isolated and the specific; the old ideal was that having put all the evidence together, we could declare that it was in fact an elephant, which is the macro-narrative, the bigger story that makes sense of our lives. But the problem with macro-narratives is that once you know it's an elephant, the game is over. Some academics are opposed to reaching definitive conclusions for philosophical reasons, but in the modern era many simply feel they can't afford to do it. There's a better shot at career advancement in saying 'perhaps the elephant perceives itself to be a snake' or 'the elephant is a tree and a racist. Let's shoot it.' History has become a game of seeking 'new perspectives' and 'marginalized voices', 'interrogating' our 'problematic' narratives, which are invariably 'contested'. You'd imagine that in the contest to win taxpayer money, universities would focus on the things that interest the taxpayer, or that historical studies would at least have something nice to say about the society that bankrolls it – instead the history business has become, in many quarters, not only divorced from its consumers but critical of much of what they hold dear or regard as being beyond politics. Literature, history and science courses are decolonized; the hunt for prejudice has filtered down to schools and heritage bodies, even gardening and zoos. In June 2021, the assistant director of Cambridge's Museum of Zoology argued that Australian animals, including kangaroos and koalas, were the victims of a cruel legacy of 'subconscious colonial bias': calling them 'weird', as apparently we often do, is 'just another way of othering these animals ... [denigrating] them through hierarchical language.'[21]

In October 2020 the National Maritime Museum in London decided it was time to 'review' the heroic status of Lord Nelson as part of an effort to challenge Britain's 'barbaric history of race and colonialism', particularly those 'aspects of slavery relating to the Royal Navy'. Nelson's defenders accused the museum of casting an elephant as a jackal.[22] Yes he was a supporter of slavery, but he also helped beat Napoleon, a dictator, and the Royal Navy spilt a good deal of blood fighting the Atlantic slave trade. Decolonization strikes many as an attempt to delegitimize the present order by finding fault in the past, making it impossible to be proud of anything the West has done – exploiting our well-intended fears of thinking or saying the wrong thing, particularly on sensitive issues like race, to persuade us to do as the French did in the 1790s, tear everything up and start all over again. A series of arson attacks on Canadian churches in the summer of 2021, following the discovery of the graves of indigenous children taught in church-run schools, raised the stakes. Nothing it seems is beyond deconstruction. Not even the sacred. Prime Minister Justin Trudeau condemned the vandalism but called the anger behind it 'real and fully understandable', capturing the impotence of liberal leaders who are as critical of the past as the protestors are but also cling, almost cowardly, to old-fashioned concepts like the rule of law. Trudeau, a Catholic, offered a curiously utilitarian reason not to burn down a church: it would deprive people in need of 'healing' of somewhere to go.[23]

The brutal killing of a black man by police in Minnesota the previous summer triggered a wave of cultural destruction. In Bristol, England, the statue of a slave trader was dumped in the river. In Poole, the local council considered moving a statue of arch-imperialist Baden-Powell, at risk of a dunking, to a safe location, until locals got wind of it and turned out in their old Scout uniforms to defend him with a fanaticism normally reserved for a condemned tree. Baden-Powell not only stayed put, he was granted police protection.[24] Conservatives accused the vandals of declaring war on history, but this was unfair.

The vandals had done their research, deciphering precisely what their targets thought and what they had done; they treated them as real people, not artefacts. Defenders of the statues said, yes, these men were imperfect, but it is unjust to put the dead on trial; useless, even preposterous (when Winston Churchill's statue was labelled racist by protestors, conservatives wondered if they'd heard about the German fellow he beat?). The vandals replied that a debt was still owed to historic victims, that crimes have consequences and must be accounted for. This philosophy, far from being anti-history, approaches the past seriously and morally, as a thing of consequence.

But should we judge a statue on one crime or the full record? George Washington, who was toppled by a mob in Portland, Oregon, owned slaves, unquestionably – but he is principally remembered for leading America to independence. Does one moral failing eclipse all else? Perhaps it should; it was a terrible one. But what do we think about contemporaries of Washington who didn't own slaves yet opposed abolishing slavery, or supported abolition but thought African-Americans were an inferior race, or who simply sat out the debate? Those who want to preserve historic memorials ask: 'where do we stop?' We could reasonably ask, 'where does one begin?' By the standards of today, it's very hard to find an eighteenth-/ nineteenth-century white voice that wasn't to some extent racist, including many of those who pushed for black civil rights – even Lincoln was defaced with red paint in Washington state – and if we tore down every 'problematic' statue, the nuance of history would be lost. It would be told not as a series of steps, forward and back, but in leaps and bounds, straight from oppression to liberation, from Genghis Khan to Nelson Mandela, with no moral ambiguity in between, or compromise, or growth. Remove every statue of America's Founding Fathers, fine; replace them all with statues of Malcolm X, okay. But that's not history, it's not even necessarily 'relevant' to the local audience. A statue of Fidel Castro dropped on a hillside in the Lake District, surrounded by disinterested sheep, would be as meaningless as unveiling a statue of Beatrix Potter in downtown Havana.

Vandals sometimes make a similar mistake to fundamentalists: they read historical symbols literally, without appreciation of how meaning changes over time. This is where the editing quality of nostalgia plays its part. If the defenders of Baden-Powell's statue fondly remembered him exactly as he was, with all his maddest and most unpleasant opinions, that would indeed be unhealthy. But they don't. They admire him for what he stands for today, namely Scouting, and its relevance to their lives. An attack upon Baden-Powell was interpreted as an attack upon their own values and memories, of teamwork and loyalty and cooking marshmallows at camp. Another example, one that I walk past several times a week in London, is the statue of Oliver Cromwell that stands outside the Houses of Parliament, like a bouncer guarding a nightclub. When MPs first debated erecting Cromwell, in 1895, he was hugely controversial. Conservatives regarded him as a regicide; Irish MPs remembered his brutal suppression of Ireland. The parliamentary motion to provide funds was defeated and the statue was only completed, in 1899, after an anonymous donor stepped in to save it.[25]

But as the decades passed, as Ireland gained its independence and British democracy had to be defended against aggressors, so Cromwell's reputation gradually evolved. By the 1960s he was widely seen as an egalitarian figure, even as the pre-eminent defender of parliamentary sovereignty, an impression reinforced, no doubt, by the location of his statue. Cromwell also became, quite simply, part of the landscape. Most tourists don't notice him; I'm sure nine out of ten Britons couldn't name him. The irony of the anti-statue movement is that most of its targets were anonymous until they were torn down, and the real objection of those who wanted to save them was probably not political but environmental. They don't like change. Even change to something they hadn't noticed before. It's amazing how possessive we can become of things we never knew we had when someone tries to take them away.

Compromise is possible. Controversial statues can be put in a museum or even, as in several East European countries, collected together and relocated to an outside park, where thousands of Lenins and Stalins now gather moss, the terrifying re-contextualized as kitsch. If all else fails, vandalize but do it creatively. In 1882, the factory owner Theodore H. Bryant commissioned a statue of the Liberal prime minister William Gladstone to stand in London's East End, a hand outstretched, beckoning in the future. It was meant to be a symbol of Enlightenment and progress, but a rumour spread that Bryant had paid for it by docking a shilling from the wages of the women who worked in his match factory. The women turned up to the unveiling armed with stones and pelted the statue. According to local legend, the workers cut their arms and let the blood run onto Bryant's hand. To this day, the statue's hand is repeatedly daubed with red paint – without official sanction and by whom, no one knows. It's a tribute to the extraordinary power of class consciousness, of how an event can be so unjust, and the people so angry about it, that the fury is tended for centuries like a flame of remembrance.[26]

III

'Those who do not learn from the mistakes of history,' goes the saying, 'are doomed to repeat them.' Given the low level of education in the West, we must be doomed. A poll of British youngsters found that 28 per cent of them had never heard of Stalin, half had never heard of Lenin and 70 per cent of Mao. With that level of ignorance, there's not only a risk that history will repeat itself but that no one will be sufficiently informed to notice.[27]

The 'mistakes of history' cliché, credited to Burke but originating from George Santayana, presents the past as a catalogue of errors – yet it contains models of good behaviour as well as bad. In Britain this is reflected in our contrasting attitudes towards the First and Second World Wars. The First was a bad war: 'lions led by donkeys'; Britain won it, but only just, and many of us think we should have stayed out. The Second, was a good war: a 'people's war' that we fought because we had to and because our side was the right side. Historians tear their hair out over these simplifications and contradictions, not least the paradox that the First war teaches us not to use military force too early whereas the Second warns us not to leave it too late.

Nostalgia is concerned less with facts than the broader truth they are interpreted to mean, and as it edits out nuance, so it transforms memory into a moral compass: 'this was the right thing to do last time, so let's do it again.' The Second World War has the twin advantages of ideological clarity – Hitler was unquestionably evil – and tangibility; the war is memorialized in song, book, photograph and, crucially, film, some of it now colourized, which brings it closer to us than any conflict before. For Britons growing up post-1945, the war is inescapable; we are often accused of being obsessed with it. And why wouldn't we be? It's the best thing we ever did, and I'm clearly not alone in thinking that because the war is deployed constantly in politics to make the case for, again, quite contrary positions. During the EU referendum campaign, Leavers said Brexit was the logical continuation of Britain standing alone.[28] Remainers said the EU guaranteed the very peace and justice we had fought for.[29]

War nostalgia returned during the coronavirus pandemic, when the lockdown was compared to the Blitz and health workers to soldiers, while the fight to roll out hospital beds was our generation's Dunkirk. In one TV bulletin, a journalist said the virus was 'determined to divide us', as if it had the mind of Joseph Goebbels. On one level, this nostalgia was deeply unhelpful because it led to people misreading the pandemic. We needed to learn to live with the disease, not imagine we could defeat it, and most of us were not called to be heroes, just to sit indoors and wait for the all-clear (I rediscovered jigsaw puzzles). The West hadn't endured a pandemic on this scale for decades, and, in order to understand it, we reached back to the closest thing it resembled and fell upon an inexact analogy.*

---

* An interesting question is why the West didn't talk about the Spanish flu of 1918–19 instead? As a pandemic, it was more relevant to the coronavirus than military combat – and it surpassed the death toll of the First World War. One explanation is the way it was reported at the time. Newspapers did cover the flu but they tended to present it as a logistical challenge, as a war on disease, rather than a human-interest story: there were relatively few published accounts of living with or recovering from the sickness. Photographic technology was also too limited to capture the tragedy, so that when the survivors died decades later, the memory was lost. The historian Guy Beiner, who has researched its legacy, argues the Spanish flu demonstrates that

Yet war nostalgia did promote duty and resilience as civic standards, useful qualities when asking citizens to make a sacrifice. One of the popular heroes of the pandemic was a 99-year-old veteran called Captain Tom Moore, who raised millions for the NHS by doing a sponsored walk up and down his garden. By chance, the virus took hold during the 75th anniversary of Victory in Europe, and people covered Facebook in photos of their relatives, observing that if Granddad and Grandma could endure bullets and bombs, then we could sit at home till the all-clear. Blitz spirit, stiff-upper lip, keep calm and carry on: British identity is wrapped up with an inherited ideal of unflappability crystalized in the old joke, a favourite of Ronald Reagan's, that when a cockney was dug out of the rubble of her bombed-out house, a fireman found a bottle of brandy nearby and offered her a drop. 'Are you round the twist?' she said. 'That's for emergencies!'[30] A few historians, spotting a myth to deconstruct – pay dirt! – pointed out that the Blitz had triggered despair and depression, that Churchill's government feared very much that the British couldn't take it. Why pretend the war generation was perfect and expect their descendants to imitate an impossible standard?[31] But, to repeat, people are not naïve about the past; they know full well that their ancestors must have panicked. The point is that they persevered. Had Captain Moore's generation been robots, enduring the war would have been almost quotidian; it's the victory over their own doubts and fears that made it so admirable and instructive. A frequent refrain during the coronavirus was 'if they could do it, so can you'. A question that haunts the British is 'are we the same nation that fought the

---

historical events do not remain lodged permanently in collective memory – with one fixed form or meaning. Rather, they ebb and flow, and change their significance depending upon the context in which they reoccur. We only think about past plagues and pandemics when we ourselves are going through them; the two world wars are drawn to our attention on an almost weekly basis by movies, TV and commemoration. Scott Hershberger, 'The 1918 Flu Faded in Our Collective Memory: We Might Forget the Coronavirus, Too', *Scientific American*, 2020. https://www.scientificamerican.com/article/the-1918-flu-faded-in-our-collective-memory-we-might-forget-the-coronavirus-too/, last accessed 25 November 2020.

war?' The answers during the pandemic were mixed. Yes, because we mostly obeyed the lockdown in a spirit of civic responsibility; no, because some of us didn't. Yes, because we were happy to give up our freedoms to serve a common goal; no, because we gave up many of the freedoms our relatives fought for. In a broadcast to the nation, Queen Elizabeth II drew upon her own memories of the war – exploiting the authority of great age – to reassure us that 'the attributes of self-discipline, of quiet good-humoured resolve and of fellow-feeling still characterise this country'.[32]

Whether she was right or not, the key point is that the nostalgic past – the past scrubbed up into an ideal – is a yardstick by which to judge the present. 'They died so that we might be free' is technically rubbish: universal suffrage in Britain had nothing to do with the Second World War – it's more closely linked to the First – and Britain was actually fighting to defend its empire. But the sentiment sacramentalizes democracy, baptizing it in blood. When a Briton behaves in a way that is deemed 'unBritish', they are judged not only to betray themselves and the country, but the millions who came before us and made Britain what it is. This sentiment completely fails the Enlightenment reasonableness test, of course: why care about the feelings of dead people? They're dead. They can't experience hurt or disappointment, and even if they did, what are they going to do about it? In an increasingly secular society, with declining belief in God or an afterlife, this lingering loyalty to the past is confounding, yet to dishonour the war dead remains a taboo, and to question the 'land of hope and glory' image of the Second World War makes most of us feel very uncomfortable. When foreigners complain about British war obsession, they must understand that we return to these events not only to feel good about ourselves but to feel good about having done good, that we use this conflict as a textbook on how to behave. The further we move from the war era and the more our country changes, as we become wanderers lost in a culture of permanent reinvention, the more precious memory becomes. It is free, yes; crucially, it is also portable.

IV

When I told my friends I was writing a book about tradition, several of them threw their arms up in the air and sang 'traditionnn!' They were referring to the musical *Fiddler on the Roof* whose main character, Tevye, is obsessed with the subject. A Jewish milkman in tsarist Russia, he has five daughters he loves very much, and his greatest desire is to see them married off to five good Jewish boys. Life in his village is precarious. The threat of an anti-Semitic pogrom hangs over them, and Tevye compares their situation to a fiddler balanced on the roof of a house: an impossible thing, but he keeps his balance thanks to the ancient rules of the Jewish people. 'We have traditions for everything,' Tevye tells the audience in the opening number, for what to eat, how to work, how to dress. 'We always wear a little prayer shawl,' he says. 'This shows our constant devotion to God. You may ask, how did this tradition get started. I'll tell you. I don't know.' But so long as you know what you're supposed to do, you'll keep your balance. Men toil; women run the house; sons study Hebrew; and daughters wait patiently for a husband, recommended to their father by the village matchmaker.[33]

That's how it's supposed to work, but *Fiddler on the Roof* is set in a world on the brink of great change and Tevye struggles to keep his footing. One daughter turns down an arranged marriage in favour of a childhood sweetheart; Tevye is offended, but he gives in. Another daughter wants to marry a revolutionary in Kiev; Tevye is furious, but at least they ask for his blessing, so he allows it. Finally, his third daughter says she wants to marry a non-Jew, a Russian Christian – and it's too much. 'If I bend that far,' says the milkman, 'I'll break.' His prejudice against non-Jews is irrational and the audience is minded to sympathize with the love-struck couple, but when, in the second act, the Russians turn on the Jewish population and drive them out of their village, his conservatism is contextualized. If the Jews give too much of themselves away, will there be anything left?

Fiddler on the Roof explores the ambiguities of cultural conservatism. Tevye is sympathetic and intelligent, but he routinely misquotes scripture to justify what he wants and he argues with God when he doesn't get it ('I know we are the chosen people,' he shouts at the sky, 'but once in a while, can't you choose someone else?') The institution of arranged marriage is presented as unfair and inefficient, and the matchmaker is motivated less by altruism than her finder's fee. Nevertheless, when Tevye realizes that custom stands in the way of his daughters' happiness, he finds solutions that are rooted in tradition. When his second daughter announces that she's marrying the revolutionary – like it or lump it – Tevye reaches into the Bible for a precedent. They met without a matchmaker, he reasons, but who was the matchmaker to Adam and Eve in the Garden of Eden? Perhaps it is God, thinks Tevye, who has brought this couple together, and maybe their union is an innovation; but then again 'our old ways were once new, weren't they?'. To save his future, Tevye looks even further back into the past, digging beneath the layers of custom applied over time, to get to the very root of what the creators of *Fiddler on the Roof* believe marriage is about: love.

As the Jews load up their carts to leave the village, Tevye makes a peace, of sorts, with his third daughter; at this time of misery, he cannot reject his own flesh and blood. The Tevyes will go West, to America, the promised land – and as they set off, they are trailed by the fiddler playing his tune. Balance is maintained. They leave the village, but they take their traditions with them, and that way they remain true to themselves – as Jewish in America as they were in Russia, never completely lost because when you carry your home with you, it is never far to hand.

Part Two

FIGURE 10 Actors Craig Cowdroy, (*left*) and Richard Hollick, (*right*), recreate a scene from Dracula ahead of a light display illuminating Whitby Abbey on 24 October 2018.

5

Hurrah for the Old

I have taken a holiday to the Yorkshire Moors, a break from the book. As I write this, a notepad on my knee, I am looking at Whitby Abbey, or what remains of it: its broken walls rise from the grass like the freshly revealed bones of a dinosaur. The Abbey was suppressed in 1539, during the English Reformation, and some of its buildings were torn down to repurpose the materials; the rest crumbled with neglect. Today, school children play among the skeleton of the Abbey, fascinated by its alien appearance. Do not assume that it landed here from outer space, all in one piece. Like Notre Dame, it exhibited many styles, grew in times of wealth and shrunk in times of decay (a disciplinary visitation in 1320 found that the monks had run up huge debts and spent most of their time hunting). Even now it casts a shadow over the town of Whitby, nestled in the bay below, such that when Bram Stoker came to write *Dracula*, he located it here; just over the wall from the Abbey is the graveyard where the count sunk his teeth into Lucy.[1] To some Victorians, the Gothic Revival was as ominous as it was intriguing. The heroes of Stoker's novel are men of the Enlightenment, rational and scientific; Dracula represents an exotic, subversive past, lurking in the corpuscles, waiting to return.[2] When the count purchases an estate without seeing it first, Jonathan Harker, his agent, feels obliged to warn him that it is a ruin. The vampire is pleased.

> I am glad that it is old and big. I myself am of an old family, and to live in a new house would kill me. A house cannot be made

habitable in a day; and, after all, how few days go to make up a century … The walls of my castle are broken; the shadows are many, and the wind breathes cold through the broken battlements and casements. I love the shade and the shadow, and would be alone with my thoughts when I may.[3]

This is a monster after my own heart. I, too, have a prejudice for the old. I like old clothes, crackling LPs, black-and-white movies and the smell of must. I particularly like things that are handmade and worn: love went into them, love made the most of them. Take luggage. Luggage today is plastic, cheap, nasty – designed to be tossed around an airport. Suitcases a hundred years ago were so handsome, crafted from luscious brown leather, that the middle class now bid for them at auction and stack them in the living room as *objets d'art*. These gorgeous old things were generally made for the rich when travel was sedate and few could afford to do it, it's true. But who decided that modern convenience must be ugly? Can't we mass-produce loveliness?

One afternoon in Yorkshire, I took a steam-drawn Pullman train from Pickering to Grosmont – a return trip with three-course meal and a bottle of wine. So magnificent is the Pullman that people will pay good money to take it to the end of the line and back, not to get anywhere but to experience the ride. Nobody put their shoes on those seats; it would be like wiping your feet on a Rembrandt. I suppose the utilitarian electric train, or the sleek but featureless bullet that ferries the Japanese from Kyoto to Tokyo in a couple of hours, must have seemed exciting once, a vision of the future. But that future hasn't aged well and, from the looks of things, it won't be a patch on the past.

'I was never a *young* man,' says a character in John Osborne's *West of Suez*. 'I think I always felt old.'[4] Growing up, I felt bored in the presence of my own generation because they only knew what I knew. I much preferred the company of adults, of human beings who had seen things I hadn't and understood things I had yet to learn. This put me against the tide of a society that finds youth compelling. Adolescence was arguably invented in the nineteenth century, when farm machinery and child labour laws gave us a breathing space between being a child and a grown-up. In the 1950s, thanks to James Dean, it became a veritable cult. Once, teenagers had aspired to be like their parents; by the 1960s, parents were acting more and more like their children. Today maturity is delayed for as long as possible – children are actively protected from responsibility and risk – yet, at the same time as the education of children has declined into 'everyone gets prizes!', we apply to our kids more moral weight than ever before, as if they know something we've forgotten. The writer Anthony Esolen observes, with horror, that some societies are seriously considering votes for 16-year-olds: 'There was a time when a fourteen-year-old John Quincy Adams could act as the effective American ambassador to the Russian court in Saint Petersburg because he spoke fluent French and the official ambassador could not; even he was not so foolish and self-satisfied as to believe that he merited the franchise. But in our day, the typical sixteen-year-old ... would find it hard going to read Quincy's letters back home – in English.'[5]

Yes, youth has a mystery. The older I get, the more its imperviousness to cold and disease seems miraculous, but the one thing adults have forgotten that teenagers do know is how confusing and unpleasant growing up is, that most of us spent it hating our bodies, unsure of ourselves, full of lust and unable to act on it, and dreaming of escaping Mum and Dad so that we could do what we want. Had we realized how tough it is in the real world, we might have stayed under their roof a little longer. Today's young may imagine themselves to be greener, more tolerant, less judgemental than their fathers and mothers, but it's hard to take the utopian ideals seriously of a generation that has yet to experience reality. Most of them don't yet know the real struggle to be a good person, or its costs, and this is why their beauty is superficial. Beauty is truth, truth is lived, life is one part joy and nine parts pain – and a person who hasn't yet lived cannot know that pain, so they cannot truly be beautiful.[*]

---

[*] Any child who has experienced these things has usually endured a tragedy, and when innocence is lost, childhood goes, too.

A conversation in John Cassavetes' movie *Opening Night* captures my attitude. Its hero is a middle-aged actress crawling past 40, terrified of old age, putting it off with alcohol. 'When I was 17,' she tells her husband, 'I could do anything. It was so easy. My emotions were so close to the surface.' Now that she is no longer attractive by the standards of the acting profession, now that she can no longer play a 17-year-old, she's not sure of how to be herself. This is not a crisis limited to women. Her husband, who understands it all too well, shows her the photograph of an old lady with a wrinkled face. 'I do love older people,' he says.

'Why?'

'I can look at this woman, this old lady, and I can count every wrinkle on her face. And for every wrinkle there is a pain and for every pain there is a year and for every year there is a person, there's a death, there's a history, there's a kindness.'[6]

Our society is becoming dangerously anti-old age. The old, we hear, are reactionary, and by living too long, too well, they suck up welfare and hoard the housing stock. It's true that the aged do have to make way eventually – the next part of this book will emphasize that in life we are always in death, that many traditions are designed, at heart, to prepare us for the end. Too many churches forgot this during the coronavirus pandemic. Rather than offering us the comforts of eternity, they closed their doors before the state had even asked them to, and when they reopened, they advised people not to come and subjected those that did to a bizarre regime of hand gels and forced distancing. 'You've got to understand,' one priest said to me, 'that many clerics don't believe in God. They've been worrying for years that they're wasting people's time. The chance to supervise our health and safety makes them feel useful again.' The more theologically conservative a person was, I noticed, the less likely they were to wear a mask: 'If it's my time, it's my time,' they reasoned, as long as your soul is in good order, you have nothing to fear (except an agonizing death). I saw the priest give a sermon to some children in which he offered a perspective that I heard nowhere else: 'like animals and flowers, people grow old and die, but that's not the end. Just as winter is followed by spring, the old gives way to the new and the world is replenished.' This is progress within a cycle; a way of seeing life that tradition embraces but modernity rejects, because if you only live life in the moment, you wouldn't want that moment to end.

The young do not progress in a vacuum. They grow in wisdom by listening to the old – even to the dead. What I want to illustrate in Part II of this book is the usefulness of ancient ideas and values. Personally, I find their beauty self-evident – like a steam train or a nice piece of luggage – but I recognize this is a subjective judgement. More objective is the question of utility: does tradition make life easier or better? I think it does.

The job of the old is to inculcate tradition, while the job of the young is to bring energy and creativity to it, while remaining true to its essence – true to its truth. The philosopher Peter Kreeft points out that in our obsession with novelty, measured in how dramatically something breaks from the past, we overrate our own cognitive abilities. We value the new because it is new: it must have something to it because it's different, fresh, and I invented it! Never mind that older values have been 'tested by time and by millions of other human beings ... [Surviving] the tsunami of forgetfulness that obliterates most of the memories of each generation, [they] have been judged precious and preserved by tradition.' Hell is full of novelty, says Kreeft; it is also grindingly repetitive, an eternity of having a pitchfork shoved up your bottom. The mind of God – the mind towards which so much great learning has striven to understand – created Mount Everest, the dandelion and J. S. Bach. The hope of many a guardian of tradition is that by understanding that tradition, we could retrace our steps all the way back to the beginning – like Theseus following a piece of string back through the maze – and, who knows, perhaps at the end of our journey, find our origin, our purpose?[7] To quote T. S. Eliot:

We shall not cease from exploration
And the end of all our exploring
Will be to arrive where we started
And know the place for the first time.[8]

FIGURE 11 Aboriginal Elder Aloysius Narjic with grandson Lachlan Narjic in Australia on 2 August 2006.

6

Tradition and Identity

Why raise a child in a tradition? Well, it's more than just a 'nice' thing to do. If that's all it was, it wouldn't be so controversial, so open to the charge of indoctrination. But it is natural, it is universal and, with obvious exceptions, it pulls off the impressive feat of simultaneously conferring identity *and* moral purpose. It's also hard to avoid doing it.

The philosopher Marshall McLuhan observed that 'the name of a man is a numbing blow from which he never recovers'. My parents called me Tim. Although I'm not sold on the theory of nominative determinism, that you grow into the name you are given, I was frequently called 'Tim, nice but dim', and people still assume that I am well-meaning but largely unreliable. I have internalized this prejudice. When I heard that Britain was sending a man into space called Tim, I thought: 'Dear God, don't let him touch any buttons. He'll crash the rocket and kill us all.'

Our parents make thousands of little decisions on our behalf that will shape our future: traditional culture is simply honest about it. There is a Chinese ceremony called *zhuazhou* (literally 'pick' and 'anniversary') that takes place on a child's first birthday, whereby Mum and Dad select various objects that represent character traits or career options – pen for scholar, phone for technician etc. – lay them on the floor and let the child choose one. If he picks up a cake, he will never go hungry. If he picks up a stethoscope, he will be a doctor. The game is rigged: the range of options is limited and, I'm told, Mum and Dad will frequently tempt the child towards the career they already have in mind by cooing and clapping. Children, however, can be wilful. *The Dream of the Red Chamber*, China's first great novel, recounts a *zhuazhou* ceremony for a baby boy that didn't go to plan:

> On his first birthday, [his father] tested his disposition by setting all sorts of different objects in front of him to see which he would select. Believe it or not, ignoring everything else he reached out for the rouge, powder-boxes, hair ornament and bangles. His father was furious and swore he'd grow into a dissolute rake.[1]

Christians baptize, Jews and Muslims circumcise boys and Hindus pierce the ear so that a child can hear the sounds of the spirit world; in all cases, the infant is welcomed into the community and stamped with a badge of identity that, whether physical or spiritual, is intended to last a lifetime. Many in the modern West recoil from this. Some countries have even flirted with outlawing male circumcision as a violation of human rights: if a man wants to do that later in life, goes the logic, fair enough, but a baby has no choice – and to mark him physically is an assault upon his autonomy. It contradicts the Enlightenment ideal of human beings as free agents, starting out as a blank sheet of paper and, as we gather knowledge and experience, writing our own story as we go. It seems axiomatic that in a liberal society, no one should have their religion chosen for them.

But our origins are inescapable, whether they are embraced or resisted, and even the decision of parents *not* to make certain choices is itself a choice that shapes identity.[2] My mother decided very early on that I should learn the piano. I hated it; she had to bully and bribe me into doing it – and after I left home, I don't think I touched it for a decade. But the result is I can now read music. I have friends whose parents didn't want to force them to learn an instrument: they cannot read music. The absence of decision in their childhood has reduced their options as an adult. My parents also made the choice to expose me to Christianity, and the church they picked, the Baptists, has a very interesting take on baptism.

Most Christians perform this ritual shortly after birth. The purpose is to free the child from the sin they were born with, sin committed in the Garden of Eden when mankind disobeyed God, and to welcome them into the life of the Church, which is why the ceremony is public and godparents are appointed to help raise the child in the faith. When the baby has grown up, one hopes, they will make the promises of baptism their own. The Baptists reject this, arguing that a believer has to choose baptism to mean it, so the idea of baptizing a baby is not only absurd but offensive – to the individual, whose free will is traduced, and to God, whose gift of baptism is dished out like a birthday present. The Baptists have a deeply emotional and instinctual faith, but with their emphasis upon an individual relationship with God and their respect for reason, they are very much children of the Enlightenment.

Having grown up among them, I find their faith in free will a bit of a stretch. When you spend your childhood attending church, studying the Bible and praying to God, you do not approach baptism with an open mind, especially given that Baptist communities are so tightly-knit (if you missed a Sunday service, the elders called to check you were still alive). And Baptist children operate at the very heart of their churches; some are even credited with powers of religious inspiration. When an 8-year-old declares 'Jesus is Lord!', it can be said that 'out of the mouths of babes' comes great wisdom – yet it's highly likely they're recycling something the pastor said on Sunday, a pattern of imitation interpreted as intuition that one sees a lot of on social media. Liberal mums and dads are forever reporting that their child just denounced racism or homophobia before they could even spell the words – and because liberal parents believe they are raising their little darlings free from prejudice, they assume that when 4-year-old Jeremy says, 'I won't have a future unless we ban fracking!' he must be speaking from the heart. The conclusion: children are natural environmentalists.

It's far more likely, of course, that Jeremy is repeating something Mummy and Daddy said over a vegan cutlet – because every upbringing, every system of education, reflects the values of the community in which it is located. When schools go out of their way not to indoctrinate children in so-called traditional values, they inevitably indoctrinate them in liberal ones instead. According to Jonathan Haidt in his popular book *The Righteous Mind*, the consensus among Western educators is that children develop in two stages, that at first they do as they are told because we tell them to, and later they develop a mature morality for themselves. They evolve from obedience to self-governance. Ergo, an education system that stresses discipline, hierarchy or authority is counterproductive because it traps children at a lower level of development. Much more useful are play and role-playing, so that children can put themselves in each other's shoes and develop a moral structure based upon empathy. Children are apparently very good at distinguishing between harm-based morality and social convention: they understand that you should never push a friend off a swing because it hurts, whereas wearing a school uniform might be what 'we do at this school' but not necessarily the done thing elsewhere. The implication is that social convention, though it might be deemed appropriate by family or community, is not absolutely essential to a child's moral development – and that children instinctively understand this.

As Haidt argues, the liberal picture of childhood is remarkably unemotional. It imagines kids to be like little philosophers, sitting in the sandbox at playtime, debating the issues of the day – and isn't it strange how every one of them crawls out of the sand thinking the exact same way? Well, actually, they don't. Haidt's research shows that in other parts of the world, children do not make a distinction between personal morality and social convention. Muslim children in Pakistan believe, as their parents do, that nudity is an offence to God; Hindu children believe, as their parents do, that it's a sacrilege to eat beef. Non-Westerners tend to see these conventions as rules set by God, applicable to all. Westerners tell themselves that we don't do universal rules – that would be imperialism! – yet we regard freedom, as we understand it, to be a universal right that encompasses the whole of humanity. Liberalism presents itself as critical of convention, but it is itself a convention of individualist societies.[3] It has to be. If a school is going to try to inculcate objectivity, you are going to have to neutralize, perhaps even contradict, the values and traditions that a child brings into the classroom from their home, with the result that the contemporary school has become as much a place of forgetting as it is a place of learning. We think we're raising children without a prepacked identity but we're really not. We are giving them the alternative identity of a person in search of an identity.

Educating a child to think and act independently is a good thing, obviously, but if the individual is to be anything other than an aimless wanderer, they need to be instilled with a sense of self that is beyond the self – be it the transcendence of music or the community of a church. This is what we do when we raise a child in tradition. Let's take one of the most controversial examples: infant male circumcision, as practised by Jews and Muslims. I seek not to condone or condemn but to understand this determined attempt to stamp an identity on an individual long before he could have any say in it. What is the rationale behind the ritual? What does it represent?

I

The first known record of a male circumcision is found on the doorpost of an Egyptian tomb on the west bank of the River Nile. Probably created around 2400 BC, it illustrates the genital cutting of two noblemen. In the first scene, an assistant restrains the arms of a young man as a priest operates with a stone knife; the inscription reads: 'Hold him and do not allow him to faint!' In the second scene, the patient tells the priest to 'thoroughly rub off what is there'. The priest replies, 'I will cause it to heal' – and as I write this, my legs have involuntarily crossed.

In her celebrated 1966 book *Purity and Danger*, the anthropologist Mary Douglas noted that the rituals of primitive societies often revolve around the themes of dirt and hygiene, and it's no coincidence that male circumcision tends to have been practised in arid societies where it was perhaps seen as a practical response to the threat of infection. But we mustn't judge ritual solely by its outward appearance, wrote

Douglas, for dirt has a symbolic significance, too. It 'offends against order. Eliminating it is not a negative movement, but a positive effort to organise the environment … making it conform to an idea.' In the case of male circumcision, 'what is being carved in human flesh is an image of society'.[4] Today, the rite is generally performed on babies, either for religious reasons or perceived health benefits, but in the ancient world it might be carried out on much older boys as an initiation into adulthood, and pain was part of the journey. The rite depicted on the Egyptian tomb appears voluntary. The priest talks to the boys almost as if he were their doctor, for there was no distinction in this world between medicine and religion, and the Egyptians believed that unguarded openings on the body could collect impurities or be penetrated by bad spirits. Circumcision may also have been a status symbol, possibly an induction into the priesthood, so the goal perhaps was to render the penis less sensitive, to allow greater concentration on prayer. Finally, the ceremony was probably seen as a form of blood sacrifice, a test of endurance. The stoicism of the patients proved that they were very brave boys.[5]

The ancient Egyptians were celebrated as sophisticates of science and magic; if they did it, there had to be something to it – hence circumcision spread across the Near East. It is possible that the Jews picked it up from the Egyptians. The early Christians divided over whether or not to maintain the practice: for St Paul, this debate reflected a tension between the flesh and the spirit, the old and the new relationship with God. In the new, Christian church, circumcision was replaced by the more metaphorical rite of baptism with water. Islam, on the other hand, not only stuck with and promoted circumcision, but the custom might have made it more appealing to the pagan cultures it encountered. 'Many converted peoples look back to aboriginal animist traditions that include genital cutting,' writes historian David Gollaher. 'By allowing these traditions to flow freely into its reservoir, Islam in effect modernizes them, and enables them to connect with a sacred global order.'[6]

One of these cultural artefacts is female genital mutilation, which (contrary to far-right myth) is practiced by Christians as well as Muslims in parts of the developing world. Condemnation is widespread and many states have outlawed it; it is not only more harmful and dangerous than male circumcision, but is also intended to mark women as inferior. It's better not to think of it as circumcision, say critics, but as mutilation. Others find the West's tolerance of one form of cutting over another paradoxical, maybe even a form of cultural snobbery – insisting that female and male circumcision are similar means to similar ends, namely a sadistic theatre of belief.

In Australia in the mid-twentieth century, anthropologists encountered rituals among some Aboriginal groups that struck them as deliberately raw and dramatic. According to Charles P. Mountford, who studied the tribes of the Central Desert, up to a certain age a boy lived a carefree life largely under the supervision of the women. This ended abruptly one evening, when the women turned on the boy and drove him out of the camp with fire sticks. Now he had to wander about for a year with gruff old men, speaking only when spoken to, even then in a whisper. When the time for his circumcision arrived, children and women were banned from the ceremony; the boy waited his turn lying face down in the sand, because this was men's work and only men could witness it. Once his penis had been cut, he was inducted into the history and beliefs of his tribe – and when he had learned enough, and his beard had begun to sprout, he underwent a final, excruciating rite of passage known as sub-incision.[7] The young man was seated on a rock and his penis was split along the underside with a stone knife; it was then pressed flat. In some instances, a red blossom was placed inside the wound to ensure that the penis was as red as possible on the inside, perhaps in an imitation of menstruation – to evacuate any blood that was deemed feminine.[8]

Aboriginal Australians have also been known to practise scarification, whereby cuts are made on the body and filled with sand, or other materials, to produce pictures in flesh. This urge to turn the body into a canvas is found in practically all societies. Light-skinned peoples practise tattooing; dark-skinned societies tend to prefer scars, presumably because they stand out better than ink. In the villages along the Sepik River in Papua New Guinea, when boys come of age they are taken to the 'spirit house' by their uncles and transformed with knives into imitations of the crocodile: their backs, shoulders and upper torsos are sliced with razors to create patterns of welts that do indeed look reptilian. The blood they lose is believed to belong to the mother; the body, thus drained, is now entirely male. Here we are thousands of miles and thousands of years away from ancient Egypt, and yet we encounter the same themes of initiation through cutting, to test strength, to mark adulthood, to initiate into mystical learning and to designate social status.[9]

And, again, the trauma is part of the package. In the case of the Aboriginal Australians, wrote Mountford, the tribesmen sought to exorcize adolescence by acting it out in public. First, the child was permitted to be a child and roam free; at the point when the hormones kicked in and he began to withdraw into himself, he was separated from the women and handed over to the men, where the tests of discipline broke down his ego and, through wandering and ritual, he learned who he was meant to be – along with the socially sanctioned purpose of his body.[10] In the Jewish tradition, observes Gollaher, the penis is compared to a tree; the capacity to bear fruit comes with maturity, and circumcision represents the pruning and preparation of the generative organ and its direction away from pleasure and towards reproduction, just as the Aboriginal boy, by 'beautifying' his penis, was prepared for marriage.[11]

'Initiation, in an aboriginal society,' explained Mountford, 'marks the transitions from carefree youth to disciplined manhood; from irresponsibility to obligation; and from ignorance to enlightenment. Its rituals are designed to teach the young ... the rules and philosophies of the tribe, and the prohibitions that accompany them.' Importantly, these rituals not only looked forward, to sex and reproduction, but also backwards, by instructing the youth in history and tradition, so that his nascent individual identity was rooted in that of the tribe. He learned the origins of things; why the landscape looks the way it does, why the kangaroo jumps and the beetle scurries. Singing was critical. Mountford compared it to Wagner's operas: 'By his incomparable media of music and acting he immortalised the mighty deeds of the gods and Demi-gods of the ancient Nordic race, and, by their age-old chants and strange rituals, the aboriginals … keep alive the epics of their heroic times.'[12]

Wagner could only evoke the past. The Aboriginal Australian has the ability to revisit it. Aboriginal and ancient Egyptian culture do not operate by our modern, linear notion of time, but instead see history as a series of repeating cycles: birth, life, death and rebirth. The Aboriginal understanding of time, called The Dreaming, defies definition, but an imperfect way of thinking of it is that past, present and future can be experienced simultaneously and in one sacred location. The modern, Western mind sees land as a commodity to be used or repurposed at will; the Aboriginal person sees the landscape as timeless and populated by ghosts.

One anthropologist compares The Dreaming to a person reading a book while, in the street outside, children play and cars go by. The book is the present; the noises are the past. The reader is conscious of both, but chooses to focus on the book; they can switch between the two at will. As for what is most worthy of focus, that's decided as much by the community as the individual. Something personal that happened recently, like having breakfast, might not be considered as immediate as something that happened thousands of years ago to the tribe, like a great hunt. The hunt happened; through The Dreaming it is also ongoing; when an Aboriginal person re-enacts an event, it's as if it were happening right now. For example, a Westerner who attended an Aboriginal re-enactment of the crucifixion of Christ reported that some of the older men did not enjoy the ceremony because they found it all too real: 'One Warlpiri man said that it made him sad to keep on killing God … Instead of merely dramatically portraying a historical event, the crucifixion was, to some Warlpiri, if not all, a contemporary reality.'[13]

This is not a simplistic take on religious symbolism but a highly sophisticated one, and it strikes a chord with this Catholic writer. Most Protestants believe that communion is a commemorative feast, a re-enactment of the Last Supper, when Jesus took wine and bread and declared them to be his blood and body, 'given for you', just as his life would be given for the world when he was crucified. In this theology, Christ died once upon the cross; it happened two thousand years ago; it cannot happen again. Catholics, by contrast, believe Jesus is present in the Eucharist, that he was speaking literally when he said the wine was 'my blood spilt for you' and the bread was 'my body, broken for you' – and thus the consecrated wine and wafer become, not just in principle but in substance, the blood and body of Jesus Christ. A similar metamorphosis occurs when a baby is baptized with water: baptism begins the transubstantiation of the person, of their transformation into a member of the Church and part of the body of Christ. As Mary Douglas argued, however simplistic, alien or brutal the rituals of primitive societies might appear, they speak to very familiar themes within Western religious tradition, including the relationship between God and the natural world, individual and community, identity and sexuality.

A consideration of the role of genitalia in faith might strike some as prurient but it underscores the point that religious tradition is, contrary to its reputation, neither sterile nor puritanical. It celebrates the human body; it is intimately concerned with fertility and reproduction. When I was a boy, in the happy days before the internet, the only two places to learn about sex were my parents' 1950s medical dictionary and the Bible; of the two, the Bible was probably the more accurate. Contained within its onion-skin pages were frank discussions of virginity, pregnancy and birth, as well as a whole dessert trolley of sins. For medieval Christians, Jesus' circumcision was a matter of fact and commemoration: they literally revered his foreskin, working on the principle that if he was physically raised up to Heaven at the end of his ministry on Earth, then this must have been the only piece of him left behind. The Protestant reformer Martin Luther, who had a low opinion of relics, marvelled at the sheer number of foreskins dotted around Europe. They were often believed to help with conception and birth: Catherine of Valois, Henry V's queen, borrowed a holy foreskin from the Abbey Church of Coulombs in the early fifteenth century and was so satisfied with the results that she and the king built a special sanctuary for the relic when they returned it. In one version of the life of the fourteenth-century mystic Catherine of Siena, Catherine had a vision of Christ in which he offered her a wedding ring made from his foreskin.[14]

Despite this, it's striking how many medieval paintings represent the infant Jesus as uncircumcised. Anti-Semitism is no doubt to blame. The Christian tradition was drawn from the Judaic one, yet medieval Christians remained emotionally ambiguous about the Jewish identity of their Messiah. They speculated that Jesus submitted to circumcision to hide his identity from the Devil (who assumed that the Son of God didn't require it), to prove his obedience to the law, to demonstrate he was human by shedding blood and as an act of sacrifice that would be bookended with his final wounding on the Cross.[15] In Andrea Mantegna's 1464 painting *The Circumcision of Christ* (see Figure 12), a Christian reimagining of circumcision, the emphasis is upon pain. Jesus looks up at his mother for help; she returns a sad gaze. A woman directs a boy's head away with her hand as if to say 'not for you', and the boy clutches a broken ring, representing, presumably, the death of one religious tradition and the arrival of another. The literal circumcision of the Jews will later be replaced by what St Paul called the 'circumcision of the heart', and thus Jesus submits to this agony so that no one in the future need go through it again.

II

These rationalizations lead the viewer of Mantegna's painting away from what circumcision really was, and what Mary and Joseph would have believed it to be: a joyful statement of religious and moral belonging. When a Jewish boy is circumcised, he is made part of a historical covenant with God, a covenant that carries with it obligations, first, to carry on the Jewish line and, second, to be a good Jew, that is to obey the Jewish law. All of this has universal significance, because God is believed to be the god of the Jews but also of mankind in general. Jews in the modern era have been drawn towards progressive movements by the radicalizing experience of anti-Semitism, no doubt, but I'd argue that a sense of social, almost

FIGURE 12 The Circumcision, ca 1463–1464, by Andrea Mantegna (1431–1506). Found in the collection of the Galleria degli Uffizi, Florence.

cosmic responsibility is imprinted on their very identity: raising children in this tradition is about delineating who they are and who they are not, assigning them a personal role within a vast moral narrative that has implications for all of humanity.

According to the book of Genesis, God told Abraham, the patriarch of Judaism, that his offspring would multiply and inherit the land so long as they remained faithful to the Lord. Just as covenants between human beings would be marked with the sacrifice of an animal, so this contract between God and man was marked for eternity by male circumcision. The agreement was tested when God commanded Abraham to take his son Isaac up Mount Moriah and offer him as a human sacrifice, a scene depicted in a mural in the top left-hand corner of *The Circumcision of Christ*. Abraham, dagger in hand, is poised to slit his son's throat. God stops him.

It's one of the most 'unreasonable' bits of the Bible. God asks Abraham to do something that would be bad enough if Isaac were a stranger – but he is Abraham's flesh and blood, and God's request turns the father/son relationship inside out. Abraham should be a protector; instead he contemplates infanticide. Some biblical commentaries insist that Abraham knew he wouldn't have to kill Isaac. God had promised him that his sons would inherit the land, therefore God would have to break his own contract to go through with it, which he presumably wouldn't do. I find this unconvincing: it turns a traumatic situation into a game of bluff. I prefer to see the story as a comment on parenthood and familial responsibility and so, I suspect, does Mantegna, for in the top right-hand corner of his painting we can spot another mural, this time of Moses holding the Ten Commandments, one of which is 'Honour thy father and thy mother'. The instruction is not a blank cheque. Parents cannot mistreat their children and expect automatic respect; always implicit in this commandment is that for a parent to be honoured they must be worthy of being honoured in turn, that 'father' isn't just a title but a state of 'being' and of 'doing' – being a good dad, doing the right thing – and parental authority stems not only from blood but the honouring of obligations towards the child. God is the father in this scenario; Abraham is the son. Abraham trusts his father enough to follow his most impossible order; God proves himself as a father to Abraham, and all mankind, by stopping the sacrifice. We mustn't over-psychoanalyse the story of Abraham and Isaac because what really matters is the outcome. Son trusts father; father comes through for son. The covenant is upheld and the rewards and responsibilities that flow from it pass down through the generations. Jewish tradition conforms to Burke's definition of the historical contract, a pattern of inherited obligations, not only between the living but between the descendants of Abraham, Abraham himself and God.

By the time the Romans annexed Judea in AD 6, the Jews stood out not only for being circumcised, although this was certainly the subject of comment, but also for having a coherent identity that defied assimilation into cosmopolitan, polytheistic Roman culture. Greco-Roman gods were all around us – up mountains, in the air, in the sea – and had walked among us, too; they had human qualities, which meant they could be bargained with, flattered, even fooled. The gods were rather like Marvel super-humans, incredible but recognizable. The Jewish God, by contrast, was out of sight and, to a large extent, beyond comprehension. When the Roman general Pompey sacked Jerusalem in 63 BC, he broke into the inner sanctum of the Jewish Temple, the 'holy of holies', expecting to find the usual loot of treasure and idols. He found almost nothing. This was the house of the Lord and the most precious thing inside it was God. Pompey was duly impressed and decided to leave the Temple as he discovered it, which was a compliment of sorts. The Jews took it as an insult. Pompey's action implied that their God was just one of many; as far as the Jews were concerned, he was the only God, and the invasion of the Temple was not 'a little local difficulty' but an event of importance to the entire world. The Jewish God was the God of the Romans, too, even if Pompey didn't know it, so this temple deserved more than just a tourist's respect. It required worship.[16]

The building was located on Mount Moriah, site of an earlier temple, constructed by King Solomon, that had housed the Ark of Covenant, itself containing the Ten Commandments (all now lost). The faithful would come here three times a year for the pilgrim festivals to 'feel themselves in the presence of God'. In Jewish culture, theology, ethnicity and geography commingled – in which case, what were they to do if the holy space was conquered and the faithful were scattered? This happened a lot: Jerusalem was occupied by the Babylonians, the Persians, the Greeks and now the Romans, who would destroy the Temple altogether in AD 70. The solution was to inculcate tradition within the individual, the community and the synagogue. While away from the Holy Land, Jews could attend their local synagogue where they could study their stories, laws and prophecies; and rather than travelling to the Temple in Jerusalem, festivals became religious meals located increasingly in the home. The genius of this portable tradition, writes Tom Holland, is that it could not be 'easily stormed. It was not constructed out of wood and stone, to be levelled by a conquering army. Wherever Jews might choose to live, there the body of their scriptures could be present as well.'[17]

Their covenant helped the Jewish people to endure invasion, migration and pogroms: it's why any discussion of tradition invariably returns to the Jews because they are history's most compelling case study in its strengths. But it also imposed burdens. One was the question of fidelity: the Jews were anxious that they might have broken the covenant and they divided into different schools of thought over the proper way to maintain it (one might even interpret Christianity not as a rupture but an attempt to develop Jewish tradition in new circumstances, according to new revelations). Another quandary was that whatever made Jewish identity resilient also made it a target for persecution. Greek Seleucid ruler Antiochus IV Epiphanes (175–164 BC) forbade circumcision, and when the order was ignored, mothers were executed and their infants hung around their necks. Today many secular Jews circumcise their sons not for religious reasons but to preserve an identity long under attack. By so doing, they commit their offspring to the perpetuation of difference. Jews participating in ancient Greek athletic contests ran into the problem that Greeks performed in the nude and strongly disapproved of the display of the male glans (the Greeks would actually bind the foreskin with string to protect their modesty, which is ridiculous when you consider that they were running and boxing, naked as the day they were born). Desperate to fit in, some Jewish athletes might have stretched the skin on their penis forward to affect a foreskin, or even undergone corrective surgery. This caused a scandal. It was the opinion of religious leaders that being Jewish meant being circumcised, and thus, when circumcision was undone, the covenant went with it and the person was no longer Jewish.[18]

This opens the door to a very difficult question: what defines ethnicity? Is it a state of being or of doing? Today, many Jews feel that their Jewishness is inherited, that they can be perfectly Jewish without observing Jewish laws or customs. But religious Jews might counter that Jewishness is defined by obedience to the laws of God – so the uncircumcised forfeit their identity. The implications of either side of the argument are hurtful to the other. A secular, ethnic Jew can face ostracism among the religious; a religious convert to Judaism can do their best to observe all the rules but, because they don't have the right lineage, they struggle to find acceptance. I know this well as a covert to Catholicism. I recall a conversation with a Scotsman who told me, with regret, that I could never be a 'proper Catholic' because I hadn't been born one. In the course of interrogating this theory, he admitted that he hadn't been to church since school.

III

The idea that you can belong to a tradition without participating in it plagues the West. An Anglican priest once said to me that christenings were the most depressing service of all, because he knew that for most babies this was both the first time they would see inside a church and the last. The meaning of this ceremony, if parents even bother with it, is in danger of being lost – yet it is absolutely not an end in itself ('a celebration of new life' as the cliché goes) but the beginning of a moral journey in the company of an entire community. As with any journey, we have to proceed with a destination in mind.

A horrible story: a few years ago, I got a phone call in the middle of the night from a friend whose wife had gone into labour prematurely. The child, very weak, had survived – but his father wanted to perform a baptism in case he didn't live, so he asked if I could recommend a priest. I'm pleased to say that I could, and delighted to add that the baby lived, is well and is now my godson. The application of baptism in that distressing circumstance really brings home what it's all about.

The ritual is not just a preparation for life but a preparation for death, just as my pledge to raise my godson in the faith is a pledge to help guide his path to Heaven. If you are uncomfortable with this theology, and it is rather morbid, then strip away the religion and what you find underneath is a recognition of the link between the fate of the individual and the health of society, between being welcomed into the tribe and the development of moral character.

Belonging can be a wonderful gift. Yet many people who don't have it – or choose to reject it – cling to nothing as if it were something special: 'Oh, we decided to let our child choose for himself!' Well done, but the absence of rooted identity is felt more painfully the older one gets. In his novel *Submission*, Michel Houllebecq imagines a future in which France elects an Islamist president. It's not a dystopia: the election is fair and the Islamist candidate is probably the best choice. The triumph of Islam in the West, Houllebecq suggests, comes because Christianity has died and secularism offers no alternative, so Islam fills the vacuum. The narrator of *Submission* is a modern type that Friedrich Nietzsche called 'the last man' – an overeducated wimp – and he submits to the new regime not out of belief but the absence of any good reason not to. He has a girlfriend who is Jewish and she tells him that, fearing for her future, she has decided to move to Israel. The narrator asks what he is supposed to do if secular France vanishes. He says: 'There is no Israel for me.'[19]

Jews were historically slandered as a race of wanderers – but as Christian civilization has rejected its past and turned its back on its religious traditions, it is the Jews who appear enviably grounded and self-aware, while the liberal Westerner is lost in a permanent state of juvenile existential crisis. The West is wandering without progressing, searching without finding, and even the once most settled aspects of our lives, even our very bodies, are now up for debate.

FIGURE 13 Two transgender people take a selfie prior to a protest in defence of Hijra rights, Dhaka, Bangladesh, 10 February, 2021.

7

Tradition and Order

I read the last chapter to Mum in the tea rooms on the high street and asked her what she thought. She said: 'So when are *you* having a baby then?' The woman has a one-track mind. To her it's a question of justice. 'I had you, you grew up and left home, now I've got nothing to do. You're supposed to have children of your own so I can help look after them.'

'Probably right.'

'Well then.' She crossed her arms. 'Where's my grandchild?'

Sorry, Mum: it's a generational thing. My friends are waiting longer and longer to have babies, if they choose to, and the fertility rate is falling across the world. In 1950, women had an average of 4.7 children in their lifetime; today, the number is 2.4 and it's expected to fall below 1.7 by 2100. The figure at which the number of human beings starts to decline is approximately 2.1. Those who worry about 'overpopulation' are right short term, wrong long term. China, for instance, is predicted to hit 1.4 billion a few years from now but, by 2100, will probably halve to around 732 million.[1] Pope Francis describes our future as 'houses full of things but empty of children'.[2]

Most people regard the falling birth rate as a success story. It has come about largely because women are better educated, they go out to work and they exercise control over their fertility. When the Catholic Church complains about a 'culture of death' destroying the West, it reads as an insult: it suggests that anyone who uses contraception or abortion, or is in a same-sex relationship, is complicit in an act of mass suicide, and the implication that we all have a duty to reproduce places a medieval burden on women. It's not men who have the baby. It's usually not men who do the bulk of the work raising it.

Nevertheless, I want to explore how tradition interacts in a positive way with some of the most dynamic, personal aspects of our nature – particularly sexuality and gender – and if I do touch upon the Catholic perspective, it's because the Church, by resisting liberal fashion, has made itself a leader on this subject. In the 1960s, Catholicism could've followed the rest of Western society and torn up its moral rulebook, embracing feminism or sexual freedom. Instead, it chose to stick to its guns. As a consequence, it is now defined in many Western minds by a deeply unfashionable commitment to traditional values, dismissed as 'patriarchy' – and there's no denying that, in the wrong hands, social conservatism can be reduced to a fetish for a past that never was, or at least was short-lived, and which seems wilfully blind to our needs, wants and taste for transgression. A tradition that operates at complete odds to our instincts is no use to us at all.

On the other hand, the tension between Christianity and non-religious morality is nothing new – it's one of the defining elements of the Christian tradition – and, as I hope I've demonstrated, true tradition is rarely puritanical, never naïve. How could it be? The Catholic Church has had two thousand years to study human nature, and, far from being unworldly, it sees with upmost clarity the conflict between freedom and order. We all want to be free to define ourselves, to do what we want – and God, according to Christian teaching, did give us the free will to make our own choices. But there are certain practical realities that we have to acknowledge, facts of life that place responsibilities upon us that we might not like but we cannot escape.

I've started here with reproduction because – Mum would agree – it is essential. If the world continues on this path, we're going to end up with a gigantic cohort of old people being supported by a vanishing number of youngsters, which is unsustainable and unfair. Moreover, this isn't just about what's good for society, it's also about what's best for the individual, and when it comes to having children, there's a tension not just between freedom and order but also freedom and happiness.

I

Sexuality and gender are sensitive issues and conservatives often make a hash of talking about them. A classic mistake is to present the 1950s as the last gasp of a historical norm, the 1960s as the decade the world went mad. In reality, the fifties were in many regards an aberration and the nuclear family unit – of husband, wife and several children – obviously had its flaws or else it would've persisted longer. This is a rule of thumb. You can test the strength of a social ideal by how long it lasts: if a golden age gives way to a sharp decline, it probably wasn't that golden.

The shape of the family is contingent upon economic and social conditions. In America at the turn of the last century, there was a popular ideal of hearth and home, of marital stability, but the family was also buffeted by disease and mortality, war, abandonment, female emancipation and a rising rate of divorce. The eminent psychologist John B Watson predicted, 'in fifty years there will be no such thing as marriage', and Theodore Roosevelt, observing that old stock Americans were breeding at a slower rate than immigrants, remarked in 1903 that the white middle class was committing 'race suicide'.[3]

If the fifties were different, it was partly because they could afford to be different. The post-war boom, as Pat Buchanan reminded voters, made it possible for a man to support his entire family on a single income: in 1950, most women walked down the aisle before 19, few got a job outside the home and a majority were pregnant within seven months. The American Dream was intimately bound up with consumerism, and families not only worked but purchased their way into the rising middle class – new home, new car, barbeque for Dad, vacuum cleaner for Mum. The more Americans spent, the higher the profits, and the greater Dad's take-home pay. But were they happy? In 1957, a journalist called Betty Friedan conducted a survey of her former classmates at Smith College and found that 89 per cent of these brilliant young women had graduated into homemaking; they were expected to dedicate themselves to cooking and sex. Friedan called it the feminine mystique, and 'each suburban housewife struggles with it alone … afraid to ask even of herself the silent question, is this all?'

Her findings were nuanced: her interviewees regretted missed opportunities and disliked housework, but most said they did not regret getting married or having a child, and they were active in politics and the local community, displaying initiative and creativity. So, perhaps it wasn't widespread dissatisfaction that blew up the nuclear unit, but technology and economic change. In 1960, the US Food and Drug Administration officially licensed the sale of the oral contraceptive known as The Pill; by 1962 well over a million women were using it. Policymakers assumed that if families could decide when to have children, the institution of marriage would be strengthened because husband and wife would have more income. The opposite happened. The Pill severed the link between sexual pleasure, childbirth and marriage; sex before and outside of marriage shot up, while women who got married by the end of the seventies were far more likely to stay in or to seek work. Employment could be liberating, no doubt, but it was also a matter of necessity: as the post-war economic party came to an end, women increasingly had to work to keep the family one step ahead of rising bills. Conservatives clung to the nuclear unit ideal and accused big government liberals of trying to undermine it, but feminists insisted that they weren't anti-family at all, they were just realistic. In this new economy, what was needed was equal pay and free daycare. It takes a village to raise a child, argued Hillary Clinton. The idea of Mum and Dad operating as an independent unit, let alone on a single, diminishing income, was for the birds.[4]

Some conservative intellectuals have reached a similar conclusion. Surveying the current, utterly depressing scale of single parenthood and loneliness in modern America, David Brooks argues that the nuclear unit has been part of the problem. 'A detached nuclear family ... is an intense set of relationships among, say, four people. If one relationship breaks, there are no shock absorbers.' The system is too rigid; too vulnerable to misfortune and people falling out of love. By contrast, Brooks argues, traditional societies depend upon a larger family, which means that when a mother dies or a father absconds, there are aunts, uncles and grandparents to fall back on, as well as a wider web of adults who are more than just friends. 'For the Ilongot people of the Philippines, people who migrated somewhere together are kin ... The Chuukese people in Micronesia have a saying: "My sibling from the same canoe"; if two people survive a dangerous trial at sea, then they become kin.' The Iñupiat of Alaska name their children after dead friends, 'and those children are considered members of their namesake's family'.

For hundreds of years, Westerners relied on extended families, too; the big disruptor, says Brooks, was capitalism. The industrial revolution lured men away from the farm and into the city, where they married much younger. Living in cramped apartments, surrounded by strangers, husband and wife formed tighter, smaller family units, and the moment their children grew up they were expected to move out and do the same. Children were raised, says Brooks, 'not for embeddedness but for autonomy' – embedding into everyday life the individualism of the Enlightenment.[5]

Via an argument for tradition and community, Brooks leads us to a similar argument deployed by supporters of the identity politics movement, namely that the way we behave – and the roles we are assigned – are not entirely natural but shaped by the economic or political structures that we find ourselves living in.[*] Take the question of what makes a man a man or a woman a woman. Most of

---

[*] This includes Black Lives Matter, which found itself in hot water for wishing to 'disrupt the Western-prescribed nuclear family structure'. The point, I believe, was not that traditional families are inherently evil but that they don't reflect the reality of black people's lives today – single-parenthood rendered unsustainable by poverty and low welfare support – or historically, given that African-descendant families typically relied upon extended families to help raise children. BLM might be critical of the Western tradition but it is not anti-history: it seeks to revive an older tradition that it believes was eradicated by colonialism.

us would accept there is a distinction between sex and gender: sex is biological, the parts you are born with, gender relates to how we behave as a male or female, so is closer to being socially constructed. Gender can be akin to being cast in a play against your will, forced to hide your true self behind a stylized mask. In the 1950s, women were compelled to 'act' as mother, homemaker, concubine, which was obviously invidious for the woman, but it could also be hard on husbands required to 'act' masculine. Not all of us want to be a 'master', and the psychological strain of playing these roles must have been considerable.

Some contemporary social conservatives insist that sex and gender are inseparable, that imagining them to be different concedes too much to people who want to eliminate altogether the distinction between male and female.[6] But experience suggests that while sex is fixed, gender has, at many times and in many places, been up for negotiation – that sex is the pole around which gender dances. In the United States, conservatives have campaigned against the phenomenon of 'drag queen story hours' held in public libraries: it is what it sounds like – drag queens read books to kids. The charge is sexualization and indoctrination of children ('This is demonic,' tweeted columnist Sohrab Ahmari. 'To hell with liberal order'!) but the bigger shock is that a drag queen would want to do something so banal.[7] Somewhere there's a gay bar missing the entertainment. Right-wing Americans might regard cross-dressing as a threat to the social order, and in the suburbs of Wyoming perhaps that's how it seems, but in other cultures it is customary and fun. I grew up in a prim, middle-class society in which, once a year, children attend pantomimes starring men dressed as women and women dressed as men – and when Shakespeare was first performed in Merrie England, the female roles were played by men, too (this was also the case in ancient Greece where, to add to the confusion, actors wore giant leather phalluses, false bottoms and a padded stomach). Figure 14 illustrates a famous fencing-match between the Chevalier de Saint-Georges and the Chevalier d'Éon, at the court of the Prince of Wales in the 1780s. Saint-Georges was a mixed-race man from

DUEL BETWEEN MLLE. LA CHEVALIERE D'EON DE BEAUMONT AND M. DE ST. GEORGE.

FIGURE 14 Illustration of a fencing match between the Chevalier de Saint-Georges (*left*) and the Chevalier d'Éon (*right*), on 9 April 1787.

Guadeloupe; d'Éon was a French diplomat and spy who lived as a woman, and the image depicts him/her wearing a natty black dress. Trans-people have always been around. Some cultures have been better than others at finding space for them.[8]

This is certainly true of India. According to Hindu folklore, when Lord Rama was exiled from the city of Ayodhya, his retinue began to follow him into the forest but he stopped them, saying: 'Men and women, wipe away your tears and go away.' They did as they were told – but for a small group who were neither male nor female, so they stayed rooted to the spot for fourteen years. When Rama returned home he was so overcome by this example of loyalty that he blessed them and gave them the power to bless others, particularly at weddings and childbirths. These became the Hijra women – a mix of trans, intersex, gay men and eunuchs – who today are a common sight in the cities of northern India, tapping on car windows with a coin, offering a blessing, in charity but with a slight air of menace. They wear bright saris and loud makeup; they arrive at weddings and childbirths unannounced, dance and sing lewd songs. You pay up or things can get out of hand.[9]

During the Mughal period of domination in India, the Hijra were employed by their Muslim overlords as tax collectors and guardians of the royal harem. It was the British Empire, in the 1860s, that inserted a section into the Indian Penal Code criminalizing non-reproductive sex, importing Western categories of normal and aberrant sexuality, driving the Hijra to the margins of society.[10] So, it's easy to conclude that the Western way of life is relatively new and rests upon false categories and constructs – like race, sexuality and gender – which 'intersect' to create the hierarchy of injustice that structures our lives. Women have it bad, goes the theory; black women have it worse; gay black women really get it in the neck; and so on. The students of twenty-first-century identity politics, influenced by the writings of the French historian Michel Foucault, insist that social conservatives are not interested in history as it actually was, but in perpetuating these structures via the maintenance of an entirely artificial, quite recently invented tradition – and nowadays, who really cares what conservatives think, particularly the religious ones?

Precious few Westerners do, it seems. Religious conservatives see themselves as side-lined or despised, but the reality is that much of the public doesn't think about them at all. Deference to religious authority was challenged by the Enlightenment, undermined by Charles Darwin and almost finished off by the sixties, with the result that most churches now speak in a language that many people simply don't understand. This became painfully obvious during the debate about same-sex marriage in the 2010s. I was against legalization for theological reasons and because I don't think the state should have the power to redefine something that had, for centuries, been purely heterosexual. My side of the argument was outgunned by appeals to tolerance and love, which turned out to be far more emotionally compelling. The mistake the anti-same-sex-marriage crowd made was to assume that society shared their definition of marriage as a union blessed by God and designed (in principle if not always in practice) for the bearing and raising of children. When declining numbers believe in God, when almost everyone practises contraception, and when half of all marriages end in divorce, most people see marriage quite differently. They think it's about love, and that when love ends, it's probably for the best to end the marriage, too. Children are a happy product, but not definitional (in societies that abort thousands of foetuses every year, we can assume that being 'open to life' has been well and truly trumped by the desire to control fertility).

So, in this cultural context, it proved very hard to win the argument that gays and lesbians shouldn't be allowed to get married. 'Why can't they be as miserable as the rest of us?' went the joke, and it touched a nerve. The reputation of marriage as a 'sacrament' blessed by God had been undermined long ago – not by gays and lesbians, who actually wanted to get married, but by heterosexuals who have treated the institution with all the reverence of a mobile phone contract. Most social conservatives, myself included, now accept the equalization of marriage in civil law and wouldn't countenance reversing it. To let people build their lives around it and then snatch it away, would be cruel. It's also not on the cards. Almost as soon as legalization was enacted, the debate leaped from whether or not such unions should be permitted to whether or not religious criticism of them should be tolerated. If the state has acknowledged marriage as a civil right in one context, shouldn't it apply across the board? Should churches be allowed to discriminate? Overnight, the burden of proof switched, tipping the balance of power with it. Gay rights was once the marginal position; now it is religious conservatism. I only hope that our new overlords in the LGBTQ lobby will show greater patience towards the religious minority than the religious, when they were in charge, showed to them.

II

In the twenty-first-century West, the preference is for tolerance; people do not like being told what to do. When a social conservative speaks out, their motives are impugned, charged with bigotry or hypocrisy. As an American cleric once observed, we've become a world in which everything is permitted but nothing is forgiven – to which I'd add that guilt is increasingly presumed. It's as if the culture is so saturated with sinfulness that it leaves its mark on everything, even the innocent, like the stench of burned toast. A friend who gave up a lucrative career to become an Anglican priest told me that the first time he wore his dog collar on the Underground, a young man called him a paedophile. Most people would be appalled by this nasty act, but contemporary culture regards cynicism as sophisticated and the queue to cast the first stone winds around the block. Christopher Hitchens famously wagered: give me a Christian preaching against the sin of sodomy and it's a matter of weeks before he's caught in a motel room being humiliated by a prostitute. It's funny because it's so often true – but if you show me a liberal congressman railing against sexism, I give it 48 hours before his Mexican maid, illegally acquired, is on Fox News, accusing him of pinching her bottom.

Remember Burke and de Maistre's warning that sin is perennial, that a revolution can aim to build the perfect society but there is no guarantee that the human beings that populate it will adapt their nature according to the new constitution. They might even profess commitment to its ideals as cover for corruption or theft. In a similar vein, though from a completely different political perspective, Michel Foucault warned that bigotry and bullying are historical constants. Foucault was writing in post-war France, at a time when the left was in despair. The world had tried socialism; it had ended in Stalinism. The USSR was not only as bad as the regime it had replaced, in many ways it was far worse, and Foucault's generation of intellectuals wanted to understand why this happened and if it could be avoided. His conclusion, broadly speaking, was that political power is not solely concentrated in the state but spread out through society, and everywhere there are hierarchies. A revolution changes who is in charge but the dynamic of power is constant: under communism, the guards became prisoners and the prisoners became guards, but society was still a prison. The tsarist Cheka secret police was replaced by the NKVD and the aristocracy by the nomenklatura; if these words mean nothing to you then that, too, is an exercise of power. Knowledge of jargon helped define who was with the regime and who was not, and language helped redefine a tyranny as a utopia, to turn a communist dictatorship into a 'democratic people's republic'.*

Today, identity politics activists love Foucault – he is probably the most quoted man in the humanities – yet they seem oblivious to the possibility that they, too, are participants in a Foucauldian power grab. Consider the parallels between communism and the recent cultural upheavals in the West. Old customs have been discouraged, old ideas shunned. Anyone who challenges the order is denounced and cancelled. A whole new lexicon has been established that we must learn – 'triggering', 'intersectionality' – and if you cannot master it (let alone call a 'he' a 'she' when it prefers 'they'), you fall behind. At least the Soviet revolution achieved some redistribution of wealth and power. Under the contemporary liberal regime, a straight, white man can pledge fealty to the new order and keep his privileges; he is, to use this language, an 'ally' or even 'victim adjacent'. However rebellious identity politics might feel itself to be, it is a curious revolution that is backed by the corporations, the police, politicians and the Church of England – yet the upper hand can never be acknowledged, and the marginalization of conservative opinion never admitted, because the moral authority of identity politics stems from its claim to speak for 'victims'. It is as unwilling to concede victory as other movements are unwilling to concede defeat.

Old categories are eroded – expectant mothers are now 'pregnant people' – but categorization hasn't gone away. Oh no: it is bigger and more obsessive than ever. There is now a whole alphabet of sexual

---

* Foucault wrote: 'In the gulag, one sees not the consequences of any unhappy mistake, but the effects of the "truest" of theories in the political order.' James Miller, *The Passion of Michel Foucault* (Cambridge: Harvard University Press, 2000), p. 296.

identities, running from asexual (nothing) to pansexual (everything); the rainbow flag, which is flown from government buildings, has had so many new colours added that it resembles an artist's impression of an epileptic fit. The ambition of the sixties, we thought, was that people should be judged on the content of their character, not their external appearance, but now we are ranked by our level of victimhood, and bigotry is not beaten but evaded with segregation rebranded as a 'safe space'. On the American campus, demands have been made for spaces, events, even housing to be reserved for non-white students.[11] Some countries have introduced women-only carriages on trains to guard against sexual assault.[12] And in 2020, a British train company announced it would be running a special service staffed exclusively by non-heterosexuals.[13] Such things are necessary, we are told, because prejudice is systemic, which is code for inevitable. But if it is inevitable, on what basis can progress be achieved? Can white people ever not be racist, or men not sexist? Perhaps the future of rail transport is that everyone gets their own carriage.*

There ought to be solidarity among victims but instead there is a spirit of suspicion, and the divisions reflect what different revolution-aries perceive the ambition of the revolution to be. The baseline, of course, is destruction of the patriarchy by deconstructing gender. Fine, but why stop there? Why not deconstruct sex? A feminist might say, 'I was born a woman, it's what defines me.' A transgendered person might say, 'Well, I wasn't born a woman, but I can become one.' A genderqueer person would probably say, 'I can be whatever I want.'† Some feminists object: they have fought for rights as women and for

---

* Finally we might see the return of smoking carriages.

† Perhaps even a new race? In 2021, the British singer and influencer Oli London came out as, first, non-binary and, second, Korean, spending over £175,000 on 18 surgeries to look like a Korean boyband member. His claims to be 'trapped in the wrong body' were met with scepticism by journalists, but the ability of the media to pinpoint why his trans-racialism was spurious was undermined by several outlets compliantly describing London as 'they' rather than 'him'. Having conceded that one identity could be changed (gender), why not another (race)? The loss of a clear set of mutually-recognized rules renders us unable to agree what is fixed or fluid, reasonable or, in this case, actually offensive. Douglas Murray, 'Oli London and the Trickiness of Being Trans-Racial', *The Spectator*, https://www.spectator. co.uk/article/oli-london-and-the-trickiness-of-being-trans-racial, last accessed 8 July 2021.

women, and the notion that someone can step into that identity like a new pair of heels and claim knowledge of it is, to them, invasive and offensive. Imagine spending decades trying to establish a woman's sport as a space in which women can compete fairly, only to be told you must allow a trans-athlete to participate who dominates the contest because their muscle mass is so much larger. This argument has become hurtful with bad faith operating on both sides: although men can be utter bounders, I find the suggestion that a man would go through hormone therapy and a sex change operation just so that he could win a badminton contest ridiculous. But identity is being asked to carry too much. Until the late twentieth century, gender and sexuality were hugely important – obviously, they always will be – yet they were only part of a personality, not its defining quality: other things, such as kinship or religion, were deemed far more significant. Today it feels increasingly as if for many people their label is who they are, that there is nothing beyond the mask but more mask, or that the language they use to describe themselves has become the very substance of their lives.

What happened in the 1960s brought liberation and disruption. We are now at the back end of that revolution, having tested its ideas to destruction – and now, to bring a little order, the revolutionaries are attempting to implement rules of their own that echo many of the rules of the past because they are dealing with the timeless, universal dynamics of power and desire.

If you take the definition of social conservatism as a suspicion of human nature mixed with the imposition of rules to keep us under control, you could argue we are witnessing a conservative correction. Thanks to millennials, the divorce rate is now falling; they drink less alcohol; they are abstaining from sex on campus.[14] We could interpret political correctness as the restitution of good manners, and the #MeToo movement, which called out men for sexual harassment, as an attempt to rebuild some notion of chivalry. But all this is an uphill effort because liberals are trying to police an anarchy they have unleashed and which they cannot quite bring themselves to disavow. Our culture has become a strange mix of the puritanical and the prurient, and the message that women must be respected is undermined by a pornographic subculture that implies they are up for it 24/7.[15] What are we to make of a society in which the popular song 'WAP' (an acronym for Wet Ass Pussy), in which two ladies invite the listener to devour them like a grapefruit, is interpreted by apparently intelligent people as a statement of female empowerment? 'Lick this big fat pussy,' go the lyrics, 'swipe your nose like a credit card.' The point, presumably, is that women's bodies are their own to enjoy as they please, but have those celebrating WAP not twigged that this is a definition of autonomy that gives men exactly what they want?[16] In comparison with a contemporary culture that screams 'look but don't touch', I'd argue that the 1950s dating code – no kiss on the first date, home by ten – is not only easier to navigate but serves the feminist cause better.

It is possible that some of the rules our forebears abided by were common sense, that they weren't solely trying to create and enforce artificial categories (although undoubtedly this happened) but understood that sex and gender are incredibly complicated and powerful – and it was out of deference to this power that tradition attempted to regulate them. G. K. Chesterton put it well: 'The moment sex ceases to be a servant it becomes a tyrant.'[17]

III

Where do 'rules' come from, and how can they be made to remain relevant in a changing social and economic context? To return to the Catholic tradition, its sense of rules is rooted in doctrine, and the authority for doctrine comes from three sources: the Bible, revelation from God and the combined wisdom of the Church. For example, the Church teaches – as we see in Genesis – that when God created man and woman in the Garden of Eden, he created us with an 'equal dignity' but also with distinct sexualities. These sexualities are complementary; they are designed to facilitate procreation. 'Go forth,' said the Lord, 'and multiply.' Much of the Church's attitude towards human bodies and relationships reflects the conviction that nature is ordered by God for a purpose.

So, doctrine is immutable; but human society is not. The Church knows this. In the nineteenth century, the English cardinal John Henry Newman put forward a theory of doctrinal development to illustrate how the Church navigates social history. Development is distinct from change; a change to doctrine would imply a rupture, it divorces the Church from its own history and, thus, from scripture and divine revelation. Development, by contrast, can authenticate old teachings: teaching can grow with experience, enlarge, mature and discover new relevance. One can develop while remaining true to first principles.[18]

Those first principles were, in their own day, revolutionary – as Tevye the milkman jokes, even traditions were new once. In the Roman Empire of the first century, might made right. The strange new Christian religion, by contrast, worshipped a meek carpenter who died, quite willingly, on a cross. In the Jesus cult, victims were heroes and a slave – even a female slave – could win a place in Heaven if she was prepared to suffer. When plague hit and the pagans fled to the hills, the Christians stayed behind to tend to the sick. When the Romans abandoned their disabled babies by the side of the road or on rubbish tips, the Christians picked them up and gave them a second chance.[19]

Today, Catholic teaching on abortion is attacked as reactionary, even anti-woman – yet its roots lie in this egalitarian conviction that all life is sacred, including a baby girl's. Likewise, the Christian teaching on marriage – that a man and a woman become one flesh 'until death' – sounds so conservative, so limiting, yet it was a liberation from the sexual chaos of the ancient world. Whenever there is anarchy, the strong prevail. Tom Holland writes that in Roman society 'women were treated as vessels, to do anything with at will'. Christian marriage replaced coercion with consent, and sex became sacred. A new appreciation for celibacy was discovered, though this, too, took time to develop.[20] Today, the celibacy of the Catholic clergy is taken for granted, but there is evidence that, up until the twelfth century, some priests did marry and wealth was passed onto their sons. This posed a very practical problem. The hierarchy couldn't tolerate money intended for the Church winding up in private hands, so one could see the papacy's efforts to formalize celibacy as motivated by institutional self-interest. And yet the argument for it drew upon Christian tradition (Christ was the model) and there was some popular piety in the mix as well.[21] Northern Italy witnessed a populist, violent backlash against married clergy. In Milan, writes Holland, 'married priests had found themselves boycotted, abused, assaulted. Their touch was publicly scorned as "dog shit".'[22]

In Holland's opinion there was a tension between a church built to change things and a church built to last, and he sees much of Western history as the struggle between the revolutionary and the conservative impulses of Christianity. Whenever the Church became embedded, comfortable or complacent, a radical movement would emerge to return it to its roots – such as the Protestant Reformation, or even secular movements, like the Enlightenment or communism, which espoused Christian themes of equality or justice even as they called for the destruction of church power. One of the limitations with Holland's argument is that it implies that at some point in the journey of human progress, the Catholic Church got left behind. According to historian Ulrich L. Lehner, this is not the full picture. Catholicism did not hide behind the walls of orthodoxy; it has always sought to revivify itself via engagement with the culture of its time. During the Enlightenment, local churches demanded greater independence from Rome; celibacy and marriage were debated again; science was embraced. The Church might have entered the nineteenth century significantly reformed, Lehner argues, had it not been for the French Revolution, which destroyed the reputation of the Enlightenment among Catholics and drove the Church into the arms of de Maistre-style reaction.[23]

Some Enlightenment Catholics concluded from their historical studies that customs they had always assumed to be cast in stone had in fact evolved, surged and occasionally died away – so, if the Church had looked different in the past, why, they asked, couldn't it look different in the future? Progress, after all, is hardwired into Christianity: individuals, and institutions, can get better over time. A number of assumptions regarding sex were turned on their head. The Spanish monk Benito Feijóo, a writer whose contemporary popularity was rivalled only by Cervantes, produced an essay in 1726 entitled *Defence of Women*, which argued that misogyny was bad for both sexes. He shamed anti-women writers as bigots; he exposed alleged female vices as the product of men's abuses. He turned chauvinist logic on its head with a reinterpretation of the story of Adam and Eve. Men blamed women for their eviction from the Garden of Eden because Eve had been tempted by the Devil, but if Eve was weak for giving into Satan, what does it say about Adam that he gave in to Eve? The only reason why women were labelled stupid, concluded Feijóo, is because for centuries they had been deprived of equal education. As you can imagine, these ideas went down with many male readers like a lead balloon – but the Spanish state came around to his way of thinking. They realized that by refusing to educate half the population, they were putting themselves at a profound economic disadvantage.[24]

Capitalism transformed gender and sexual relations; the Church developed in kind. Until the eighteenth century, parts of the Church had taken a lax attitude towards premarital sex because sexual intercourse was commonly regarded as a precursor to marriage – almost like the signing of a contract, doubly so if the girl got pregnant (in Nantes in 1787, almost 90 per cent of brides gave birth sooner than nine months after the wedding ceremony). But with men moving around in search of work, they ceased marrying the girls they slept with, and there was a corresponding rise in extra-marital births. Today, critics of Catholicism blame the Church for the marginalization of illegitimate children; we can infer from Lehner that it was men who created the problem of abandonment, spreading misery and shame, and the Church tried to take a stand by preaching more strongly against extra-marital sex. What is often described as a conservative, even reactionary attitude towards sexual relations began life as a serious attempt to protect the vulnerable. The human consequences of abandonment were shocking: from 1750 to 1799, the child mortality rate in one Dublin home for unwanted babies was 89 per cent. To be born out of wedlock was almost a death sentence.[25]

As the Enlightenment emphasized the rationality of man, so female intellectuals – like Mary Astell or Mary Wollstonecraft – spoke up for the rationality of women, for their right to education or to build families on their own terms. With men behaving badly and women left to manage the domestic sphere, it wasn't such a leap for Christian thinkers to ask if women were in fact the *more* rational sex, and thus entitled to tell men how to behave. Jeanne-Marie Leprince de Beaumont, author of the most famous version of *Beauty and the Beast* along with a large number of proto-feminist tracts, advised wives in 1798 to flatter their husband's ego by reassuring him that he's the boss, all the while making the big decisions for him. 'When you are under the necessity of thinking or acting contrary to [your husband],' she wrote, 'never wound him by a flat contradiction ... contrive, if possible, such expedients as will make him believe he is following his own inclinations, while he is guided by yours.'[26] Elements of the Catholic Church were of a like mind. Missionaries in North America utilized newly baptized women to serve as lay ministers, and in Europe there was a trend towards marriage counselling, which brought the feminine values of tolerance and kindness to family life.[27]

As for the popular idea that the Church has always regarded women as birth machines to churn out little Catholics, Lehner disputes this, too.[28] The Enlightenment-era Church was indeed opposed to artificial birth control, but it urged congregants to leave themselves 'open' to pregnancy without necessarily seeking it, and it encouraged periods of abstinence and prayer in place of sex. Pressure to reproduce was more likely to come from intellectuals who were convinced the population was too low. The philosopher Montesquieu, for example, 'was quite insistent that it was the role of a woman to bear children and not to have personal ambitions'.[29] While the Enlightenment brought women some new freedoms, notably to file for divorce or to accept inheritance, it also cast them as breeders and emphasized subservience, whereas the Church preached 'mutual love and tenderness of spouses', and female Catholic proto-feminists were leading the way in claiming equal rights, especially in the area of education'. Throughout the nineteenth century, Catholicism shifted from putting men at the top of the moral tree to seeing women as the upholder of sacred Truth, culminating in the revival of the veneration of Mary, the Mother of God.[30]

The veneration of virginity is a sticking point for many modern secularists – not just irrational, they say, but anti-women because it implies that for Mary to be perfect, she had to be sexless. Yet it's possible to read in the countless stories of saints resisting sexual aggression a case for female autonomy. St Agnes, for example, was dragged to a brothel to be forced into prostitution; God made her hair grow so long that it covered her nakedness, and when a man tried to hack a path through it, the Lord struck him dead. Female saints could be sex addicts (Mary of Egypt), queens (Jadwiga of Poland) and soldiers (Joan of Arc). Not far from where I write is the well of St Edith in Kent, a self-possessed young nun who, when visited by the Devil, thumped him on the head and split him in two. 'Against much resistance,' writes Lehner, the convent provided 'new spaces of activity hitherto unavailable to [women] and championed the necessity of female education.' In the convent, they were in charge of their lives, their incomes, their bodies. There were stories of nuns allowing themselves coffee or chocolate, even vacations to spas. The cell – a word that conjures up images of straw beds and dripping ceilings – might consist of three or four private rooms with a sunroof and patio, and attempts to tighten up the regime could spark a rebellion. 'In Oberwerth, Germany,' says Lehner, 'an increase in discipline turned an already disgruntled nun into an assassin, who attempted to poison the entire convent.'[31]

The most compelling example of feminine self-will was the Carmelite Order at Compiègne. In 1790, the French revolutionary government abolished religious vows and gave the nuns the opportunity to go home; when interviewed, however, they said they wanted to stay. They regarded their vocation, like a marriage, as being unto death. In 1792, the Revolution evacuated the monasteries and nunneries altogether; the Carmelites were even forbidden from wearing their habits. They were deprived of their status, their property and their visibility – it must have been frighteningly obvious where things would end. In the summer of 1794, 16 members of the order were arrested and taken to Paris, accused of treason and sentenced to the guillotine. They went to their deaths calmly, singing a hymn to the Holy Spirit. Only the rhythmic fall of the blade punctuated the sound.[32]

In a paradox worthy of Foucault, the new enlightened state, determined to free people whether they liked it or not, became the oppressor. The Church was recast as a force for resistance. Maybe the nunneries had been a prison for some; perhaps the religious habit was a symbol of patriarchy. But the moment the state chose to remove it by force, the power dynamic shifted and the outcome was grimly coercive. France's secular state has never come to terms with this conundrum, and a similar debate in the twenty-first century surrounds the Muslim veil. France promises women liberty and one measure of success is their freedom to display their body – but what if a woman chooses to cover up? What if any of us opt to live our lives and raise our families according to traditions that contradict the prevailing liberal ethos? In the new era, social conservatism has become scandalous.

IV

At the heart of the Christian and Muslim traditions is a profound pessimism about sexuality and gender relations: human beings cannot be trusted with absolute freedom, and men unleashed will behave like pigs. Being a man, I suspect this is true, and the fruits of the sexual revolution of the 1960s go some way to confirming it. But there is also a positive affirmation of femininity and masculinity within tradition. They are distinct but interrelated, which is why conservatives will often assert that a child needs, or has a right to, both its mother and father, because they contribute different emotional characteristics that are essential to development: nurture and protection, gentleness and strength.

In contemporary Western culture, women are presented as brilliant – they can do anything – men as emotionally illiterate clowns; good for unblocking a sink, but little else. Men face the same stereotyping once endured by women and minorities; there are few aspirational templates for manly behaviour. When men do get praised, it's often for defying masculine clichés. I have, I'm sure, read far more column inches applauding Prince Harry for talking about his feelings than I have for him serving in the army, and I seem to be in a minority for believing that flying helicopters in Afghanistan is braver than 'opening up'. Courage itself has been redefined. In his excellent book *Honor: A History*, James Bowman points out that in 1914 it was considered honourable to sign up to fight for king and country, and men who refused to would be sent white feathers by women disgusted with their cowardice. Come the 1970s, when Bowman faced the possibility of service in the Vietnam War, 'honor was reserved for the draft avoider and evader, shame for the dutiful draftee or volunteer soldier' – and women held up 'signs reading "Girls say yes to boys who say no." There was a nice symmetry about it, really.'[33]

Many men today feel despised or unimportant. We are more likely than women to show signs of alcohol dependence or be frequent users of drugs, and our biggest killer under the age of 50 isn't cancer or heart disease – it's suicide.[34] We are told that we are dispensable, that a woman needs a man like a fish needs a bicycle.

But kids do want fathers. I'm not going to cite scientific evidence to prove it because I shouldn't have to. It's as obvious as the Earth is round and water is wet, and an indictment of the derangement of certain parts of society that they would insist it wasn't so.* The pain felt in the absence of fatherhood is explored in Homer's epic

---

* As Mary Eberstadt writes, 60 years of social science has documented that 'the most efficient way to increase dysfunction is to increase fatherlessness', and yet no one in the room wants to admit that the one thing they have in common is the large elephant sitting in the corner. Nelly is the link between many of the leaders of the present identity politics crusade: 'The author of the bestseller *White Fragility* was a child of divorce at age two. The author of the bestseller *So You Want to Talk About Race* reports that her father left the family and broke off contact, also when she was two. The author of another bestseller, *Why I'm No Longer Talking to White People About Race*, was raised by a single mother. The author of another hot race book, *The Anti-Racist: How to Start the Conversation About Race and Take Action*, was raised by his grandmother.' It's true that single parenthood is now so common that it might connect any group of people selected at random, but the formation of 'identitarian' groups provides 'protection and community' – an alternative family that helps its members understand where they've come from and who they are. Mary Eberstadt, 'The Fury of the Fatherless', *First Things*, December 2020. https://www.firstthings.com/article/2020/12/the-fury-of-the-fatherless, last accessed 29 December 2020.

poem *The Odyssey*. Our hero, Odysseus, leaves his wife and son, Telemachus, to fight in the Trojan wars (the mythic equivalent of stepping out to buy a packet of cigarettes). For twenty years he is missing in action, presumed dead; his island is overrun by suitors seeking his wife's hand in marriage. Telemachus goes in search of news of his father, a journey that triggers his maturity from child to adult, and what he's looking for, argues the Italian psychoanalyst Massimo Recalcati, is a father as 'master' or 'god', someone who will bring order to chaos and restore his inheritance. There are plenty of boys today who are looking for that, too. The problem, says Recalcati, is that, unlike Telemachus, they have nothing to inherit; modern culture is now so denuded that even if Daddy did show up, it's not obvious what he could restore or if he'd know how to do it.[35] Fathers who have themselves not had a father might struggle to be fatherly, for it is a tradition whose transmission has, for millions of us, been broken.

My dad, I think, struggled to be a dad. Sometimes he was cruel; at other times he was almost absent. I found this desperately hurtful when I was young, but now I'm grown up I realize that some of his flaws came from not knowing how to act in certain situations (particularly when I was being a pain in the neck) because, as the child of a single mother, he lacked a male role model to show him how. This phenomenon, and how to fix it, is at the heart of the work of the clinical psychologist Jordan Peterson, a man who has received a panning from feminists because they don't seem to understand that his books aren't written for them. They're a necessary conversation between men. Peterson is a fan of Carl Jung (as, curiously, is Donald Trump) and the theory that human beings operate in accordance with archetypes, that categories of near-mythical types – classical hero, loving mother etc. – even if entirely constructed, can be useful 'maps of meaning' to help us navigate life.[36]

For Peterson, the differences between men and women are real and self-evident; female qualities suit the new, post-industrial economy and men, to some degree, have been left behind. But don't wallow in resentment, says Peterson: pull yourself together! It's an approach summarized by the mantra 'clean your room', meaning that if your life is a mess, start with the small things, get them in order, set your goals and make changes. It's the kind of advice men can process because it's not about talking or overthinking, it's about rolling up your sleeves and doing. It's also not especially new (Jung and Baden-Powell preceded Peterson by a good century), and it's amazing how much money one can make peddling the blindingly obvious, but Peterson is a best-seller precisely because a lot of young men have not heard this stuff before.[37]

Peterson also has an important message for feminists: you do not want to live in a world of emasculated men.[38] Failed men are pathetic, self-pitying and inclined to hate women – and the link between chauvinism and extremist activity is well discussed.[39] Their anger is entirely unjustified: feminism did not destroy the manufacturing industry or trades unions, economic developments that have removed purpose and status from millions of men, and women cannot be expected to return to the kitchen for the sake of burnishing a man's ego. The case for tradition is not to resist inevitable change, especially where it has improved women's lives, but to defend the tools that help men to cope, which includes the self-assured masculinity that our present culture seems determined to erode.

Another tool for the survival of the sexes is each other. I do not mean that men owe it to women to protect them or women owe it to men to fix them, although each sex is probably imprisoned by this fantasy, but, rather, that in traditional societies, individual identity is defined in relation to others, and that from this spreads a patchwork of roles, rights and responsibilities that lead us away from the ego and towards partnership or kinship. Sexual identity is less healthily defined by preference or desire than it is by self-giving and creativity.

The fact that religions teach God created Adam and then created Eve from Adam's rib should not be interpreted as evidence of the superiority of man but the necessity of both sexes for each other. Adam was formed from common dust; chaps, we are nothing special. And as soon as we were built, it was obvious something was missing: Adam needed Eve, Eve needed Adam, and they were pulled from one another with the hope of putting them back together. Hence marriage is understood in Christian tradition to make man and woman one flesh, from which more flesh – God willing – will proceed. What most undermined this understanding of marriage, sexuality and gender relations was not contraception or same-sex marriage; it was divorce. Divorce means that one flesh can be divided, and it adds a self-defeating conditionality to the word 'forever': the marriage is contracted with a get-out clause. This might make perfect sense to the husband and wife who choose to separate, but it rarely makes sense to their children. When told that Mum and Dad no longer love each other, many a child has said, 'Have you stopped loving me, too?' Children are better than adults at identifying and sticking to first principles. If flesh can be torn one way, separating husband and wife, it can be torn a third way, too, separating parents from children – and the profound self-doubt that divorce breeds has eaten away at our culture like a cancer.

It is indulged, of course, by consumerism, by an ethic that says if you're not content with something, you can always throw it away or take it back to the shop. How can we have a culture of permanence, let alone one of mutual respect, when our economy and society has been structured around autonomy and the satisfaction of desire?

FIGURE 15 Emperor of Ethiopia, Haile Selassie, poses with two cheetahs in front of the Jubilee Palace in Addis Ababa, Ethiopia on 1 November 1962.

8

Tradition and Freedom

Ask most conservatives what they are for and they'll say 'freedom'. Some of them will shout it and wave a flag. It's a pithy answer but not quite right. If you pursue freedom pure and unsullied, it'll destroy a lot of what conservatives value most. Totally free markets eliminate old industries and the traditions that have built up around them. Totally free love erodes monogamy and marriage. Too much freedom can even undermine freedom. A man who is free to drink all he wants is free on paper, true, but if he becomes an alcoholic then he is no better than a slave: the booze rules his life. Worse still, he's likely to enslave others around him, to mistreat his wife and children.

An excess of liberty can easily lead to tyranny, and one of the paradoxes of our society is that every step towards freedom seems to be countered by a weight of costs and restrictions that leave us less free than we were before. Take driving. The car is the ultimate symbol of freedom: on TV, a driver speeds across a desert, Van Halen pumping in his ears. But no road looks like that in England. If the traffic doesn't slow you down, the lights will, and if you try to dodge the regulations or taxes that accompany car ownership, you'll wind up in trouble. As for the machine itself, it has evolved beyond our mastery. An abiding memory of my childhood is my father's legs sticking out from under his Citroën as he spent his Sunday afternoon 'tinkering' with the car. But in the 1990s, notes philosopher Matthew B. Crawford, cars got bigger, heavier and more automated. The goal was to make driving as smooth and safe as possible, to free us from having to think so much, to give the impression that we were 'being cared for by some surrounding entity you can't quite identify', which could tell us when to turn left or right, or gently beep if we got too close to another car. It was, says Crawford, like 'returning to the womb' – though not quite as safe. Between 2013 and 2015, deaths on American highways rose by their fastest rate in 50 years. The culprit was the smartphone: driving had become so easy, writes Crawford, so boring, that drivers started to look at their smartphones rather than watch the road. The solution was more regulation (ban drivers using smartphones) and more automation, until the point will be reached that the car drives the driver rather than the other way around. Driverless cars will be convenient, especially if you like a drink, but isn't freedom from the exercise of free will the very antithesis of freedom? The promise of greater security is probably an illusion, too. As the comedian Robert Webb says, 'anyone who expects to feel safe in a driverless car has never owned a printer'.[1]

This is the dance between freedom and order; a little more liberty, a little more constraint as state and business step in to clear up the consequences, and more and more this tango leads us away from freedom and towards a therapeutic authoritarianism that reduces risk to such a small degree that it's unclear how much choice we exercise at all. Tradition orders society in a different way. It balances rights with responsibilities, governing less by arbitrary laws and abstract concepts, more by common sense and institutional authority. I'm going to take as my prime example the institution of monarchy, but not because I'm a diehard fan. On the contrary, I am rather cynical about it: I take the radical view that the only true king is Jesus Christ, and all human monarchs are pretenders. Consideration of monarchy's history and philosophy illustrates that far from being divine – as some of its more eccentric supporters insist – it is the most human of institutions, that it only works in so far as it understands its rationale and limits, and, under the right conditions, it can be good for liberty. It is useful and virtuous to know one's place, to see oneself not as an autonomous individual working to selfish ends, but part of a tapestry of relationships and hierarchies in which each is given what is due to them, and no one claims more than they deserve.

I

'The best reason why monarchy is a strong government,' wrote the journalist Walter Bagehot in his 1867 masterpiece *The English Constitution*, 'is that it is an intelligible government.' One monarch meant one will, and thus the country knew who was in charge and what was what; the alternative was anarchy. Bagehot regarded the poor as a volatile bunch and feared that if they could vote on everything, they'd turn revolutionary and undermine the state. 'The excitement of choosing our rulers is prevented by the apparent existence of an unchosen leader.' Monarchy, he argued, brings stability throughout the ranks. It keeps the poor enchanted, it puts the rich in their place by denying them access to the most important office in the realm, and it is a healthy check on the ego to know that no matter how much money a man accumulates, he can never buy the crown. Monarchy is familiar, composed of a family whose stories reflect the arc of our own lives, but also mysterious; its exoticism, wrote Bagehot, its rejection of reason, casts a spell over the British state.

> That which is mystic in its claims; that which is occult in its mode of action; that which is brilliant to the eye; that which is seen vividly for a moment, and then is seen no more; that which is hidden and unhidden; that which is specious, and yet interesting, palpable in its seeming ... this is the sort of thing – the only sort – which yet comes home to the mass of men.[2]

Elizabeth II put it another way: 'I have to be seen to be believed.' Seen but not close up, because distance lends authority. Not heard either, because that can lead to disappointment. According to the Polish journalist Ryszard Kapuściński (though whether his writing is factual or allegorical is disputed), Ethiopia's Emperor Haile Selassie gave a regular audience to his subjects in the Golden Hall of his palace in Addis Ababa, and people would travel from miles around to beg for money. 'How much do you want?' he asked each petitioner. 'How do you intend to spend it?' His most Charitable Majesty would then announce that their worries were behind them. The Emperor turned to his treasurer and whispered the amount to be donated into his servant's ear, and the treasurer would dip his hand into a bag of cash, stuff the money into an envelope and hand it to the recipient, who – overcome with joy – backed out of the room, bowing as he went. Only when the petitioner had left the hall would he open the envelope to find there was almost nothing inside it. It was a cruel trick, but, thanks to the ritual of whispering, the Emperor rarely took the blame. People assumed that Haile Selassie whispered the correct amount to the treasurer, but the treasurer, being a mean and wicked man, must have skimped on expenses.

Monarchy is performance, wrote Kapuściński. Selassie's palace was his stage. When he was at home, the palace was clothed in majesty and humming with power; the moment he left, the staff got drunk and grazed goats on his lawn.[3] What the subjects see and hear has to be choreographed. 'We must not let in daylight upon magic,' warned Bagehot, who even in the nineteenth century feared the public was getting too close and the monarchy too visible. Technology complicated things further. In 1952, when parliament discussed the coronation of Elizabeth II, Winston Churchill voiced the concern that televising the ceremony might reduce the sacred to theatrics. What would it do to the mystery of the occasion if the average man or woman could watch it from the comfort of their sofa with a cup of tea?

The decision was taken not to broadcast one critical part of the ceremony. This was the Act of Consecration, an anointing that not only bestows authority upon the monarch but transforms them physically (another example of transubstantiation). To almost complete silence in Westminster Abbey, Elizabeth took off her crimson cloak and her jewellery. Clothed in a plain white dress, she sat under a golden canopy on a wooden chair that belonged to Edward I; the Archbishop of Canterbury was handed the Ampulla, a golden flask in the shape of an eagle, four hundred years old at least, and from this he poured some 'blessed oil' that he used to anoint Elizabeth with a cross on her hand, her breast and the crown of her head. He whispered: 'Be thy head anointed with holy oil: as kings, priests, and prophets were anointed, and as Solomon was anointed king by Zadok the priest and Nathan the prophet, so be thou anointed, blessed and consecrated Queen over the Peoples, whom the Lord thy God hath given thee to rule and govern.'[4]

Time is monarchy's badge of honour; everything about this coronation was designed to suggest that it was not just old but ancient, and its symbols not manufactured but handed down and curated.[5] Joseph Pieper notes that when we refer to the 'wisdom of the ancients' we cannot strictly speaking be correct: Solomon and Zadok, the ancient Jews imitated in this ceremony, knew far less than we do about the world around them.[6] Yet it is presumed that they were wise, and thus authoritative, because they were closer in their time than we are today to the origin of things. Solomon was one of the great kings of a united Israel, one of the wisest and richest, and, by imitating Zadok, the Archbishop reminded the audience that monarchy is endorsed by God, that it has always been and always will be, so there's no questioning its future. Haile Selassie claimed to be 235th in the line of rulers who were directly descended from the union of King Solomon and the Queen of Sheba, a heritage he ostentatiously name-dropped in the second article of Ethiopia's constitution of 1955, lending weight to his 'inviolable' dignity and 'indisputable' powers – 'lion of the tribe of Judah', 'elect of God'. When the communists seized power in 1974, the Emperor mysteriously disappeared; his remains were unearthed in 1992, buried under a palace toilet.[7]

Appearances are deceptive. Those who think the monarchy is rooted entirely in slavish deference need only consider the horrible way the British treat the royal family, particularly the women – and particularly the women who marry into it. Nor is the British constitutional settlement quite as old as it affects to be. In the sixteenth century, the Tudors expanded parliament's power as they nationalized the Church and robbed its property. Charles I attempted to govern without parliament and triggered a civil war in 1642; his son, Charles II, restored the monarchy in 1660, but his brother, James II – an absolutist and a Catholic – was booted off the throne in 1688, replaced by a Protestant dynasty more closely bound to parliament. The British monarchy has long been a game of give-and-take with its subjects. As for claiming authority from the Bible, that source, too, becomes more ambivalent on closer inspection. Ancient Israel, in fact, began as a theocracy, guided by judges, or prophets, who spoke directly to God. According to the Old Testament, the Jews grew dissatisfied with this arrangement, so they asked the prophet Samuel if he could petition God for a king. This displeased the loyal servant, but he passed on the message. God replied: 'Listen to all that the people are saying to you; it is not you they have rejected, but they have rejected me as their king. As they have done from the day I brought them up out of Egypt until this day, forsaking me and serving other gods, so they are doing to you.'[8]

Was God resentful? No: he just understood how human beings think, that we need tangible signs of power and authority to cling to. When Moses disappeared up Mount Sinai in the book of Exodus, the Jews created a golden calf to worship in his absence, because they wanted a god who was physically among them, a focus for their devotion.[9] Now the Jews wanted what the surrounding tribes had, a king around whom they could rally – 'then we will be like all the other nations!' God granted their wish, but it came with a warning so dire that it sounded almost republican: 'This is what the king who will reign over you will claim as his rights: He will take your sons ... He will take your daughters ... He will take a tenth of your grain and of your vintage ... He will take a tenth of your flocks, and you yourselves will become his slaves. When that day comes, you will cry out for relief from the king you have chosen, but the Lord will not answer you.'[10]

It all came true. The kings united the tribes of Israel into a single, great kingdom; then they betrayed their covenant with God, weakened the nascent state and divided their people. Even King Solomon, sitting resplendent on his ivory throne, overspent, overtaxed, kept '700 wives who were princesses and 300 wives who were concubines' and, most unforgivably, introduced foreign gods.[11] Biblical kingship has a ring of divine endorsement, but the abiding message is that monarchy by itself is not enough, that it's a poor substitute for rule by God and it only works when the sovereign defers to holy law and is of estimable character. Monarchy is a lottery.

Fans of monarchy have an obvious emotional attachment to the institution, yet they often advance surprisingly utilitarian arguments for it, such as 'it's good for tourism' or 'it brings stability'. The tourism argument is preposterous – as if the moral quality of a system is judged on the sales of commemorative mugs – and the stability claim is dubious: the rites of the British coronation and its sense of permanence belie centuries of usurpations and wars that are not incidental to monarchy but entirely its fault. The concentration of power in the court creates a zero-sum game: one is either on the throne or not, in the king's favour or not. When a king does not have a viable heir, there is a crisis. When his heir is a daughter, there is a crisis. When the king has several heirs and they all want power, there is a crisis. Royalty is privileged yet it is also a gilded cage, wherein the rivalries and anxieties of everyday life take on a Shakespearean quality, whether in the medieval or modern era. I once met an Etonian who recalled with bemusement that one of his school friends had been excused from attending chapel on the grounds that he was a living god. This was Crown Prince Dipendra of Nepal who, one Friday night, during a party at the Narayanhiti Palace, marched into the billiards room with a small arsenal of guns and massacred half the royal family, most probably because his father wouldn't let him marry his sweetheart. Dipendra then shot himself in the head. He was crowned king while lying in a

Non est potestas Super Terram quæ Comparetur ei Iob. 41. 24

FIGURE 16 Detail from the title page of the 1651 edition of *Leviathan*, by Thomas Hobbes (1588-1679).

coma and ruled his country as a vegetable for three days, before succumbing to his injuries.[12]

II

What, then, is the best argument *for* monarchy? A common answer is: 'the alternative'. The bridge between the sacred monarchies of the medieval era and the popular monarchies of today was a period of revolution and constitutional innovation extending from the mid-seventeenth century to the French Revolution. In 1651, the philosopher Thomas Hobbes, living in exile in France, published a masterful defence of monarchy called *Leviathan*. Hobbes concluded from the anarchy of the English Civil War that man is by nature selfish and violent and that, without proper government, things descend fast into a tyranny of the appetites, creating a world without law, culture, industry or peace, a life that is 'solitary, poor, nasty, brutish, and short'. Fine principles won't save us; a principle only has power if it is backed by force. Therefore, what man requires is a state of sufficient authority to terrify him into being a good subject – a leviathan, depicted on the frontispiece of Hobbes' book as the colossal shape of a king who rises above the city below him, with a sword in one hand (secular power) and a crosier in the other (divine authority).

The image, shown in Figure 16, was created by the French printmaker Abraham Bosse, and one important detail is that while the crown sits on the monarch's own, giant head – it is his will, in other words, that is in charge – the rest of his person is composed of the bodies of his subjects. Hobbes' argument for a strong state was not exclusively monarchical; in theory, it could apply to an aristocratic republic or a democracy. But monarchy was best, he argued, because it brings a unity of purpose: the king knows his own mind, so there cannot be a civil war because he cannot go to war with himself. Bosse's image is a vivid illustration of the theory of the 'body politic', that the monarch has both a literal body and a figurative one that belongs to the nation. In a well constituted state, 'A Multitude of men, are made One Person, when they are by one man, or one Person, Represented; so that it be done with the consent of every one of that Multitude in particular.' To a modern audience this might sound alarmingly totalitarian – all is one and one is all – but it can also be read as one of the first examples of a theory of 'social contract', of a form of government that is justified by giving everyone a stake in the system, by integrating us all into the body politic.[13]

For Hobbes, monarchy isn't solely a mystical institution, there because God wills it; it is a practical necessity. It exists because mankind is weak; it exists to manage our flaws. In other words, Hobbes justified monarchy with reason. From the French Revolution onwards, several thinkers rejected this outlook, arguing that it is self-defeating to give utilitarian arguments for institutions whose authority rests upon a notion of the sacred. To do so, wrote the German philosopher Hegel, is 'to drag down the majesty of the throne into the sphere of argumentation, to ignore its true character as ungrounded immediacy and ultimate inwardness, to base it not on the idea of the state immanent within it, but on something external to itself'.[14] If Elizabeth II had put her rule to a referendum in 1953, she would have won by a mile, but the monarchy would also have been irreparably damaged. She would have been reduced to the status of a democratic politician, whose job is permanently on notice, and she would have given so much of herself to the electorate that she would have given herself away, destroying the mystique of monarchy. There is also some truth in Joseph de Maistre's warning that the moment a monarch explains his or herself, the magic is gone, because the authority of some of the most important roles in life rests on the assumption that they never have to be justified. When a child asks, 'Why do I have to do what you say?', the most compelling answer is, 'because I'm your mother!'

De Maistre believed that republics were built to fail. 'Institutions are strong and durable to the degree that they are, so to speak, deified': the republic is invented, thus unendorsed by God and untested by time. To make matters worse, because republics tend to endorse the values of equality and reason, being geared towards maximizing freedom, they commit the cardinal error of trying to reflect the desires of mankind rather than the will of God. Man cannot create anything of value, argued de Maistre, unless he acts in harmony with the Creator: 'Mad as we are, if we want a mirror to reflect the image of the sun, would we turn it towards the Earth?'[15] Here was a moral argument that went beyond the expediency of saying 'the monarch prevents anarchy'. The historical record, insisted de Maistre, also shows that monarchy guarantees the greater degree of freedom. The French Revolution tore down absolutism, wrote a constitution promising liberty – and then suspended it in order to persecute its enemies. The France of Louis XVI, by contrast, had been governed by 'fundamental laws' that even Louis could not touch because they were inherited. His power was restrained by custom and by the influence that had been granted over time to the nobility and the Church. Old France had been a nation 'too noble to be enslaved' yet 'too impetuous to be free', and in the sense that the king ruled as a conduit for God's law, his office was an inherently moral exercise.[16]

Like the authors of the Old Testament, de Maistre argued that monarchy is a display of obedience: not only of the subject to the king but of the king to God. Some rulers will fail this test of character, of course, but that doesn't invalidate the principle of monarchy itself. The contrary is true: the example of a bad king or queen reminds us of what a good king or queen should look like. For example, says de Maistre, when a court declares that a father is too cruel to raise his son and his son is taken away from him, the court doesn't undermine the principle of paternal authority with its ruling. By making an example of a bad father, the court reasserts how a good father should behave, and by removing the child it re-establishes in society's mind what a proper father–son relationship should look like.[17] For this reason, it would be quite wrong to regard the socio-drama element of monarchy as a wholly modern by-product of its irrelevance: it's part of the package.*

Royal scandals have implications for the rest of us. If a king moves his mistress into the palace, it outrages all women because their husbands could do the same. If a queen is denied her claim to the throne simply because she is a woman, it horrifies both sexes because the principle of inheritance is in jeopardy. Any assault upon the monarch is an assault upon the social order of which they are part, which is why some weep even for rotten kings when they face

---

* When a royal behaves particularly badly, such as Prince Andrew was accused of doing over the Epstein affair, it can lead to calls for abolition of the monarchy. At the same time, the prosecution or shaming of rule-breakers helps reassert norms – in this case of royal vs non-royal behaviour. Andrew's alleged impropriety was not just a bad way for a human being to behave but was judged particularly unbecoming of a *prince*. Moral binaries are common. When Prince Harry and Meghan Markle left England in a blaze of publicity in 2020, their behaviour was contrasted with that of Prince William and Catherine Middleton, who bore the burdens of their office quietly and got on with their duties without a fuss. Good prince vs bad prince is the stuff of Jungian archetype. Not only can a monarchy endure transgression, illicit behaviour is almost woven into the fairy-tale logic.

the executioner. Charles I was an incompetent and intransigent ruler, but even after many years of a civil war he had caused, his critics were reluctant to prosecute him – let alone cut off his head. The Lords wouldn't sanction his trial of 1649; the House of Commons had to be purged. Of the 135 men nominated to the High Court of Justice to try the king, barely half showed up and only 59 signed the death warrant (perhaps under pressure). One MP, Thomas Hoyle, committed suicide on the anniversary of the king's death. According to legend, Oliver Cromwell stood over Charles's headless corpse and muttered 'a cruel necessity'. Cromwell was at heart a monarchist; his fight was with this king, not kings in general, and the constitutional invention of a republic that Cromwell forced on the nation was forced on him. The case against Charles was that the king of England was 'not a person, but an office' and that its occupant must obey the law of the land.[18]

Awaiting trial, Charles tried to keep tradition going by observing the feast of Christmas, which was now illegal in England: 'He dined on 25 December under a canopy of state and dressed in a new suit. There were no traditional mince pies or plum puddings, however, and he read the service to himself from the banned Book of Common Prayer.' The king refused to offer a defence. He argued instead that the trial was nonsensical because no one had sufficient authority to examine him – certainly not the Commons, which had taken into its hands power it could not lawfully hold. If the Commons can do this to me, Charles said, then it could do it to anyone. 'If power without law, may make laws, may alter the fundamental laws of the Kingdom, I do not know what subject he is in England that can be sure of his life, or any thing that he calls his own.' One could retort that when he was king, Charles acted unlawfully himself – but that was beside the point. The moment the king was clapped in irons and dragged before a court, he became a potent symbol of how fragile our freedom is, even for the person at the top of the social pyramid.[19] Charles as tyrant was an abuser of liberties. As prisoner, he was a surprisingly eloquent defender of them.[20]

Regicide was perceived as an act of sacrilege.[21] High office is often imbued with a sacred quality, and when we harm the individual in the office we hurt the office itself and commit a kind of desecration – an offence that is hard to define, but we know it when we see it, just as we know there are hierarchies of crime defined by their wider implications. Graffiti a school textbook, and you deserve a reprimand. Graffiti the *Mona Lisa* and not only have you ruined something that millions enjoy but you have committed a crime against all art in principle by attacking a prominent work noted for its exceptional beauty and excellence. Likewise, to kill a monarch is to commit a crime against all humanity; to storm a palace and trash it is a crime against all property. The body of the king, his family and his things are inseparable from the institution, and the institution inseparable from the social order that revolves around it. Subjects thus rely upon respect being shown to the monarchy for the maintenance of the hierarchies in their own lives.

III

'Social order.' It sounds depressingly restrictive, especially if it validates the English poison of class. Writers like to think they can rise above it, to be part of society yet objective and critical at the same time. The powerful, vain as they are, welcome our attention, but they don't let us in. No writer can be entirely trusted. This understanding was made clear to me when I was invited to Buckingham Palace to report on a 70th birthday party for Charles, Prince of Wales; I was told I could go wherever I wanted but I was not, under any circumstances, to talk to His Royal Highness. I did a good job of staying out of the way for most of the evening, being present but unseen – until, just when I'd started to relax, Charles rounded the corner and walked towards me. He smiled. Had he mistaken me for a guest? Did he want to shake my hand? Our worlds were in terrible danger of colliding, until my breeding as an Englishman kicked in and I deftly stepped behind a giant fern. The prince passed by, unmolested.

After that, Charles had a strange habit of popping up at events I was covering; I said 'hello' to him once. He replied: 'And what do you do?'

'I'm a journalist,' I said. He giggled like a naughty schoolboy and moved on.

I was less interested in the Prince than the effect he has on other people. He is the opposite of a politician. He has nothing to say, yet everyone, great and small, hangs on every empty word. There's a similar effect when people are introduced to beautiful women and chimpanzees: their exoticism casts an egalitarian spell, all eyes in the room are on them. I found one exception to this rule at a garden party in Rome to celebrate the canonization of John Henry Newman. The prince was at one end of the lawn, surrounded by admirers; standing by himself at the other end was a cardinal in a bright red cloak. He looked very still and noble, as if in a theatrical pose, waiting for a scene to begin. 'What are you up to, your eminence?' I asked.

'I am waiting for the Prince,' said the cardinal. 'There is no way I am going over there to speak to him. He must come to *me*.'

As the spatial hierarchy of the garden party showed, everyone has a sense of place. It can be snobbery to point this out; it can also remind the powerful of their limits. Charles might be a prince of this world, but the cardinal was a prince of the Church, and, when in Rome, bishop takes king.

As the philosopher Peter King argues, if we are told 'you are out of place', we can easily take offence – but it suggests there is somewhere we do belong, somewhere that someone else doesn't have a right to be and where they, too, are out of place and uncomfortable. When we are accused of 'overreaching', says King, again this might be an insult – but it also suggests that 'we always have a level' of our own, 'that there is somewhere that is more properly ours. There is a level that is correct for us.' It's not uncommon to hear people say that their place is better than everyone else's, even if this is improbable. Birmingham cannot possibly be nicer than Paris, but I dare you to tell a Brummie otherwise.[22]

Life is full of complex hierarchies of place. If you dine in a restaurant, you cannot wander into the kitchen to find out how the food is doing, even though you are paying for it. You cannot march into your boss's office at work, uninvited – conversely, if he walked into the staff room when you were trying to take a break, it would feel like an invasion of what is supposed to be your space. I had an embarrassing experience of this when I was a schoolteacher. I was only 19; the oldest students were 13. I had zero authority and the little monsters knew it. On one occasion, one of them followed me into the staff room when it was empty. I ordered him to leave; the boy stood his ground. A senior teacher walked in and was horrified. First, she castigated him, then, when he was gone, she unleashed the wrath of God on me, and quite right, too. There was nothing special about the staff room; it contained a kettle and some romantic paperbacks. But it was for the staff, not the students, and the fact that the children couldn't go in it gave it an air of mystery that added to the authority of the adults. The boy was in the wrong place. He had overreached. His transgression turned the structure of the school upside down and threatened the order of our little universe.

Space and authority are connected. When I go to see a doctor, I tap politely on his door and wait for an answer before entering. I defer to his advice – and I do so on trust in his title, because he could be a miracle worker or he could be an incompetent butcher. A critic might say that the difference between a doctor and a monarch is that the doctor has earned respect through study and experience – yet not only do most monarchs have these, too, but by dint of being in the job for life they've probably been studying and practising their vocation longer than a doctor has medicine (I'd wager that monarchs kill fewer of their subjects, too). The respect shown towards a monarch is a barometer of social harmony and a mirror of the respect we show towards others and expect to be shown towards us in turn. An analogous relationship is between parents and children. You need no experience, no qualifications, to be a parent; it's a status you acquire through birth, and it's a status that commands due respect and an authority that is, again, often spatial. I would never dare to go into my parents' bedroom uninvited when I was a boy; I never sat in my father's chair.

Christian tradition dictates that the commandment to honour thy father and thy mother is a case of the particular speaking to the universal, that pupils should honour teachers, employees their employers, subjects their monarchs. But the commandment includes and presupposes the duties of teachers, employers, monarchs and parents to all those placed below them. The places we occupy are not islands but linked to each other by reciprocal rights and responsibilities. To know thy place is to know what you owe and are owed.

One of the most interesting thinkers on this subject is Simone Weil, a French writer of the early twentieth century whose biography reads like a confusion of intellectual fads (far-left, anarchist, Catholic) but whose insistence that politics be above all human achieved a synthesis that appealed to the defenders of tradition. T. S. Eliot called her 'more truly a lover of order and hierarchy than most of those who call themselves conservative, and more truly a lover of the people than most of those who call themselves Socialist'.[23] Weil spoke less of human rights than of human needs, and therefore a hierarchical system, if it met those needs, could conceivably be just. The subject is obedient to the monarch, but in turn the monarch has to be obedient to the subject, by recognizing their liberties and the monarch's responsibility to protect, defend and consult them. Weil argues that the hierarchy of obedience does not end at the monarch; they are also obedient to God, obedient to their conscience and, crucially, obedient to the office. She returns us to the theme that tradition requires a sacrifice of ego, suggesting that the best monarch was not a colourful individual but a personality that has become submissive to the office, like a body defined by its uniform.[24]

When I speak to a policeman, I speak to a *policeman* – not an individual personality but the embodiment of their job and rank. Would you feel comfortable with a copper who had a ring through his nose? No more than I'd board an aeroplane flown by a pilot with gin on his breath. Respect for the authority of a complete stranger cannot be based upon what we know of them – obviously – so they have to project a certain character associated with their office. I want a doctor who not only is a doctor but looks and sounds like one, someone whose manner encourages trust. The French Romantic François-René de Chateaubriand described the perfect priest as 'the interpreter between God and man', therefore,

> an air of holiness and mystery should surround him. Retired within the sacred gloom of the temple, let him be heard without being perceived by those without. Let his voice, solemn, grave and religious, announce the prophetic word or chant the hymn of peace in the holy recesses of the tabernacle. Let his visits among men be transient; and if he appears amid the bustle of the world, let it be only to render a service to the unhappy.

The otherworldliness of a priest, we can infer, is a performance. But it's not a mere contrivance; it's necessary to do his job. If a cleric were too familiar, drunk or, God forbid, lecherous, he would instantly forfeit that authority.[25]

A weak person fails to fill their office and loses respect; a tyrant is too big for the office and generates fear. The ideal monarch, thought Weil, is a proportionate model of obedience to nation, tradition and the hereditary principle: 'The effective rulers, rulers though they be, have somebody over them; on the other hand, they are able to replace each other, each in unbroken continuity, and consequently to receive, each in his turn, that indispensable amount of obedience due to him.' We all have a need, she wrote, to have someone to look up to, and while this can lead to a dangerous veneration of charisma – Hitler worship – if married to a traditional understanding of institutional authority it becomes veneration not of a person but of their office and the ideals that office embodies.[26]

Here we run headlong into the cultural contradictions of liberalism. Liberalism has torn down or discredited many of the traditional structures of hierarchy. It says that we can be whatever we want to be; the notion of 'place' is discouraged.[27] The irony is that liberalism does try to impose a hierarchy of its own, based upon its own ideal of government by reason. Liberals generally believe that the most reasonable men and women – the most technically adept – should run society, ergo they have done their best to elevate and empower the expert. The problem is that for expertise to command authority, we need people to appreciate the mystique of office; we need the public to trust scientists, obey the police, swallow what a doctor prescribes and believe what a teacher tells them. Surveys suggest that there is still ample trust in teachers and the medical profession. The police, however, are on thin ice, and faith in many of the institutions that liberalism venerates most – politics, business, journalism – has fallen through the floor.[28] This is partly because a liberal culture erodes deference and deconstructs authority, and its self-centred, narcissistic qualities render it hard to command respect.

In June 2018, President Emmanuel Macron of France attended a parade to mark the anniversary of the Second World War. This was an important day and a formal occasion, so imagine his horror when a longhaired boy in the crowd addressed him by his nickname: 'Manu!' Macron gave him a dressing down and tweeted a video of it *pour encourager les autres*. 'Call me Mr President of the Republic,' he said, 'or sir.' The world laughed.[29]

My heart went out to Macron. Whatever you think of him – and he is pompous – it ought to be possible to dislike him personally but respect his office, especially on an occasion that contains a ring of sanctity. But Macron embodies a generational crisis of legitimacy in liberal politics. Unlike his predecessors, Charles de Gaulle or François Mitterrand, he has no connection to the Second World War. He did not serve in the army; he isn't a father figure; he isn't known for his religious devotion. Macron is highly intelligent but not an honoured intellectual, like Foucault. His primary qualification for politics is that he's good at politics, and his greatest achievement was winning. Like Tony Blair or the Clintons, he represents politics as an end in itself, an expertise – and what such people don't realize is that beyond the world of politics, politics commands very little respect, even a little contempt.

Populism falls into this trap, too. The populist claims, accurately or not, that they are popular – and too often this becomes the sole criteria on which they are judged. As a journalist, I grew mightily sick of writing articles with the headline: 'Will Trump win again?' The more important question was 'does he deserve to?' One count against him was that he was shamelessly unpresidential, but then that was the point. Republicans nominated a trashy candidate to protest against how trashy politics had become. They blamed the decline in presidential standards on the Clintons: Bill's adultery had destroyed whatever dignity the White House once had as a temple of the republic, and the perception that Hillary tolerated his philandering undermined both her authority and the credibility of the feminists who supported her. 'Do as I say, not as I do' is the motto of a bankrupt elite. It was on display during the coronavirus pandemic, when a number of officials were caught breaking the very restrictions they had authored or enforced. Professor Neil Ferguson, an epidemiologist at Imperial College London, produced the modelling that the UK government followed when it ordered its initial lockdown; Ferguson took to the airwaves to tell us to stay indoors and away from others. A few weeks later we discovered he had been meeting his lover on the sly. The public was outraged; some would've put him in the stocks.[30] I thought he deserved a medal for courage in pursuit of passion. It reminded me of when Winston Churchill was told, during a harsh winter, that one of his ministers had been caught in flagrante with a man on a park bench at three in the morning. 'In this weather?' said Churchill. 'My God, it makes you proud to be British.'

Just because Professor Ferguson had ignored his own warnings didn't mean they were inaccurate, but his adventurism cast doubt on his word – and on the reputation of data scientists in general. It is not enough to call yourself an expert, you must act like an expert – yet our society is managed by people who occupy their offices *without being changed by them*. They cling to their own tastes and personality, expecting the office to adapt to them rather than the other way around.[31] We have clergy who avoid the subject of religion, teachers who think they can learn from the kids, doctors who ask, 'what do you think is wrong?' and police who want to be hip. In 2017, budget cuts forced Avon and Somerset Police to cut their special burglary unit, which had only solved one in ten cases – yet its officers, male and female, found time to publicize the fight against modern-day slavery by painting their nails and posting photos of their handiwork online. Taxpayers were indignant; one civilian asked, 'How about nailing some criminals?' Avon and Somerset Police responded with a threat: 'If anyone found these comments offensive, please report them to Twitter. If you feel you were targeted and are the victim of a hate crime, please report this to us. We take this issue extremely seriously.'[32]

Avon and Somerset made the same mistake as Macron: when authority collapses, it's easy to resort to bullying, which is why Britain's liberal and tolerant police force has gained a reputation in recent years for being heavy-handed and nasty.* But, as G. K. Chesterton reminds us, 'bullying is almost the opposite of authority ... Authority simply means right; and nothing is authoritative except what somebody has a right to do, and therefore is right in doing.'[33] The police have struggled to enforce the regime of political correctness because precious few citizens take it seriously – they don't think it's *right* – and the more authoritarian the cops have become about it, the more their authority has weakened. The moment authority has to throw its weight around, it is lost, just as the moment that someone utters the words 'Don't you know who I am?' we know they are going to be humiliated by the reply. If you have to ask, the answer is no. Genuine authority is seen and believed.[34]

IV

The need for hierarchy, for social order, is not contingent upon monarchy, of course, and is perfectly reconcilable with a

---

* Put another way: when force is no longer implied it has to be applied. That's why fat American cops shoot suspects who run away. They couldn't catch them if they tried.

well-constituted democracy. America proves it. Its revolution swept away kingship and its egalitarian spirit is still felt by English visitors centuries later. It's one of the reasons why I fell in love with the country. Britain is my faithful old wife, I joke; America is my exciting younger mistress. The English, tired and jaded as we are, are concerned primarily with where you came from – and will never let you forget it. The Americans want to know where you're going and if they can tag along. It is a society that, in principle at least, has no snobbery but also no envy. Donald Trump could never be elected in Britain because he is both too common and too rich.

Unquestionably, America was fashioned by the Enlightenment and its political culture is essentially liberal, but as we've seen in the case of the Catholic Church, conservatism and the Enlightenment rubbed off on each other. Edmund Burke sympathized with the grievances of the American colonists; de Maistre prayed their new republic would work. Both men saw a parallel with Britain's Glorious Revolution of 1688, which they regarded not as a revolution but a correction. The real innovation in the 1680s, said Burke, had been James II's absolutism – another monarch who didn't grasp the limits of his office – so the coup that dethroned him wasn't innovatory, it was a step back.[35] De Maistre agreed: the men of 1688, he wrote, 'activated their old constitution and took their declaration of rights from it'.[36] Likewise, the proximate cause of the American Revolution was that the British crown had overreached itself and tried to impose on the colonies taxation without representation. The key difference between the French and American revolutions, argued Roger Scruton, was that the French invented liberties that previously did not exist, whereas the Americans were fighting for rights they felt they already had and which were threatened by the crown. The downside of this relatively conservative revolution is that the Americans also protected ways of life that were quite wicked. The French abolished slavery. The Americans did not. It would take another war, in the 1860s, to begin the process of guaranteeing full equality for all Americans.[37]

As the philosopher Isaiah Berlin wrote, the United States constitution rested upon a notion that de Maistre should have found agreeable, namely that rights are not invented but divinely ordained and therefore inalienable. This makes the American concept of liberty very hard to tinker with. As an Englishman, I look across the ocean and see a new society, but also a country that, probably because it broke away from us, has retained certain qualities that the old world has lost. No socialism for America; no whiny self-doubt. Church and state are separate, but faith and public life are not. Its constitution evolves, thank heavens, but slowly and piecemeal, whereas parliament can, in theory, do whatever the majority wants. The United States is not a pure democracy, it is a republic, and it has done a better job than any monarchy of promoting self-governance.

So far. Why in recent times has America's political leadership fallen so far from its ideals? Why is the country no longer governed by people of the calibre of the Founding Fathers? On this point, we should avoid nostalgia. When I hear complaints about the partisanship and cruelty of modern politics, I like to point out that in 1804, the vice-president of the United States, Aaron Burr, shot the former secretary of the treasury, Alexander Hamilton, in a duel (Hamilton probably fired first – and deliberately missed; Aaron Burr shot Hamilton in the abdomen and left him to die). A few weeks later, Burr was back at his desk, chairing the senate. President Thomas Jefferson, who hated Hamilton, invited him to dinner.[38]

These were proud, stubborn, petty men, some of whom owned slaves and, in the case of Jefferson, fathered children by them. But they were exceptional. They defeated the British Empire, created a state and put the tiny republic on its Manifest Destiny towards the conquest of the continent – their documents are hallowed and their principles remain near-biblical to both Democrats and Republicans. One reason for their brilliance, suggested Russell Kirk, is that they were British, steeped in Britain's parliamentary tradition; another is that they were a 'natural aristocracy', that they had talent and virtue, cultivated by education, religious literacy and, crucially, the spare time to debate great questions and come up with inspired answers.[39] Leisure is essential to culture: a society that works its fingers to the bone, or is distracted by the narcotic of technology, hasn't the opportunity to contemplate progress.

The death knell of this culture was the birth of republic itself and its erosion of deference to aristocratic values. 'As the common man rose to power in the decades following the Revolution,' writes Gordon S. Wood, 'the inevitable consequence was the displacement from power of the uncommon man, the aristocratic man of ideas.' The Founding Fathers 'helped create the changes that led eventually to their own undoing, to the breakup of the kind of political and intellectual coherence they represented. Without intending to, they willingly destroyed the sources of their own greatness.'[40] Again, let's be cautious about this thesis. Privileged oligarchy did not die out overnight (the Kennedys, the Bushes) and for every demagogue (Andrew Jackson) there was a poet of the common man (Abraham Lincoln). But there is a growing tension between the spirit of modern democracy, which is increasingly about asserting what government must do according to the will of the majority, versus the republican foundation of America, which stressed what government cannot and should not do for fear of destroying the capacity of the individual to manage their own affairs.

The Founding Fathers, broadly speaking, dreamed of self-governance: for the republic, for the states (as far as was practicable) and for the individual. But this is impossible without virtue. Give a virtuous person freedom and they will thrive, and their society will flourish. Give an unvirtuous person freedom and they will destroy themselves and their country. John Adams, the second president, stated: 'Public virtue cannot exist in a Nation without private Virtue, and public Virtue is the only Foundation of Republics.'[41] A government is only as good as its electorate. The most honest answer to the question 'how did the 2016 election come down to Hillary Clinton vs Donald Trump?' is 'that's what the people wanted'. There were perfectly acceptable alternatives. The voters rejected them. There are those who see politics as a conspiracy against the citizen, as if the only way Trump could win the White House was with Russia's help – and conspiracy thinking is often an attempt to rationalize an irrational world. But the voters are perfectly capable of making a bad decision without being tricked into it.

For society to cohere and freedom to survive, we need a healthy culture, one that has a shameless bias for virtue and which promotes it at every turn. The American right, more so than its European variant, has grasped the importance of this, which is why it has waged a culture war for the last few decades – railing against education and art that, in the opinion of conservatives, undermines the very basis for an enduring republic. But Harvard and Hollywood are not the only culprits; American conservatives have for too long been strangely blind to the corroding influence of the area of life to which they have given too much liberty and demanded too little responsibility. One of the greatest enemies of truth, beauty, excellence, authority and self-government is the untrammelled free market.

FIGURE 17 Margaret Thatcher meets a pack of Cub Scouts from Wakefield on the steps of Ten Downing Street, London, 24 October 1979.

9

Tradition and Equality

I once had lunch with a senior Republican (too senior to be named) the day that an English court ruled against the construction of a new runway at Heathrow airport. The Republican was outraged: it would be bad for business, he said. 'Hang on,' I replied, 'you do realize that in order to build that runway they were literally going to bulldoze an ancient village? As conservatives, aren't we supposed to want to preserve the landscape and our way of life?'

He said: 'But you can't stop progress.'

I used this as an opportunity to lay out my patented Grand Theory of Western Conservatism, of which I'm rather proud. 'Okay, let's imagine that we have to build a road between two towns,' I said, 'and standing in the way is a beautiful oak tree, a thousand years old. Now, it seems to me that we have three options. We could not build the road, but that would be bad for jobs. We could cut down the tree, but that would be vandalism. Or we could do what I suspect Edmund Burke would do and spend a little more money to build the road around the tree so that we can have both.'

The Republican looked at me as if I was mad. He said: 'Or you could just cut down the tree and plant five new ones elsewhere.'

'But, but—' I stammered, 'it's a very old tree! It's been there for centuries, children have played in it, lovers have carved their names into it. Isn't the whole point of conservatism to save it?'

'Yeah, but my way you get five new trees.'

There was no arguing with him. It was odd because, like almost all American conservatives, he was a very religious man who peppered his conversation with Jesus' best lines, yet the sanctity of a tree – its uniqueness in design and character – was beyond him. I imagine that if someone suggested building a runway across the Grand Canyon, he would sign off on it so long as five more canyons were dug further down the road.

In recent years, some conservatives, particularly populists, have become critical of this attitude: they talk not just of conservation but preservation, of saving jobs and a way of life, and they are prepared to use government to do it. They have called for trade protection, investment in infrastructure, government-financed childcare and even put 'big business' on their list of culture war enemies.[1] The left calls this cynical. The right is as privileged as it's always been, they say, it's just learned to clothe its greed in language that appeals to the working class. Some on the right argue that this proves populism isn't conservative at all; real conservatism, they claim, is in favour of keeping government small and helping people get rich, so populism is a historical deviation, a mutation of the philosophy, or even socialism in disguise.[2]

A simpler explanation is that, while conservatives see their primary function as preserving traditional culture, big business does not. In fact, it benefits materially from integration to the European Union, free trade with China and mass migration. Novelty is essential to consumerism and diversity is a cash cow. In 2019, reported *Newsweek*, several corporations decided to mark the 50th anniversary of the Stonewall riots – when gays, lesbians and transgender people protested against police brutality in New York – by launching a celebration of 'love, equality and diversity'. One could buy rainbow-coloured vodka from Absolut; a rainbow-coloured cup from Starbucks; rainbow-coloured cake from Bouchon Bakery; rainbow-coloured trainers from Doc Martens; and a rainbow-coloured Mickey Mouse rucksack from Disney. These companies were 'giving back' to the LGBT community, said *Newsweek*, although it's a strange definition of 'giving back' to churn out a high-end product for people to buy. That sounds more like cashing in.[3]

To say that conservatives have come to loggerheads with business because the 'woke' have suddenly captured the boardroom is shallow analysis.* These tensions have flared up many times before. In the early twentieth century, religious conservatives smashed up shops that sold booze; in the 1970s, at the height of détente, anti-communists were horrified to discover that corporations were happy to trade with the Soviet Union. Business does what's good for business, short-sightedly at times, and it doesn't always translate into a conservative cultural tradition. If there's a tree in the way, cut it down, plant five new ones. Charge the kids a dollar to climb it.

Capitalism, like liberalism, has been shaped by the ideas and aspirations of the Enlightenment, so it's another example of a tradition that erodes tradition: it doesn't just create and enrich, it also destroys and impoverishes, and as it drives society apart into extremes of rich and poor, so it erodes the environmental balance necessary to sustain it and the social consensus necessary to tolerate it. Capitalism unfettered is like a fox loose in a hen house. Unless it exercises self-discipline, or has discipline imposed upon it, it will either eat all the hens in one go, and later starve, or else the hens will finally realize who their common enemy is and fight back. Someday, we shall eat the fox.

---

* Corporations almost certainly believe in the cause but, as *Forbes* magazine pointed out, they swing both ways. The chemical giant Pfizer was a sponsor of World Pride in New York City in 2019, yet only the previous year it gave nearly $1 million to politicians who voted against gay rights initiatives; Pfizer said: we are pro-gay, but those politicians are pro the chemical industry, so we were happy to bankroll them. Money was also paid out to right-wing politicians by fellow donors AT&T, UPS, Comcast, Home Depot and General Electric. Across the ocean, the organizers of the rather more modest Pride festival in the English county of Surrey announced that the lead sponsor of their inaugural event would be BAE Systems – an arms dealer that supplies weapons to Saudi Arabia, where one can't drink vodka straight, let alone rainbow-coloured. A spokesman for Pride in Surrey acknowledged that the sponsorship was 'controversial' but added, 'We'd say it's fab to see them wanting to make a difference, break down industry stereotypes and build a more diverse and inclusive community.' Three cheers for BAE Systems: an equal opportunity killer. Dawn Ennis, 'Don't Let That Rainbow Logo Fool You', 24 June 2019. https://www.forbes.com/sites/dawnstaceyennis/2019/06/24/dont-let-that-rainbow-logo-fool-you-these-corporations-donated-millions-to-anti-gay-politicians/, last accessed 20 October 2020; Nick Duffy, 'Arms manufacturer BAE Systems named lead sponsor of Pride in Surrey', PinkNews, 1 February 2019. https://www.pinknews.co.uk/2019/02/01/arms-manufacturer-bae-systems-sponsor-pride-surrey/, last accessed 20 October 2020.

The 'cultural contradictions' of capitalism help explain how conservatism came to lose its way in the mid-twentieth century, and why today's populism, far from being novel, returns to a more tradition-oriented outlook. If some of populism's methods sound like socialism, that's no coincidence. Not only have defenders of tradition and socialists sometimes turned to the state to protect what they value, but they have also often valued similar things. Acknowledging this fact has implications both for conservatism and for socialism – because just as conservatives have lost some collective memory of their tradition of social reform and state intervention, so socialists have become almost totally divorced from their earlier cultural commitments to religion and rural life. Socialism has a strong tradition of its own. In its desire to protect the hens against the fox, one might almost call it conservative.

I

When I was at Cambridge, studying twentieth-century history, a lecturer told the class: 'By the way, we all know Margaret Thatcher was evil, but don't write that in the exam.' This was how many left-wingers see Britain's most important post-war prime minister, not just wrong but dynamically wrong – an active force for wrongness. Before she came to power, in 1979, conservatism was regarded as passive. Britain had a social democratic consensus: the Conservative Party mostly preserved it. Major industries remained nationalized and the welfare state continued to be bankrolled by high taxation. The rationale behind this consensus was egalitarian but also subtly conservative. The unions were bought off; mass unemployment was kept at bay. The Conservatives feared that joblessness would drive the country even further to the left, but full employment was also something they felt they owed to the generation that fought the Second World War. They believed in *noblesse oblige*, that the rich and powerful have an obligation to help the poor.

By 1979, however, over one million Britons were out of work, the unions were out of control and inflation was eroding wages. Margaret Thatcher was elected to change things, and she shifted the tone of British conservatism away from the One Nation romanticism of Benjamin Disraeli, with its alliance between the aristocracy and working class, and onto territory that sounded far more like an Enlightenment liberal – aimed at a solidly middle-class constituency. She advocated freedom and personal responsibility; the locus of her conservatism was the individual, not the collective. Over 11 dizzying years in office, she cut taxes, privatized state assets, let businesses fail, deregulated markets and crushed union power. Some people, like my parents, did well and climbed the property ladder; others slid down. Whole communities, often very traditional – defined by work and church – collapsed into poverty and addiction. In 1987, Mrs Thatcher gave an interview to the magazine *Woman's Own* in which she was asked if free-market capitalism had, in the end, torn society apart. 'There is no such thing as society,' the prime minister replied, there are 'individual men and women'. Some readers wondered if this woman was a conservative at all.[4]

Her defenders insisted that she was. It was the Britain of 1945–79 that had been the revolutionary regime, they argued; Thatcher was returning things to the way they were before socialism tampered with the natural order. Free markets, they said, were rooted in tradition; in fact, they exemplify it. Markets function according to lots of little decisions – what my customers want, what manufacturers should make, what shopkeepers should charge – that feed off local knowledge and customs, amounting to a giant web of human relationships far too complicated for any state to compete with, let alone replace.[5] By trying to decide what people need and to provide it for them, the post-war British state subverted the traditional market, much as it had undermined the charitable impulse by replacing voluntarism with welfare. When Thatcher said, 'there is no such thing as society', she did not mean we have no responsibility for each other. Quite the opposite. If you say that poverty is society's problem, she argued, you take the burden off your own shoulders and hand it to an anonymous bureaucrat. A truly social being wouldn't do that: they would ask, 'what can I do to help?' Thatcher elaborated: 'There is a living tapestry of men and women … and the beauty of that tapestry, and the quality of our lives, will depend upon how much each of us is prepared to take responsibility for ourselves … and help by our own efforts those who are unfortunate.'

Thatcherism represented the defeat of the politics of 'we' – of socialism, the masses, the attempt to build heaven on Earth – and the victory of 'I', wherein it became the vocation of the individual to try to build their own private slice of paradise. But do not assume that Thatcher didn't care about society or didn't operate within a framework of traditional morality. 'Economics is the method,' she once said, 'the object is to change the soul.' She was deeply religious, like many of her contemporaries in parliament – in fact, you could argue that politics in post-war Britain was a battle between two strands of Methodism, Primitive and Wesleyan. The Primitives stressed service to the poor and found a natural home in the Labour Party. Thatcher was raised in the Wesleyan branch of Methodism, which emphasized the doctrine of free will – that we must be free to choose to do the right thing.[6] She maintained a liberal attitude, too, when it came to alternative religions and therapies; in fact, once every six weeks, she would get herself electrocuted. In 1989, an article published in *Vanity Fair* revealed that the prime minister would visit the flat of a Hindu practitioner called Lady Price, and that Lady Price would 'poach Mrs Thatcher in herbs in a hot tub and then literally electrify her … Standing at the foot of the tub, Madame would turn the amps up to .3 on the baffle plates which lined the bath … After an hour's electrification she would rub down the tingling body with natural flower oils.' Following a particularly difficult meeting with Thatcher, one of her ministers was heard to joke: 'She must've had the full 240 volts this morning.'[7]

'There are certain rules by which to live,' Thatcher told *Woman's Own*, 'certain courtesies, certain conventions, certain generosities to other people.' These traditions, she argued, were essential to the maintenance of a free society. The interviewer did not disagree, but he put it to Thatcher that by unleashing the free market and encouraging people to get rich quick, the prime minister had accidentally undone the very rules she cherished. The 'divorce rate under 35 is nearly 50 per cent', he pointed out, and abortion had almost doubled since the Conservatives came to power. There was violence among strikers and the poor, but also violence among the rich, who now celebrated excess where once it was the fashion to disguise it. 'We have competition and free enterprise and it seems somehow to go together with greed.'

This observation could have been made in the 1890s or the 1920s, and it was a problem explored compellingly by Daniel Bell in his 1976 book *Cultural Contradictions of Capitalism*. Bell argued that capitalism began life as an economic method by which one makes as much money as possible so that it can be reinvested for future return. This gave birth to an admirable new cultural ideal: the delay of gratification for long-term benefit, through work, thrift and savings. The Protestant work ethic, almost personified by Margaret Thatcher, became the moral identity of the emergent middle class, a new bourgeois cult of self-denial.

Unfortunately, said Bell, capitalism also unleashed forces that undermined this ideal. For capitalism to work, it had to persuade us to consume, to buy things we don't necessarily need, and as the nineteenth century wore on, a countervailing ethic of profit for profit's sake – for pleasure and desire – took hold. As Western man became more acquisitive, he naturally became more materialistic. A new standard was set for judging the success of a society that lacked spiritual foundation: each generation should be richer than the last.[8]

In America, the early conservative bourgeois ideal was captured in Frank Blackwell Mayer's 1858 painting *Independence* (see Figure 18). The subject, Jack Porter, was a wealthy man – he'd made a killing out of coal – and was depicted wearing a nice pair of boots and a smart waistcoat. But the overall aesthetic of Mayer's portrait was homely: Jack smoked a corncob pipe while sitting on a roughly hewn bench, with his wife's knitting balanced on the windowsill, looking like an everyman pioneer. What mattered most to the mid-nineteenth century American Dream was being independent, and if independence was to be sustained, one must be as careful with one's money as possible. Cut to 1925, and the American Dream was now embodied by F. Scott Fitzgerald's Jay Gatsby, a self-made tycoon whose wealth was ostentatious. It was also mysterious (possibly criminal) and, in the new world of the stock market and salesmanship, it must have seemed as if one could turn the base

FIGURE 18 *Independence* (Squire Jack Porter) by Frank Blackwell Mayer.

metals of talent and good luck into gold. This rags-to-riches fantasy colonized Europe, including Thatcher's Conservative Party, which cooked up its own British Dream of ceaseless growth up for grabs, even though the proposition was illogical and unsustainable.[9] If a free market is truly free, then there will always be winners and losers, generations that add wealth and generations that lose it. The notion that we can all make it, and go on making it, is absurd, especially if the implication is that there is no upper limit with no regard for the impact upon the world around us. Such an economy must necessarily eschew self-denial. The American Dream, said right-wing columnist Ann Coulter, 'is Jet Skis, steak on the electric grill, hot showers, and night skiing'.[10] If the ecological cost of this fantasy is that half the world becomes a dustbowl, one must ask by what definition the American Dream is conservative at all? The trouble with capitalism, concluded Bell, is that it has triggered a civilizational switch from 'restraint' to 'release'. In 1848, Karl Marx and Friedrich Engels observed:

> The bourgeoisie cannot exist without constantly revolutionizing the instruments of production, and thereby the relations of production, and with them the whole relations of society … All fixed, fast frozen relations, with their train of ancient and venerable prejudices and opinions, are swept away, all new-formed ones become antiquated before they can ossify. All that is solid melts into air, all that is holy is profaned.[11]

This helps explain how the bourgeoisie, even though triumphant politically and economically in the nineteenth century, came to feel as if they had lost. Bell's argument goes like this: you want people to buy stuff, okay, but what stuff? To tell consumers what to purchase, capitalism endorsed the notion of 'taste', to generate a sense of excitement around products and their associated lifestyles. The more exotic and exciting a product was, the better it sold, so norms in art were broken down and novelty was celebrated. The nineteenth century saw an explosion of celebrity culture, as personality triumphed over character and sensation squeezed out sobriety. When the industrial revolution began, economics still shaped culture – but culture increasingly determined taste, and as culture encouraged acquisition, so the West became more acquisitive, the culture corroded and the cycle continued into the hideous mess of a culture we have today.[12]

According to Bell, the bourgeoisie tried to navigate this with a new formula: they were 'radical in economics' – i.e. all for capitalism and free trade – but 'conservative in morals and cultural taste'.[13] Margaret Thatcher was not its only salesman. In 1980, Ronald Reagan was elected president on the promise that he would simultaneously unleash the free market and put God back into public life. He was supported by an ecumenical council of religious conservatives called the Moral Majority. The name said it all: majorities shouldn't require pressure groups. The American right saw itself, paradoxically, as representing the masses yet also at war with mass culture, with popular music, popular movies, pornography and sexual licence. The contradiction between the cultural message that 'sin is bad' and the economic dogma that 'greed is good' slipped the right's attention.

One of the most prominent faces of American capitalism in the 1980s was Donald Trump. Married three times; profiteer from gambling; he once joked that avoiding a sexually transmitted disease was 'my personal Vietnam'.[14] There was no restraint in Trump's personality, only release. 'I play to people's fantasies,' he wrote in his memoir *The Art of the Deal*. 'People may not always think big themselves, but they can get very excited by those who do. That is why a little hyperbole never hurts. People want to believe that something is the biggest, the greatest and the most spectacular.' And yet Trump, despite his elephantine ego, was at least sensitive towards the consequences of free-trade economics – because he understood the game and what it takes to win it. In 1987, he paid nearly $100,000 to run a newspaper ad complaining that America was bankrolling the defence of Japan at the same time as Japan was deliberately operating a weak currency, allowing Meiji's heirs to outcompete the United States. Trump's primary objection was not moral but reputational: the world was laughing at his country and he didn't like it. But he raised an important question. What was it that conservatives wanted to conserve? The principle of free trade? Perhaps – yet this came at the cost of other things that conservatives are supposed to like, such as jobs, communities and a strong nation state. It took two decades for the American middle class to put two and two together and realize that untrammelled free trade has unconservative outcomes, and the fact that they turned to Donald Trump to fix it, a man barely capable of governing himself, let alone an entire country, was the crowning irony of the cultural contradictions of capitalism.

If you want to see just how confused American conservatives are about what they want, you could pay a visit to Trump Tower on 5th Avenue, Manhattan (the food is quite good). In a past life it was a department store, a limestone tower erected in 1929 that featured a stunning art deco front with classical friezes and an ornate grill – like a cathedral dreamed by Gustav Klimt. The store was closed in the late seventies. Manhattan, cash-strapped and crime-ridden, accepted Trump's offer to knock it down and rebuild as a mix of shops and apartments, on the understanding that he would at the very least treat the art deco with care. He did not. Trump cut every corner possible, including using illegal Polish labour, and on his orders 'the demolition workers cut up the grillwork with acetylene torches … jackhammered the friezes, dislodged them with crowbars, and pushed the remains inside the building, where they fell to the floor and shattered in a million pieces'. Trump called the fittings 'garbage' and recycled them for scrap.[15] The new tower he unveiled in 1980 was innovative for its time – but the striking thing about it today is its complete absence of character. It is tall, black; the glass is like the reflective windows of a limousine, letting the residents look out, but no one see in. It's a sort of flat-pack, ship-and-assemble design that, because it belongs nowhere in particular, could conceivably be built anywhere – indistinguishable from a thousand glass towers in Dubai, London or Kuala Lumpur. And on the inside, gold everywhere – yes – but also the same cream and tan bland that you can find in some of the better Marriott hotels. Rabbi Jonathan Sacks once argued that in a globalized world, the nation state has become a place people migrate to and do business in, essentially transactional and transient. His observation that places that were once homes now feel like a hotel is reinforced by the efforts of men like Trump to make everything actually look like a hotel, pushing a corporate aesthetic down our throats that destroys any semblance of the local, the quirky or the eccentric.[16]

In 1964, the *Daily Telegraph*, my newspaper, expressed its dismay at the arrival of modernist architecture in London, at the transformation of Victorian splendour into a drab landscape of prefabricated buildings and concrete blocks. The playwright John Osborne called us hypocrites. In a furious letter to the newspaper, he wrote that the death of beauty 'is precisely the price you Tories have always been willing to pay for a society run by moneymakers … You can't have your free-for-all enterprise, your shareholders and chairmen of money-grubbers and decency, taste, comfort and honour as well … You don't want beauty. You never have, you never will. Not if it costs you anything.' The *Telegraph* replied, correctly, that it was socialist authorities that had built some of the most hideous estates in Britain and expected poor people to live in them, while the old houses that Osborne mourned were constructed by the rich and the privileged. That's true, said Osborne in a second letter, but these great houses were built 'at a time when the aristocratic and classical virtues' of the past 'had not yet been betrayed' by the capitalism endorsed by the *Telegraph*. 'The inescapable remains: supporters of your sort of newspaper will always sell out even traditional Tory values like loyalty, taste, the enjoyment of beauty and craftsmanship ... even tradition itself – for a good old fast, easy buck.'[17]

The accusation as directed at the *Telegraph* was unfair and inaccurate, but as a comment upon the tension between radical economics and cultural conservatism it touches a nerve. Conservatives of the last century or so have protested against the collapse of the family, the desecration of culture and the loss of religious faith, routinely overlooking the responsibility of their own wealth and ambition. What conservatives dare not confront is that capitalism is part of the problem.

II

Does the left have its cultural contradictions? Absolutely. Every year in England, thousands of left-wing activists and unionists gather in the city of Durham to mark the Durham Miners' Gala, an event that has been taking place since the late nineteenth century. Highlights include the parading of union banners – illustrating the history and ideals of the working-class movement – and the performance of colliery bands. It's the closest thing the British left has to a Mardi Gras, and a surprising locus for activism given that the environmentally conscious left hates fossil fuels; coal mining was dangerous and unhealthy; and the last pit in Northumberland, next door, closed in 2005. Journalist James Bloodworth, writing in 2016, called the Gala a 'carnival of nostalgia' that illustrates how an obsession with the past 'can act as a dead weight on meaningful action in the present'.[18]

Friedrich Engels described pit conditions in 1844: 'The working-man lies on his side and loosens the coal with his pick ... The women and children who have to transport the coal crawl upon their hands and knees, fastened to the tub by a harness and chain ... The shafts are wet, so that these workers have to crawl through dirty or salt water several inches deep, being thus exposed to a special irritation of the skin.' There was nothing to mourn about this industry, and its impact upon human behaviour, as Engels encountered it, left little room for class pride: 'To church they go seldom or never ... Their morality is destroyed by their work itself. That the overwork of all miners must engender drunkenness is self-evident. As to their sexual relations, men, women, and children work in the mines, in many cases, wholly naked ... The number of illegitimate children is here disproportionately large.' We are still arguing today over why the poor smoke, drink or eat bad food: Engels pointed out that these are the indulgences of people who have few pleasures besides sex, and too little time to raise their children to middle-class standards.[19]

So it's no surprise that when, in 1871, the Durham bourgeoisie heard that a Miners' Gala was going to be held in their city – seat of a great cathedral and university, a bastion of Anglican respectability – they imagined themselves being overrun by savages. On the day, however, they were pleasantly surprised. 'A more well behaved body ... could no well be found,' reported the *Durham Advertiser* the following year. 'There was an entire absence of all drunkenness and no ill-spoken word never offended the ear of the spectators in the streets ... The pitman has become a respectable and peace loving citizen and his conduct proved so.'[20] The transformation of the working-class culture over the course of the nineteenth century, argued the historian E. P. Thompson, was thanks to its growing organization and self-consciousness, to an emergent class identity that both looked forwards and backwards. This is not a contradiction:

> The conservative culture of the plebs as often as not resists, in the name of custom, those economic rationalisations and innovations ... which rulers, dealers, or employers seek to impose. Innovation is more evident at the top of society than below ... It is more often experienced by the plebs in the form of exploitation, or the expropriation of customary use-rights, or the violent disruption of valued patterns of work and leisure. Hence the plebeian culture is rebellious, *but rebellious in defence of custom*.[21]

There was an obvious influence of radical ideas at the Durham galas – socialist, atheist and evocations of the French Revolution – expressed through campaigns for political representation and fairer working practices, but the mining villages around Durham had also been heavily evangelized by the Primitive Methodists, who had their own distinctly Christian tradition of mass gatherings. Early banners pleaded for social reform couched in biblical authority (Examples of modern equivalents are illustrated in Figure 19) and tried to appeal to the better, God-fearing nature of the pit-owners. Gradually, the Anglican establishment came to give its blessing to events, too.[22] The unions reached back into the folk memory of the medieval guilds – trade and mutual aid organizations for craftsmen that functioned like a proto-union – evoking their language and rich pageantry to elevate their own labour to the status of a craft.[23] The Durham Miners' Gala was a celebration of courage, a display of numbers, an attempt by working people to claim a role in the national narrative: did they not power the industrial revolution and fuel the empire? Wasn't it coal that made the difference in the Second World War? Thanks to their political organization, by the turn of the last century the miners had become the shock troops of socialism. Michael Foot, a man on the left of the Labour Party, disagreed with the Gala's relatively conservative politics yet found its customs 'sensational … The whole city absolutely throbbed with the thing from early in the morning right through until you left. And you left absolutely drunk with it – the music, the banners and all in that beautiful city. It overwhelmed you.'

By the time Foot became minister for employment in 1974, the coal industry was already in serious trouble. Attendance at the Gala fell thanks to the rapid closure of pits, reports academic John Tomaney, but the conservatism of its organizers didn't help matters: only the miners' banners could be paraded. In 1979, the organizers were asked if other unions could join in. The answer was sniffy: 'As you will gather, we are jealous of our traditions … If you understand [them] you will have half expected a "no".' The final nail in the coffin was the Miners' Strike of 1984, a brutal struggle with the government that split the movement and crippled trade union power. It is possible

FIGURE 19 Banners on display at the Durham Miners' Gala, 8 July 2017. They are local, historical and, in the case of the one on the right, religious. The image evokes the book of Isaiah: a lion lies down the lamb and a little child leads them.

that the Gala almost *had* to endure this nadir before it could undergo reinvention and recovery. Attendance today, without any local mines in operation, has sprung back from its decline in the 1970s – and banners are still central to the event, although modern imagery and participation is more diverse, tying together the historic working-class struggle with campaigns for gay rights, gender equality or environmentalism. By rooting these modern struggles in old-fashioned imagery, they repeat the nineteenth-century trick of citing the guilds and the Bible, lending a movement that could easily fracture a sense of historical coherence. Nostalgia is the glue. It gives a dead industry remarkable relevance. Divorced from the reality of life down the pits, which really could be nasty, brutish and short, mining is now associated with camaraderie, solidarity, community and masculine pride. Mining is popularly remembered as a 'proper job'; the kind of work advertised in the contemporary service economy can't match it. Just as veterans of the Second World War are 'the likes of which we shall never see again', so the mining unions represent the mythical heroes of organized labour.[24]

Industrialization weakened tradition; the union movement revived it, only for globalization and de-industrialization to corrode it all over again. One wonders if the Conservatives were on the right side in 1984. They wanted to break the unions because they saw them as overpowerful, which they were – and it's true that some in the labour movement wanted to destroy capitalist democracy and institute a Marxist alternative. But most of the men who joined the Miners' Strike did not want a revolution, they wanted to preserve their way of life, an instinctual conservatism that put them at odds not only with Thatcher but also the Marxists in their own ranks – a perennial problem for a radical left that often finds itself at loggerheads with the traditional cultural values of its own constituency.

Karl Marx had contempt for nostalgia, dismissing it as a 'worldwide necromancy'. He recognized the traumatic destructiveness of capitalism, but hoped it might uproot the old, aristocratic order and radicalize the workers. There were possibilities even in imperialism. What Britain did in India, eradicating local tradition, was 'actuated only by the vilest interest' but it spread modernity and would trigger a social revolution. The bourgeoisie were an 'unconscious tool of history', digging their own graves, and Marx and Engels wanted them to get on with it, so it made no sense for the working class to resist upheaval. 'It is better to suffer in modern bourgeois society,' they warned, 'which by its industry creates the means for the foundation of a new society that will liberate you, than revert to a bygone form of society which, on the pretext of saving your classes, thrusts the entire nation back into medieval barbarism.' The salvation of the working class, they concluded, lay not in reversing the industrial revolution but seizing control of industrial property. Don't stop technological advance, they argued: take control of it.[25]

This was the Marxist view that took power in Russia in 1917 and which still shapes our assumptions about socialism today. Socialism existed before Marx, however. It, drew upon the tradition of Christianity and had many schools of thought and approaches to history. A notable body of nineteenth-century intellectuals sympathized with Marx's critique of capitalism but saw industrialization as a dark cul-de-sac into which man should proceed with caution. Progress, they argued, was not measured in growth or technology, or who owned what, but in morality, and rather than wiping the slate clean and starting over again, they suggested it was better to ask what had worked in the past and what we might revive. They associated exploitation with cultural decay.

A key characteristic of the nineteenth century, wrote the contemporary historian Thomas Carlyle, was that 'Men have lost their belief in the Invisible, and believe, and hope, and work only in the Visible ... The infinite, absolute character of Virtue has passed into a finite, conditional one; it is no longer a worship of the Beautiful and Good; but a calculation of the Profitable.' That was why Victorians were so horrible to one another, he deduced, why the rich exploited the poor, for 'our life is not a mutual helpfulness; but rather cloaked under due laws of war, named fair competition, and so forth, it is a mutual hostility'. An ugly society produced ugly things; taste was deformed. William Morris, a writer now most celebrated for his textile and wallpaper designs, drew a link between cruel working conditions and the shoddiness of the goods that rolled off the assembly line. The Medieval era, he believed, had been capable of incredible beauty, such as Notre Dame, because its artisans, enjoying freedom in their work, were moved to create wonders. Morris and his friends in the Arts and Crafts movement tried to replicate older aesthetic ideals through their own use of embroidery or woodblock printing, as well as making stained-glass, even illuminated manuscripts (tradition, once again, being repurposed as a consumer product), and they sketched out fantasy factories of the future that would be democratic in spirit, providing libraries, schools, and theatres for the enlightened workforce. The proletariat, given time and decent pay, could be 'natural aristocrats', too. Morris had no intention of recreating feudalism, yet he admired, some suspect 'envied', the men and women of the Middle Ages 'to whom heaven and the life of the next world was such a reality, that it became to them a part of the life upon the earth, which accordingly they loved and adorned'.[26]

The melting pot of Romanticism, reaction and socialism was not a coherent movement, on the contrary it contained plenty of eccentricity, perhaps a drop of madness, but it did represent a compelling dissident ethic that defied the clichés of left and right to argue that man's fundamental problem was not material but spiritual – or, rather, that our very real material problems have a spiritual root. The proposition was this: capitalism had put profit before God and fellowship.[27] The dissidents were not opposed to initiative or effort, in fact William Morris's friend, John Ruskin, an eminent art critic and lecturer, persuaded his students to help mend a road in Oxford, under the supervision of an elderly gardener nicknamed Professor of Digging (one of the amateur navvies was Oscar Wilde). The finished road was a mess, even Ruskin had to admit, but he was convinced that hard lifting should be a branch of education like any other; enriching, ennobling.[28] The ideal mode of labour, however, was a craft – skilled and talented – eschewing vanity in favour of a collective enterprise for collective gain, which, the dissidents imagined, is what had happened under the guilds. In medieval Europe, the rhythms of the year were dictated by the seasons; rest and charity by the church. The bulk of work was done in the home or nearby, which made the family, not the individual, the preferred economic unit. Labour and spirit were integrated: sculptor Eric Gill described craft as the 'training of persons for the end envisaged by religion … to see all things in God'.[29]

Capitalism degraded work. The worker was divided from their family, their place of birth, their talents and their soul: workers on the assembly line were treated as employees, not fellow human beings, almost as a piece of equipment. It's true that we no longer generally work on assembly lines here in the West (and where they still exist, they are largely automated), but the rise of the modern service economy would have been regarded by most of the dissident thinkers as another step in the wrong direction, never mind the proposition that a product could be manufactured in a sweat shop and sold several thousand miles away from its origin, at several times the price it cost to make. Trade has always happened, argued the Catholic conservative G. K. Chesterton, and trade can be very helpful at getting us what we want, but it only exacerbates our alienation from God's creation. Writing during the Great Depression of the 1930s, Chesterton noted that before the rise of capitalism, 'the universal habit of humanity has been to produce and consume as part of the same process; largely conducted by the same people in the same place'. It might have been on a feudal manor, where the serfs were little different from slaves; it might have been among guilds, where the sharing of property and profit bordered on communism. 'But none of these many historical methods, whatever their vices or limitations, was strangled in the particular tangle of our own time; because most of the people, for most of the time, were thinking about growing food and then eating it; not entirely about growing food and selling it at the stiffest price to somebody who had nothing to eat.'

To Chesterton, and again to many of the dissidents of the nineteenth century, capitalism seemed insane. It was lunacy, he wrote, that the world could be brought to ruin by an excess of production: by what Alice-in-Wonderland logic could there be too many good things? When a tree produces an abundance of apples, wrote Chesterton, this is usually regarded as a blessing, yet in the twentieth century a society could actually be pushed to the brink of starvation by abundance – and the only solution, insisted economists, was a dose of austerity. God, by contrast, is never austere in his gifts. Nature is not efficient. In the gospels, the usual hierarchies of power are inverted – the rich man, we read, has less chance of getting into Heaven than a camel has of passing through the eye of a needle – and Christ's teaching is full of images of fertility, of mercy and second chances.[30] In that spirit, Christian socialists called not for the end of productivity but greater collective control of it, for fairer distribution and a more creative allocation of resources. Invest in that which gives life, they said, not that which destroys. It would be better to have a surplus of orchestras than a glut of guns. 'There is no wealth but life,' declared Ruskin. The fact that capitalism insisted upon behaving in such an unnatural way, in defiance of the very reason it purported to exemplify, implied that its branch of economics had become a form of religion, with its own dogmas, priests and sacrifices upon the altar of profit. Ruskin described himself both as a 'violent Tory' and a 'communist of the old school'; idiosyncratic, yes, but between them Ruskin, Morris and Carlyle probably had at least as great an influence upon the miners and the emergent labour movement as Marx or Methodism enjoyed. In 1906, when the first Labour MPs were returned to parliament, a survey was circulated among them that asked what books most shaped their thinking. The winner was *Unto This Last*, written by Ruskin in 1860.[31]

The dissidents were hopelessly nostalgic; they were also prophetic. Ruskin decried the mechanization of agriculture, for example, because of its impact upon the environment. If the land is used solely for one purpose, and farmed to the point of exhaustion, he warned, it loses its soul just as surely as the man who is worked to death in the mill. Ruskin warned of the risks of a 'silent spring' – a countryside devoid of wildlife – a hundred years before it became a common concern:

> No air is sweet that is silent; it is only sweet when full of low currents of under sound—triplets of birds, and murmur and chirp of insects, and deep-toned words of men, and wayward trebles of childhood. As the art of life is learned, it will be found at last that all lovely things are also necessary:—the wild flower by the wayside, as well as the tended corn; and the wild birds and creatures of the forest, as well as the tended cattle.[32]

Man does not live by bread alone, he reminded readers, but by all God's natural gifts, a theme picked up in Pope Francis's famous encyclical *Laudato Sì* over a century later, wherein the pontiff argued that nature is a 'magnificent book in which God speaks to us' and that 'everything is connected'. Even the most casual sin against nature in Britain can have horrific consequences elsewhere; as the West consumes, the poor choke on our detritus.[33]

Ruskin's bucolic language, and Chesterton's dream of most men living as farmers, lead us to the reasons why the dissident strand of socialism, or anti-capitalism, did not triumph: it was out of date almost as soon as it began. It might have connected with a generation of workers forced to move to the cities, but the British working class tended to become less revolutionary the longer that industrialization took hold. By the mid-nineteenth century, they were more interested in taking control of the means of production than returning to the land. But certain themes endured that made Christian socialism distinct from Marxism. For a start, it was sceptical of state power. Second, even though collectivist and utopian, the Romantic or Christian socialist assumed that change proceeds through the actions of the individual. While the Marxist tends to judge progress in terms of the interest and actions of the group, or class, the Christian believes man has a personal relationship with God and thus a personal responsibility to do the right thing. Ruskin's vision of socialism has some sympathy with Thatcher's ideal of self-governance, or the modesty of Mayer's painting *Independence*: 'We need examples of people who … have resolved to seek … not greater wealth, but simpler pleasure; not higher fortune, but deeper felicity; making the first of possessions, self-possession; and honouring themselves in the harmless pride and calm pursuits of peace.'[34]

Finally, the dissident socialists had an attitude towards the past that provides a necessary rebuke to the view of the Durham Miners' Gala – or any commemoration of labour history – as the dead hand of nostalgia. In 1871, when the Parisians rebelled and formed a commune – an embryonic socialist revolution – Ruskin was hopeful. When the revolutionaries burned the Tuileries Palace and damaged the Louvre art museum, he was disheartened. This was wrong, he said. The past should not be swept away but preserved, maintained and studied as a means of placing the people of today within a tradition of human progress – just as Vaughan Williams argued that only by understanding folk music could one appreciate the glories of Bach or Wagner. 'Arising out of Morris's developing socialist understanding,' writes John Bellamy Foster, 'was a sense of history as constituting endless strivings to create a new present. The precious remnants of the past, revealed in artistic production, were records of these strivings; speaking to us as a ghost of the present in spite of the irreversible changes that had taken place.'[35]

III

An interesting question is why socialism didn't emerge as a serious electoral force in early twentieth-century America. The elites conspired to destroy it – unions were broken and radical leaders were deported or imprisoned – and it didn't help that in a country that still romanticized its agricultural past, socialism of the Marxist sort was easily caricatured as urban, atheist and foreign. Yet the state in the Union where socialism enjoyed its greatest expression wasn't New York or Illinois, it was Oklahoma. Historian Jim Bissett writes that economic factors came into play – recession and the rising cost of credit drove farmers to the left – but Oklahoma's socialists also did a clever job of celebrating farm work as a dignified route to independence. They presented socialism as more authentically American than capitalism.

Many Oklahoma activists were also evangelical Christians who saw socialism as the fruition of Jesus' teachings, as their best shot at building heaven on Earth. 'One party member,' according to Bissett, 'estimated in 1912 that a majority of the ministers in his county supported the socialist movement' and that it was gaining more members among clergy than any other profession; another reported that 'most of the Baptists' in his area 'were socialists'. Opponents found this surprising and alarming and did their best to recast the Socialist Party as damnably atheistic, but the charge didn't stick because it was packed with ministers and its rhetoric was so reassuringly conservative. Weren't the Democrats the party of slavery and alcohol? Didn't the polygamous Mormons vote Republican? The Socialist Party proclaimed itself 'the great bulwark of society, Christianity and the home'. Of course, many socialists outside the state were atheist and found this language strange and reactionary, which helps explain why the success of socialism in Oklahoma is not a well-known part of the story of the American left. It has been overlooked by historians because it defied the narrative.[36]

And yet, the Christian tradition runs like a thread through America's history of social progress, most notably the civil rights movement – and it's in the DNA of the British labour movement, too. Karl Marx, ultimately, was a materialist: what mattered was who owned what. Keir Hardie, Labour's first leader, was a moralist: what mattered was how we treat each other, and for him socialism was 'a question of ethics or morals … a handmaiden of religion and as such entitled to the support of all who pray for the coming of Christ's kingdom on earth'. The nature of Hardie's faith is contested by biographers. His theology 'was not divinely based on God but on a human Christ' argues one, and he was scathing about established churches. Many Christians have left the Church, he said, in order to join socialism and become better Christians. But whether Hardie was using Christian imagery to articulate socialist ideas or the other way around, what matters is that the early Labour Party found a means of translating complex economic ideas into a language that cast socialism as a part of British tradition, as if it was capitalism or the ruling class who were the recent invention. In 1885, addressing a group of miners, Hardie beautifully summed up the political implications of a mankind made in God's image: 'You are God's children. Your work is mining, but the blackest work to which a man may put his hand can never disguise or blot out the image of him in whose likeness he was made."[37]

Today, the left struggles to speak to the very constituencies that have historically sustained Labour in power. The lesson of early socialism is that it helps to tap into memory and history.[38] I understand why the left is reluctant to do this: they don't want to

---

[*] Christian equality was one way to connect poetically with the voter; patriotism, another. Much of the British Labour movement opposed membership of what would later become the European Union because it was a 'capitalist club', detrimental to the interests of the global working class, and because it was undemocratic and unpatriotic. The old Left could be internationalist and militantly parochial. When, in 1969, parliament debated making it easier to take currency abroad, facilitating tourism, one Labour MP, Hector Hughes of Aberdeen, who had written the national anthem of Ghana when it became independent, suggested it was borderline treason to want to holiday anywhere other than the British Isles. There were plenty of holiday camps to go to in the UK, he said, and if you want to see what Spain or Italy look like, plenty of travel programmes on television. 'In our modern libraries there are [also] books of a descriptive character,' he added. 'Foreign Travel Allowance debate', Hansard, 30 June 1969. https://hansard.parliament.uk/Commons/1969-06-30/debates/1d070ea6-46a3-4015-be22-a0792550dc01/ForeignTravelAllowance(%C2%A350Limit)?highlight=currency%20overseas#contribution-e5f72361-67bc-4b5f-a13e-f3f6c627fe00, last accessed 13 July 2021.

validate nostalgia, to confirm the fantasy that things were better in the past when there was less immigration, gays were in the closet, women were subservient and the workers 'knew their place'. Yet the past is not just a land of reassurance; it is also a source of moral learning, and the early Labour Party used Britain's Christian identity to shame the country and to challenge it to change.

Were they alive, the Romantics and the Christian socialists would probably accuse the modern left of individualism, of abandoning the unity of class in favour of micro-identities. Social liberalism undermines solidarity in some of the places working people value it the most: nation, the community, home and the family. What too few twenty-first-century left-wingers realize is that whatever the current culture of their movement might be, historically it was subtly conservative. Roger Scruton, reflecting upon his father's lifelong commitment to the Labour Party, believed that he had supported it in the faith that it was the one institution capable of saying no to forces of iniquitous change, be they property magnates chewing up the countryside or financial speculators robbing Britain of its wealth: 'Only through the Labour Party, he thought, could we safeguard an England which belonged to the people, who in turn belonged to it ... Deep down his passion was a religious one, a protest against a world which placed material prosperity before spiritual need, and which ignored the fact that the soul of a man is a local product, rooted in the soil.' If Scruton's father was correct, then it's a wake-up call to left and right. Conservatives have too often sided with forces that brought devastating change.[39]

They need to ask themselves what they actually want and how to get it: which policies destroy and which preserve? Politicians, more sensitive than intellectuals to the mood of the people, have started to recognize this and conservatism has begun a tectonic shift away from shrinking the state and towards exploiting it for conservative ends – to promote some vague concept of the 'common good'.[40] Defining that common good will be difficult; avoiding the trap of enlarging the state to the point that it squeezes out civil society is vital. But at least there is a tacit acceptance that capitalism as we presently practise it is doing more harm than good, that inequality, if you don't address it, could lead to revolution; free trade, if you don't regulate it, could strip away everything; pollution, if uncontrolled, could destroy the ecosystem. And you cannot expect people to marry, settle down and have lots of kids if their pay is low, the rent is high, they could be sacked any moment and childcare, or healthcare, is prohibitively expensive. If the 1950s is your go-to decade for tradition, your theme park of nostalgia, it's worth remembering that taxes were much higher back then and society more equal by force of redistribution. The kind of world that conservatives want has to be paid for, probably by wealthy conservatives.

The work that has gone into constructing traditions, wrote Thomas Carlyle, is underappreciated because it took centuries, like the growth of a tree. Revolutions are celebrated because they are loud, exciting, transformative, but in truth they are a singular event, and a devastating one, too. 'The oak grows silently, in the forest, a thousand years; only in the thousandth year, when the woodman arrives with his axe, is there heard an echoing through the solitudes; and the oak announces itself when, with a far-sounding crash, it falls.' Centuries gone in a moment of madness. That is why we mourn the tree.[41]

FIGURE 20 A family member delicately dresses the body of a deceased relative, adding an oh-so-important cigarette, in North Toraja, Indonesia, 25 August 2020.

10

Tradition and Faith

This brings us to death. One of the most essential questions is, what happens next? The thought that the answer might be nothing is frightening, not just because oblivion is incomprehensible but because the idea that all this was for nothing, that once we're gone, and the memory erodes, we disappear like sandcastles on the beach, is awful. To defeat this, we build legacies; we have children, we write books. We also memorialize the dead, so that we in turn won't be forgotten, and we make a taboo of speaking ill of them in case that should happen to us, too. Traditional societies honour their dead and, in a sense, never quite let them go. This is neither morbid nor backward looking. It is magnificently human. Through custom and ritual, we transcend our physical limits, and our fears, and bring life to death.

For the Egyptians, death was a hazardous journey; you had to pack well. The deceased pharaoh, after being embalmed and mummified, was buried with food, furniture, spells and weapons, even a cat for company, and rode a raft through the underworld to the Hall of Truths where, following a trial by 42 judges, his heart was placed on a pair of scales and measured against the weight of a feather. If his heart was out of balance, the pharaoh failed the test; his soul would be devoured by Ammit, a goddess with the head of a crocodile, the torso of a lion and the bottom half of a hippo. Journey and judgement are frequent themes of mythologies of death, with a concern to take the right steps to attain the right outcome.[1] Many pre-modern Nepalese believed that if they died holding the tail of a cow, they went to the front of the queue in Heaven.[2]

The goal of Pure Land Buddhism is to escape the cycle of mortal existence and be reborn in a paradise fit for the enlightened: to get there, one must be in the right frame of mind. At the death-bed, as the consciousness departs from the body, there is chanting and sublime concentration. In one legend, a virtuous monk, thought guaranteed to make it to the Pure Land, at the last moment spotted a jar of vinegar on the shelf and wondered who would inherit it. He was reincarnated as a snake in the jar.[3] The Malagasy people of Madagascar believe that the spirit remains in the body after death, even after burial, until the corpse has fully decayed: every few years, their family removes it from the tomb, gives it a fresh set of clothes and brings it up to speed with the family gossip.[4] This is nothing compared to the rituals of the Toraja people in South Sulawesi, Indonesia, where funerals are of such importance that an entire lifetime's work can go into paying for them. We live, say the Toraja, to die. Such is the cost, so elaborate are the rituals – so far do family members have to trek to be there – that it can take months before a funeral takes place. While waiting, the deceased is embalmed, dressed and placed in the home, where life continues as normally as possible. The corpse attends meals sitting in its usual chair; at night, it is laid out in its bed. It is treated with kindness and respect. In 2016, the journalist Amanda Bennett visited South Sulawesi and discovered a dead village chief who had been lying in state in her bedroom for over a year, still receiving guests who came to her for blessings and her permission to marry.

The daughter of the village chief said: 'My mother died so suddenly, so we weren't ready to let her go.' Bennett tried to get locals to explain the theology behind their beliefs, and undoubtedly one exists, but it's striking how human their responses were, more emotional than spiritual. A family who brought their dead father food four times a day said they did it because 'we love him and respect him so much … Before, we used to eat together. He's still at home – we should feed him.' At the funeral itself, wrote Bennett, 'everything … is hierarchical, cementing the status of the dead person's family, the people who attend, and many who don't.' Fifty-five buffalo were slaughtered; the Toraja watched the massacre 'unfazed'. 'The buffalo's obligation … is to provide meat to ensure human existence. People in turn, must care for the species and make sure it endures.' Slowly and symbolically, the body is separated from the family home; placed in an ancestral building until it is carried to the communal crypt in a lavish coffin, where it is guarded by a wooden effigy of the deceased. August is the month for reunions: the body is taken for a walk around the town. It receives fresh clothes, even – the most tender of gestures – a brand new pair of glasses.

A man showed Bennett his family crypt, which contained more than ten relatives: 'My father is in here,' he said, 'but I am here, so he is not really dead. Mother is in here, but I have daughters, so she is not really dead. My daughters have been exchanged for my mother. I have been exchanged for my father.' Bennett: 'The important thing, the Toraja say, is that they are not just individuals. The death of one person is only the dropping of a single stitch in an intricate … canvas winding backward through ancestors and forward through children.' In other words, by making ourselves an integral part of what came before – by tending to our traditions in the present – we pass something on that we have helped shape, and achieve for ourselves a kind of immortality, of which the deceased Toraja, sitting at dinner with his living relatives, is the most tangible example. We should not run away from the question 'what happens next?'; we should think about it and prepare for it. Religious tradition helps us to do this: it not just a curious thing, or a nice thing, but a practical necessity. Like most of the traditions we've explored, it not only shows us how to behave but provides an explanation for 'why'. It is also a moral bulwark against the human regimes of death – those fascist or fanatical movements that would destroy us all because they can't say 'no' to their basest desires.

I

Tourists are welcome in South Sulawesi. The Toraja regard their presence at their rites as a compliment; foreigners come looking for the exotic, but some encounter a culture that makes more psychological sense than the one they left behind. An IT consultant from Madrid told Bennett: 'When someone dies in Spain, it's the worst thing that can happen in a family … We Western people … don't think of the end. Here, they have been preparing for years.'[5] In fact, Westerners used to live a similar way. Prior to the twentieth century, when most people grew sick there was nothing that could be done: they were treated in the home, they died in the home and death was a familiar sight. Vast improvements in medicine helped us live longer, which is obviously a good thing, and the growth of hospitals, nursing homes and hospices saw end-of-life care move away from the family and disappear behind closed doors. I was 33 when I first saw someone die – my father, in a hospice. Before that, I lost all my grandparents but never once saw a body. They were there one minute, gone the next; the coffin lid screwed down at the funeral. This is in marked contrast to the custom that my grandmother's generation observed of placing the coffin at home for at least a night with the lid open so that visitors could pay their respects. François-René de Chateaubriand reported that in pre-revolutionary France, the faces of recently deceased priests and nuns would be left uncovered, so that mourners could study them and, from their expression, try to guess whether or not they had made it into Heaven.[6]

Chateaubriand is one of the most important figures in French Romanticism: his 1802 book *The Genius of Christianity* helped revive the reputation of French Catholic culture and encourage its restoration, and he achieved this not through arcane theological argument but by presenting his religion as both mystical and tangible, as a cure for the psychological malaise of post-revolutionary life. Fans of Proust will recognize his ability to 'transform everyday life, both ordinary and historical, into something immortal', along with his 'expression of involuntary memory'.[7] The sound of bells, wrote Chateaubriand, 'has a thousand secret relations with man'. There is the tolling of a death bell, 'like the slow pulsations of an expiring heart' and the bell 'rung at night in certain sea-ports to direct the pilot in his passage among the rocks'. In peace, the bell is joyous; in war, a warning. And hanging from the tower of a church, it spreads 'moral sympathy' among citizens and communicates man's events to God: a Mass, a wedding, a death – the same tone, different meanings. If Christendom didn't have bells, wrote Chateaubriand, then it would have to copy the Native Americans and use the voices of children 'to call us to the House of the Lord'.[8]

Chateaubriand travelled to America in 1791, hoping to find a new kind of society on virgin soil. The colonials turned out to be mercantile bullies; the indigenous peoples, though capable of doing wrong, at least had not jettisoned their inherited culture, as the French revolutionaries had done, and remained loyal to their customs and rituals.[9] In his 1801 novel *Atala*, his hero encounters a mother whose baby has died and, according to custom, before placing the child's body in a tomb, she first dries it on the branches of a tree:

> She selected a maple with red flowers, festooned with garlands of apios, that emitted the sweetest perfumes. With one hand she pulled down the lowest branch, and with the other she placed the body thereon; then loosing the branch, it returned to its natural position, with the remains of innocence concealed in its foliage.[10]

Chateaubriand discovered that the need to mourn is universal, that human beings across the world have constructed rituals that allow us to articulate emotions too painful to put into words. To this day, even in highly secularized Britain, many people choose to get married in church, baptize their babies and ask a priest to officiate at a funeral – including those who don't believe in God and have no intention of returning to church again. This can infuriate clerics, but it is a compliment to religion. These are the most important moments in our lives and few of us have the eloquence to express what we're going through. Ritual lends us the language of action. Put simply, in the midst of the most all-consuming emotion of all – grief – tradition relieves us of the burden of reason by telling us what to do. The Native American places her baby in a tree; the English mourner wears black. The tragedy of the French Revolution, says Chateaubriand, is that when inherited customs were washed away, France was left with a culture that was more egalitarian and informal, yes, but also shallow and inarticulate.

Liberalism has had a similar effect upon my native country. Contemporary British funerals often leave it up to the mourners to decide what they want to do even if they're not in the best state of mind to judge. In my experience, funerals are often less about the dead, more about the living – and the phrase 'it's what she would've wanted' covers a multitude of sins. My maternal grandmother was an accomplished pianist. She did not, I'm sure, imagine herself being cremated to 'Are You Lonesome Tonight?' by Elvis Presley – but that was what her loved ones wanted, so that's what she got. (The vicar said to me 'do you want to give a eulogy?' 'Yes.' 'In that case, make it short because we are in a queue.') Another common request is that the funeral service be a 'celebration of life', a nice idea in the planning stages, but when the solemnity of the moment hits you, its shortcomings become obvious. Mourners need to cry. I once attended the funeral of a friend's beloved uncle, a wonderful man who apparently 'loved bright music', so the organist was instructed to 'keep it light'. The service began and the tears, ineluctably, started to flow, but it was too late now to change the programme. As the coffin was carried in from the driving rain, the family did their best to retain a dignified composure while an old lady, sticking to her brief, bashed out 'Puttin' on the Ritz' from the organ loft.

Maybe it's because I've been to so many funerals that they've come to define for me the cultural confusion of the West – of a society living, uncomfortably, off the folk memory of a lost order, haunted by an idea of what it ought to do but not certain how to put it into practice. The institutions have no authority: 'Tell us what you want,' they say, 'and that's what we'll do.' What one typically ends up with exposes the fallacy of choice: given free rein, we all choose the exact same thing. The hymn is always 'All Things Bright and Beautiful'. The psalm is always

23: 'Though I walk through the valley of the shadow of death …' (it's what we remember from school). If it's a humanist funeral, someone will probably read W. H. Auden's 'Funeral Blues' ('Stop all the clocks…'); give it a few more years and it'll be extracts from *Harry Potter*. These things are 'chicken soup for the soul', popular because they touch upon emotional themes that lie at the heart of religion, too – and they often express the mood of the congregation far better than the officiator who, in trying not to upset anyone, deceives with platitudes. The deceased is not 'dead', we hear; they are sleeping. They have not 'died', they have passed over. A popular reading at funerals goes:

> Death is nothing at all. It does not count. I have only slipped away
> to the next room … life means all that it ever meant. It is the same
> as it ever was. There is absolute and unbroken continuity.[11]

Unsurprisingly, the full context of these words is never given. They were first spoken by Henry Scott Holland, a canon of St Paul's Cathedral, in 1910 in response to the death of Edward VII. Holland wanted to contrast the view of death as an irredeemable tragedy with its polar opposite, a passing phase, and though he sought a reconciliation between the two, his image of the dead person waiting for us in the next room is implausible and far from reassuring. What if someone died slowly and painful, or shockingly young – how can that be 'nothing'? What if this reunion takes an unbearably long time, and where will it occur? Psychologically, Holland's glib words do not help us confront the enormity of what has happened, and in supernatural terms offer no clarity and, therefore, no real hope. There is no journey to the afterlife, no judgement upon the scales, and without judgement, no justice. What if the deceased was a wife beater or a serial killer? The knowledge that he's 'waiting next door' not only lets him off the hook but sounds positively sinister.

If poetry, like Chateaubriand's bells, is intended to bring clarity by evoking mood and meaning, the purpose of jargon is to obfuscate, to dampen emotion and avoid the subject; it assumes the listener is ignorant and probably leaves us so. Michel Foucault observed that, during the Enlightenment, medicine replaced faith as the popular religion, and doctors retreated behind a professional litany designed, with its coldness and objectivity, to reduce the patient to a passive subject. We haven't a clue what the physician is saying but we take comfort in the assumption that he must be jolly clever if *he* does.[12] When I accompanied Dad to his final appointment with his cancer specialist, the doctor told him: 'I cannot recommend any further treatment to halt the advance and therefore I suggest we engage in palliative care going forward.' My father nodded. Later, when we went for a cup of tea in the canteen, he said 'What does palliative mean?' I had to break it to him that he was going to die.

When he got worse, he was placed in a hospice. Again, no one would say straightforwardly what this meant, but they suggested that I might like to move into one of the guest rooms to 'be on hand', which even then I failed to translate. Our last lucid conversation was about religion. 'I can't believe in God,' said my father.

'Why?'

'Because if God existed and he loved me, like you believe, and he can do anything, like you say he can, he wouldn't let me suffer.'

'Is that what you want him to do?' I asked.

'I want him to make me young again,' said my father. 'If God existed, he'd take away the pain and make me twenty-five.'

I don't quite know what my father wanted from me, but for all the problems in our relationship – this might have been the longest we ever spoke – I felt I owed him honesty. I told him the way I saw it: God doesn't do things like that, but he is there if you look for him. He's there in the staff who were so kind and in the friends and family who had come to see him. God is all around us, all the time, acting through other people, even if we don't always see it for what it is.

Dad said: 'Well, I'd still like to be twenty-five,' which is fair enough. Around 1 a.m., I was woken by a nurse who told me the old man was on the way out. I held his hand as he gave his last breath. I recited the rosary and the 'Our Father'.

I cannot even begin to comprehend what my father was going through or how awful and frightening it must have been, but I also saw in him the consequences of firm and rigid disbelief, of an outright refusal to contemplate what the end meant, let alone what would happen next. He didn't know what to do or how to articulate his feelings. People who are signed up to a religious tradition are no less terrified of death (you don't want to sit next to me on an aeroplane during turbulence), but at least they have a guide to how to act and a narrative to accompany them – in the Christian case, the story of a God who lived as a man and experienced every pain imaginable when he was nailed to a cross. This puts the incredibly personal and particular experience of death into a wider context. The believer, in theory at least, does not go through these trials alone.

Chateaubriand noted that, among the ancient pagans, the remains of the poor and slaves were 'forsaken almost without ceremony'. By contrast, the Christian minister is duty bound 'to bestow the same attendance on the corpse of the peasant as on that of a monarch'. The liberal age is a step back towards the pagan. Now that funerals are a matter of consumer choice, the rich and the famous have the best and those lucky enough to have a big family have the most 'celebratory'. But what if you have no money? What if you don't have much of a family? In most religious traditions it ought not to matter, for in death the individual receives not what they can afford but what they are owed: 'the great name of Christian places all mankind upon a level in death, and the pride of the mightiest of potentates cannot extort from religion any other prayer than what it voluntarily offers for the lowest of peasants.' Both secular and religious ceremonies look backwards, to identify a memory and hold onto it for as long as possible, so that the deceased will live on for one or maybe two generations until, like a faded photograph, the image is indecipherable or gone. But the religious funeral, believing as it does in eternal life, also looks forward – to resurrection. Chateaubriand found it particularly moving that the individual's life is also commemorated by a 'general ceremonial', which recalls the memory of history's entire dead – 'all those who have gone before' – thus 'the Christian soul mingles her grief caused by the loss of her former friends' with the grief of the 'entire family of Adam'.[13]

Reading Chateaubriand helped make sense of why over the years I have become less socialist, more conservative; less political, more religious. In religion, there is the basis for a more humane equality than one usually finds in Messianic politics. Marxists dream of egality, but they also divide us into classes, between which there is tension and struggle. This conflict has been used to justify theft and violence. In Christianity, by contrast, the inequalities of this world, though very real, are in sharp contrast to the revelation that God loves us all equally, and that we are commanded to do the same. This leads to a very different model of social transformation, not revolution but mission.

In September 2019, the relics of St Thérèse of Lisieux, a French nun who died in 1897 at the age of 24, paid a visit to Scotland. Thousands turned out to see the golden casket that carries her tiny body, though her popularity rests on her humility. Most saints were, in life, heroes or miracle workers, whereas Thérèse specialized in small acts of compassion, the sort of everyday kindness that you or I can emulate. One of her most famous acts was to pray for the conversion to Christ of a murderer who was apparently beyond redemption. On the day of his execution, he paused to kiss a crucifix, suggesting that God had heard Thérèse's prayer. It's now custom that whenever Thérèse goes abroad, she always visits a jail.

She arrived at Barlinnie men's prison in Glasgow like royalty. The guards, of their own volition, had put on their old-fashioned ceremonial uniforms – vastly superior to the 'supermarket security' look they normally have – and carried her on their shoulders into the chapel. The prisoners joined us for Mass. The striking thing was the silence. The bane of most Masses is babies crying and phones going off, but this was one of the most prayerful and peaceful liturgies I could remember. There was no barrier between the guests and the prisoners, which meant that at the sign of peace, when congregants shake hands, I was able to dart forward and look the convicts in the eye – peaceful, serene faces, containing evidence of grace. At the end of the service, they shuffled out, stopping to kiss Thérèse's coffin and mark themselves with the sign of the cross. At the door, four nuns gave them a flower each, and a chocolate.

Christianity urges the prisoner to repent and reform. It also obliges us to love them. It's a very difficult, almost unhuman thing to ask – but God demands it. The Christian formula is 'hate the sin but love the sinner'. I've seen the consequences of war; I've met the survivors of atrocity. I know I have no right to forgive on any victim's behalf, but to stand in a room of men who have done terrible things and feel, through Christian fellowship, not just equality but brotherhood, and not just brotherhood but a duty to love these men as if they were my own sons – I cannot imagine anything but religion that would produce such an effect, and it's infinitely more radical than the doctrines of Marx and Engels. Mother Teresa said we must 'give until it hurts'. W. H. Auden wrote: 'As children of God, made in his image, we are required in turn voluntarily to surrender ourselves to being assimilated by our neighbours according to their needs.' The slogan of Hell, said Auden, is 'eat or be eaten'. The slogan of Heaven is 'eat and be eaten'. Death is an inevitability; the question is not 'will we die?' but 'how?' and 'for whom?'. The denizens of Hell kill and are killed; the residents of Heaven lay down their lives for others.[14]

As Simone Weil argued, human beings have needs – emotional as well as material. Religious traditions try to meet these needs while directing people towards the good. No alternative system of thought has yet to be found that is nearly as benign. Many lead to disaster.

II

There are two ways to make sense of the 1930s and the rise of fascism. One is as the ultimate indictment of tradition and nostalgia. Either Christian tradition wasn't strong enough to resist fascism or, worse, fascism arose from Christian tradition. Anti-Semitism certainly ran through Christian theology and the conservative intellectual tradition like a hereditary disease.

There is, however, an alternative interpretation that accepts the complicity of Christians while challenging the idea that what Europe saw in the 1930s was a Christian phenomenon. In the opinion of several contemporary intellectuals, popular Christianity was in fact dead – or at least on its way out. Totalitarianism filled the gap it left behind.

When Lenin died in 1924, his widow assumed he would get a private ceremony at the family cemetery, with a simple headstone. This was what a good Marxist might want, but it wasn't what the people needed. 'We must show that Lenin lives,' muttered Stalin, himself a former seminarian. Trotsky likened Lenin's public funeral, during which hundreds of thousands paid their respects in freezing temperatures, to the veneration of a medieval saint. The most apt comparison was with the pharaohs. The great theorist of the revolution – a materialist and strict atheist – was placed in a sarcophagus and embalmed by two chemists who had studied the Egyptian techniques of mummification. When Lenin was pumped with a secret formula and repainted to look as youthful as possible, the scientists were happy to report that they had pulled off a trick the ancients never could: 'The embalmers contrived to impart a smile.'[15] The poet Vladimir Mayakovsky wrote: 'Lenin lived. Lenin lives. Lenin will live.' The post-Christian metaphor doesn't need spelling out. Likewise, fascism swapped the brotherhood of man for the unity of nation; loyalty to Church for loyalty to state. 'When a man stops believing in God,' said Chesterton, 'he doesn't then believe in nothing, he believes anything.' The cleric Richard Neuhaus wrote that if religion is carved out of the 'public square', the public square will not remain empty for long: 'it will be filled by the agent left in control of the public square, the state. In this manner, a perverse notion of the disestablishment of religion leads to the establishment of the state as church.'[16]

In *The Year of Our Lord 1943*, historian Alan Jacobs tells us that even when the Nazis were losing the Second World War, many Christian intellectuals – including Jacques Maritain, C. S. Lewis and W. H. Auden – were just as nervous about the future of the West as we are today. Germany had been a civilized country before Hitler came to power; what was so special about France, Britain or America that made certain what happened 'over there' couldn't happen 'over here'? Materialism was rampant; the culture was decadent and selfish. A particular form of government was clearly no guarantee against fascism – Germany had been a democracy, too – and there was nothing constitutionally to stop a majority, slipped from its moral moorings, from voting for evil. These Christian thinkers were especially worried about the legacy of liberalism upon ethics, that the growing consensus that all views are equal might have erased the clarity of Christian teaching and opened the door to cruder concepts of justice. Some put a large amount of blame on the universities, arguing that free people 'have more to fear from their professors than from Hitler, because their professors make us all the more likely, over the long run to become Hitler. Only a clearly articulated and rationally defended account of true justice can resist totalitarianism.'[17] The West was teaching a whole generation that freedom meant freedom from restraint, but wasn't that what Nazism amounted to? Beneath the uniform and the choreography ran a libertine creed: with the civilizational switch from restrain to release, the appetites had been let loose to devour the weak. Nazism was tempting. If it was to be resisted, some self-control was needed, some purpose in life other than the satiation of desire.

W. H. Auden wrote: 'In 1912, it was a real vision to discover that God loves a Pernod and a good fuck, but in 1942 every maiden aunt knows this and it's time to discover something else He loves.'[18] It's a crude account of a religious journey but an honest one. Raised an Anglican, Auden had spent his youth rebelling against the past, flirting with every fad going – communism, sexual liberation, Freudianism, pacifism – all based, according to one biographer, 'on the belief in the natural goodness of man', the conviction that if only one external source of evil could be defeated — repression, war, authoritarianism — 'then humanity would be happy'.[19] His humanism had already been tested, according to Jacobs, by witnessing the civil war in Spain: Auden experienced 'unexpected and inexplicably intense distress at seeing the destruction of churches in Barcelona'. But he moved in an intellectual circle that made it hard to stop and ask himself why. Migration to America in 1939 gave him the necessary space.

That autumn, a few weeks after Germany invaded Poland, Auden visited a cinema in Yorkville, Manhattan, where he saw a newsreel about Hitler's advance. To his horror, the German-Americans in the audience were ecstatic. Some shouted 'Kill them!' at the screen. 'What was remarkable about the film,' Auden wrote to a friend, 'was its lack of hypocrisy. Every value I had been brought up on, and assumed everybody held, was flatly denied.'[20] Fascism was not an indictment of Christianity, it was its polar opposite – and its great lie was that it said tradition was biological, inherited, that you are either German or not, and if you're not then you're fair game for domination. But the great mistake of liberalism, argued Auden, was to think that the solution to this corruption of tradition was to abandon tradition altogether: 'The whole trend of liberal thought has been to undermine faith in the absolute ... It has tried to make reason the judge ... But since life is a changing process ... the attempt to find a humanistic basis for keeping a promise, works logically with the conclusion, "I can break it whenever I feel it inconvenient."'[21] Chateaubriand had made a similar point:

> Morality is the foundation of society; but if we are nothing more than material, there truly can exist neither vice nor virtue and, accordingly, no morality either. Our laws, always relative and changing, cannot provide any basis for morality, which is always absolute and unchanging: morality, then, must have its origins in a world that is more stable than this one and consequences more certain than precarious rewards or transitory punishments.[22]

In 1944, when confronted with a treaty that put onerous obligations on the Third Reich, Heinrich Himmler, head of the SS and murderer of millions, asked almost innocently 'what compels us to keep our promises?'. In a debate on atheism in 2010, the writer David Berlinski, a Jewish agnostic, recalled those words and added an interesting allegory of his own. He said: 'I have in front of me a rather remarkable button. If you should press it, yours would be untold riches and whatever else you desire. The only consequence to pressing it beyond your happiness is the death of an anonymous Chinese peasant. Who among us would you trust with this button?'

We might not press the button because we are thoroughly decent. We might not press it because we'd feel guilt. We might be persuaded through reason, not emotion, that it is wrong – perhaps because we wouldn't want to live in a world in which people press buttons like that. Who knows? Someday a Chinese peasant might be offered the same deal in relation to us. But Berlinski's challenge is this: even if you could convince us in principle not to press the button, what actually *compels* us not to do it if there is no threat of sanction?[23] His allegory goes right to the heart of a great deal of philosophical debate since the Enlightenment: if there is no God, no weighing of the heart after death, what ultimately compels us to do the right thing? The Enlightenment encouraged the idea that we could conceive of just principles of morality through reason alone, that we don't need to be told what to do. But the problem is that 'reason is not enough'. It might be thought reasonable today to stay away from the button. Tomorrow, mankind might conclude that it is reasonable to leap on it and dance the carioca. Auden felt himself drawn back to a necessary belief in the doctrines of the Christian Church, necessary because, alone of all the structures of thought and belief, faith is the one creed that not only persuades or encourages us to love each other but tries to turn love into an obligation.

The cynic says that religious tradition treats us like naughty children, keeping us under control with the threat of damnation, that it doesn't let us grow up, we just do as the priests tell us because their stories scare us into submission. Only someone without any sympathy or insight into religion could believe this – but plenty do, and they overlook two elements of faith that make it essential to a healthy society. First, faith balances a healthy scepticism about mankind's moral integrity with the promotion of a set of ideals to which to aspire. The ideal person in Christianity is the very opposite of the fascist *Übermensch*. Jesus is Jewish, for a start. He associates with sinners and the diseased; he disregards wealth and power. He is crowned not with gold but with thorns; he is slandered, tortured and nailed to a cross, tormented by his killers. All this he endures willingly. He does not resist. He actually asks forgiveness for his murderers.

The perfect man is abandoned by his friends and his body is left to rot in a tomb. The hero in Christianity is everything the fascists had contempt for; he preached mercy where they practised hate. These ideals are hard to live up to, even a little daunting, but they are inescapable and humbling, and they offer a marvellous remedy to the greed of liberal capitalism. Very often, when I succeed by the standards of my society, I am failing by the standards of my faith: every penny made from the sale of this book puts me one penny further from Christ who, when asked by a rich man how to enter the kingdom of Heaven, replied that he could begin by giving away everything he had. I pray this book doesn't sell *too* well.[24]

Second, religion imposes its rules not only by law but also by self-governance of the conscience. Man-made laws might change; the conscience does not. Most of what the Nazis did was technically lawful, and the people who did their dirty work could legitimately say 'it was legal and I was following orders'. Most religious people cannot do that, because where temporal law contradicts divine law, one's first loyalty is to God. That law is written on one's conscience – which is why, even when bad things are legal, we feel a twinge of doubt in doing them. Listen to your conscience. The truth it contains is not a burden or a harsh restraint but a liberation, for the great revelation of much of religious teaching is that we don't have to be evil. We are so often told by this culture that being bad is the default, that we must push and shove and claw our way to the top. It's all a lie. Not only can we choose to be good, but we were made to be good.[25]

If we lose the tradition of religion then we will enter a phase in history, much like the 1930s, where there is no golden rule. There will be no divine judge to hold us to our promises. The niggling, nuisance voice of religion, with its ideals and rules that can defy even the most apparently innocent pleasure or pragmatic solution, will disappear – and, with it, the one voice that can deliver an unequivocal 'no' to that which is wrong or might lead to wrong.

FIGURE 21 Believers attend a religious service at the Cathedral of the Nativity of the Blessed Virgin in Gori, Georgia, commemorating the 67th anniversary of Joseph Stalin's death.

Conclusion

Brexit and Trump triggered a debate among centre-right intellectuals. Some said they were aberrations: a hiccup in the history of conservatism, contrary to what conservatives were supposed to believe. Others saw in them the potential for creative destruction. The conservative elites, they said, had surrendered to too many precepts of liberalism; the time had come not just to preserve the status quo but turn the clock back, and if that requires some government intervention to do it, so be it. A phrase America's right-wing post-liberals like to use is 'common good'. Individual liberty is a facet of the common good, but if it stands in the way of it, the common good comes first.[1] This logic opens the door to a world of possibilities: could we see conservative governments pushing welfare programmes that promote the family? Or measures that correct the destabilizing aspects of capitalism? Could we finally get that Romantic dream of socialism with medieval characteristics? Who knows? The question that interests this book is, can we not only rescue tradition but revive it?

Russia says 'yes'. Eastern European states experienced the very worst of modernity in the twentieth century: atheistic communism, which killed millions, followed by liberal hyper-capitalism, which worsened the condition of the poor. Both systems went to war with cultural and religious tradition. In the twenty-first century, several governments have tried to 'restore' those traditions, typically by restricting immigration, throwing money at the family and reasserting Christian identity. The regime of Vladimir Putin has attempted to achieve a synthesis between its goals and those of the

Russian Orthodox Church, reflected in socially conservative, anti-gay legislation and religious endorsement of military aggression against Ukraine.[2] Since the 1990s, the country has undergone an ambitious church-building programme, culminating in the opening of the enormous Cathedral of the Russian Armed Forces outside Moscow in 2020. The original design of the interior, which commemorates victory in the Second World War, was to include a mosaic of Putin himself; this was dropped, according to the Church, at the intervention of the Kremlin. It was 'too early' yet 'to celebrate the accomplishments of Russia's current leadership'.[3]

The goal of Putin's cultural counter-revolution is to bolster his legitimacy by saying 'this leader is authentically Russian and Russia is behind him'. We mustn't fall for it: there is plenty of opposition to Putin, including within the Orthodox Church. But reviving tradition, leaning back onto it for political support, is undeniably a Russian characteristic, and it reflects the country's historic status of being half in Europe, half out, modernizing while swimming against the tide.

You can tell this from the architecture of its two main cities. Moscow, even after the communists rebuilt it, still looks recognizably Russian; the Kremlin dominates the city centre. When you open the hotel curtains in St Petersburg, however, you'd be forgiven for thinking you were in Venice or Paris, and this is quite deliberate. Peter the Great snatched the land from the Swedes in 1703 and moved the capital from Moscow to St Petersburg in 1712. Just as Louis XIV liberated himself from Paris by escaping to Versailles, so Peter declared independence from Moscow by shifting his power base to the very fringes of his empire – to a capital constructed on canals, designed by foreign architects and artists. St Petersburg was built to face west, not east, to drag Russia into the Enlightenment by imitation. Even the new capital's churches looked Scandinavian, Dutch or Italianate. If you think you've seen the cathedral of Our Lady of Kazan before, it's because you have: the exterior, completed in 1811, is modelled on St Peter's in Rome.[4]

Over the next two hundred years, Russia swung fitfully between reform and reaction, and the more one side resisted, the more extreme the other became. Not everyone aspired to be Western; conservative clergy thought Peter, who forced his country through a mini reformation at the point of a sabre, was the antichrist. He went to war on beards, traditional clothing and monasteries, mocked the Church and was unspeakably cruel: the tsar had his own son tortured to death.[5] And some of the intellectuals who travelled to Europe to study the societies they were supposed to be emulating found themselves repulsed by the whole project. In the summer of 1862, the writer Fyodor Dostoyevsky visited Paris and London. London, with its drunken workers and bawdy prostitutes – 'half naked, savage and hungry' – made him think of Babylon: 'the polluted Thames, the coal-saturated air ... It is a Biblical sight ... some prophecy out of the Apocalypse being fulfilled before your very eyes.' The French, he wrote, 'make you sick'. Money was all that mattered to them; Catholicism was a moral veneer. In the bars and parks, among the mass of vile bodies, Dostoyevsky felt lonely: 'You feel that you are cut off from the native soil and separated from one's everyday native connections.' And yet this spiritually vacuous existence apparently appealed to the Russian bourgeoisie! 'There is no soil [they say], and no people: nationality is nothing but a system of taxation, the soul is a "tabula rasa", a small piece of wax out of which you can readily mould a real man ... all that must be done is to apply the fruits of European civilisation and read two or three books.' A hundred and fifty years before Brexit, Dostoyevsky had described the conflict between Anywheres and Somewheres.[6]

He saw Russian identity as inherently spiritual, although its conscience was not so much the Church as it was its people, who 'arguably, of all nations, are most capable of encompassing the idea of universal unity, a sense of brotherly love, and a sensible reception of things'. This cult of the Russian soul could easily breed introspection and nationalism, but it also gave the country a sense of global mission that lingers today, analogous to that of the United States. Russia was an example to the world; the defender of Christian civilization; and, like Christ, a holy sacrifice whose history was a ceaseless fire of martyrdom.[7] 'I think the most important, most rudimentary spiritual need of the Russian people is the need for suffering,' wrote Dostoyevsky, 'constant and unquenchable, everywhere and in everything. It seems they have been infected with this thirst for suffering from time immemorial.'[8]

It's easy to see how this narrative of Russian exceptionalism and capacity for pain could be exploited by a brutal elite. Tsar Nicholas I, who had Dostoevsky arrested as part of a crackdown on intellectual freedom, promoted the reactionary triad of religious Orthodoxy, Slavic unity and imperial autocracy – rule by one man with no concessions to popular participation, which was unnecessary if the tsar was appointed by God.[9] His son, Alexander II, was a reformer who abolished serfdom, but, in the absence of a proper democratic forum, opposition to the monarchy became as implacable as the regime itself. In 1881, in St Petersburg, a nihilist threw a bomb at Alexander's carriage – the seventh attempt on his life in two years. Stunned but unhurt, the tsar characteristically ignored the danger and insisted upon inspecting the crime scene. A second assassin lobbed another bomb that severed his leg. Alexander was carried to the Winter Palace where he died in his study.[10] Alexander III decided to commemorate his father's murder by building a church on the exact spot where he was mortally wounded: the Church of the Saviour on Spilled Blood. Work began in 1883 and was completed in 1907, under the last Romanov ruler, Nicholas II, and the church stands out on the St Petersburg skyline because it looks atypically Russian: multiple onion domes, an interior smothered with colourful mosaics. This was the Romanov equivalent of neo-Gothic, and the more violent the opposition to their system, the less certain their position, the more consciously the Romanovs rooted their right to rule in the past. In 1913, they celebrated the dynasty's three hundred years in charge and the tsar presented himself as the living embodiment of a timeless union between ruler and people; there was plenty of pomp, but Nicholas also appeared in peasant dress, inspecting fields and handing out black bread to the poor. Royal tat went on sale: for the first time, the tsar's face was put on a stamp. Postmasters scratched their heads. Technically, it bore the image of a living saint. If they hit it with a date stamp, they might be defacing an icon.[11]

The tercentenary was the last gasp of popular support before the heady first weeks of the First World War, a conflict that demanded too much suffering, even for Russia. In 1917, Nicholas was deposed, and murdered along with his entire family the following year. Saviour on Spilled Blood was ransacked and closed; during the Second World War, it briefly functioned as a morgue. Later, it was a food warehouse, earning it the nickname Saviour of Potatoes. Today it is reopened as a museum, and, walking around it on a visit to Russia in 2018, I had the sense of being in a restoration of a restoration, that while Russia's contemporary rulers are compared endlessly to Stalin, they are closer in instinct and method to the Romanovs. Coming from the West, a part of the world that seems ashamed of its history, it was fascinating to encounter a country where the past is being scrubbed up, edited and retold to reflect a nation's attempt to navigate an uncertain future that, in some places, sees signs of the worst of the past. In the Cathedral of St Peter and St Paul, the foundation stone of St Petersburg, what is purported to be the bodies of Nicholas and his family have been interred. Nicholas was an incompetent, an anti-Semite and a butcher of his own people. You can buy a nice icon of him in the gift shop.

Ethics aside, does this experiment in state-sponsored tradition work for the tradition itself? The answer in Russia's case is perplexing: it's estimated that around three-quarters of the population identify as Orthodox, which is impressive, yet only 6 per cent attend church each week, which is less so (certainly compared to 21 per cent of Romanian Orthodox or a whopping 45 per cent of Polish Catholics).[12] This is a phenomenon known as 'believing without belonging', and it's global: across the West, large numbers of people describe themselves as Christian or spiritual without feeling the need, or perhaps instinct, to attend church.[13] Russian Orthodoxy has not escaped this problem despite its liberation from communism, the historic link with patriotism or Putin's cheerleading. On the contrary, when faith and nation become synonymous, there's a risk that faith becomes a label of identity rather than a system of lived belief. The same happened long ago in Ireland, which still has a relatively high rate of church attendance, but where Catholic doctrine is routinely disregarded or dismissed, even from the pews. In 2015, the Irish voted overwhelmingly to legalize same-sex marriage. In 2018, they did the same for abortion. During the latter campaign, a priest in Clogherhead tried to talk about abortion at his church and several parishioners marched out in disgust. 'It was totally inappropriate,' said one of them, 'I just wasn't sitting there listening to it ... It might be the church's opinion, but it should not be said in front of children, and there is no place for it at that Mass.'[14] You might call this phenomenon 'belonging without believing' and, again, it's international. According to a staggering poll by Pew, only one-third of American Catholics believe in transubstantiation, despite it being absolutely central to the Catholic faith.[15]

Moreover, we can't put ethics aside. One thing that has destroyed the reputation of countless religious leaderships is the scandal of clerical abuse: religious institutions have failed to live up to their own standards. Likewise, if a state is committed to the promotion of a tradition, shouldn't we expect it to reflect that tradition's moral principles? Vladimir Putin has been lionised by foreign conservatives as a Christian bulwark against Western decadence, yet his regime is utterly immoral, stealing money, persecuting opponents and invading neighbours. He has broken the commandment 'thou shalt not kill' many times. A tradition is not about paying lip service to dogma or putting on a mask in public: traditions are meant to transform the lives of those who are a part of them, and if it doesn't make them happier, wiser and, crucially, more noble in spirit, then I'm not sure what the point of them is. The East must not repeat the mistake of the Soviet Union, which failed not only because it didn't work but because its idealism decayed into dogma and its traditions into pantomime. There were statues and commemorations, parades at Lenin's tomb and medals for the heroes of socialist labour – but no one believed in it, and the corruption, the dread hypocrisy, ran all the way up to an elite that preached equality but enjoyed access to special shops and luxurious dachas. It was, ironically, the point at which

Mikhail Gorbachev decided the USSR should revisit the original ideals of socialism, to see if this thing could be kept going without the threat of arrest, that its hollowness was exposed and the structure crumpled.[16]

Tradition is not rules, performance or architecture. It must have soul. If Notre Dame is rebuilt exactly as it was before, but the liturgy is ugly, the priests hypocritical and the congregation doesn't believe a word of what they hear, and don't live by the commandment to love, then the exercise would be pointless. If the faithful of any tradition want to keep it going, the trick is to live it.

I

In my lifetime I've seen two traditions decline and recover in unexpected ways: gay pride and fox hunting. The London Pride festival started life as a radical protest movement in the 1970s and reached a peak in numbers by the 1990s. In the early 2000s, however, participation fell and the event was cash-strapped; it didn't help that the mayor of London, Boris Johnson, doubled the price of meeting in Trafalgar Square. A solution was found: the City of London would bail out Pride but in exchange it became something called a community interest company, a form of privatization. Pride would increasingly be run by businessmen and saturated with corporate sponsorship, transforming a protest into a party endorsed by Tesco and Lloyds Bank. It survived and flourished, not only as a carnival of sexual freedom but a celebration of liberal identity – and nowadays there are probably more middle-class heterosexuals at Pride than gays or lesbians.[17]

Around the same time, in 2004, fox hunting was banned by law. It was a revolutionary move. Hunting was woven into English identity like tea and bad weather, and the attempt to eliminate it didn't just reflect sympathy for the fox but hatred of the hunter: this was a war on the last vestiges of aristocratic tradition. It backfired. Hitherto, hunting had been in numerical decline – not many people wanted to stand in the pouring rain watching 'the unspeakable in pursuit of the uneatable', to quote Oscar Wilde – and now it was replaced by drag hunting, by which the dogs chased a synthetic scent rather than a live animal. Who would want to follow that? Thousands, it turned out. Rural people believed their way of life was under attack and urban conservatives agreed, so they rallied around and attendance at hunts rocketed.[18] Just as Pride became a badge of identity for liberals, so the hunt was a meeting place for much of the constituency that would later vote for Brexit. At a gathering I attended in 2019, the hunt master gave a rousing speech in opposition to the EU. A tradition once endorsed by the establishment was transformed into a subversive act, proof that you don't need state sponsorship to keep customs and rituals going. A little persecution might be just what the doctor ordered.

The Pride tribe, the hunt tribe: it does feel increasingly as if our identities are shaped by politics, a development that itself concedes too much to liberalism. If one swallows the Enlightenment view that the answers to great questions can be reached best through reason and debate, then it's inevitable that we'll live in a world where everything is seen through the prism of the political, from what you eat to who you sleep with. One reason why I'm nervous about the common good project is that I feel the tradition-minded should resist this, that we should be stubbornly defending spheres of life that are separate from the state and separate from politics – because sometimes I want to listen to music, read a book or eat a meal without having to think about the political ramifications. When a liberal on Twitter says *Jurassic Park* is transphobic, or zebras are racist, that's their problem, not mine, and I'd rather turn off my phone than waste an afternoon arguing the point. Conservatives who claim to hate crudity and stupid opinion shouldn't be on Twitter anyway. It's like walking into an orgy and declaring oneself opposed to sex.

Rather than complaining about the liberal domination of the arts, conservatives would make better use of their time if they actually produced some art. Perhaps your watercolour won't win any prizes or be featured on Oprah Winfrey's Instagram, but so what? For hundreds of years, during the Dark Ages, monks worked at producing stunning illuminated manuscripts that were probably never seen by more than a few pairs of eyes. One does something, ideally, because one wants to and because it's worth doing – not for the approval of whatever elite is fleetingly in power.

On the other hand, as we've seen throughout this book, things that might have been regarded as the enemy of tradition have turned out to be its unexpected ally.[19] In the nineteenth century, consumerism brought tradition to the masses and gave them a stake in its survival. Democracy did not eliminate the monarchy but forced it to adapt to survive, becoming less about divine right, more about the duty to serve. Imperialism and globalization eroded cultures, no doubt, but also blended, added to and spread them around – because, to repeat for the final time, tradition does not stand still but develops. As for technology, I'm allergic to it, but I found out about that fox hunt online and might never had attended it if the internet did not exist. The journalist Kevin Kelly reports that when he spent time among the Amish, who supposedly spurn gadgetry for horse-drawn carts, he was surprised to discover they were 'ingenious hackers and tinkerers, the ultimate makers and do-it-yourselfers'. The Amish are happy to work with technology, they just do it in a way that complements their traditions rather than contradicts them: 'They don't adopt everything new, but when they do embrace it, it's half a century after everyone else does. By that time, the benefits and its costs are clear, the technology stable, and it is cheap … As one Amish man said, "We don't want to stop progress, we just want to slow it down."'[20]

We need to treasure our traditions, but do not see them as fragile antiques – as if the only thing that can protect a nation or a religion is to build a wall around it – or make the mistake of judging an alteration in appearance as evidence that the interior life has died. In 2018, the American journalist Andy Ngo wrote an account of walking around a London transformed by Muslim migration, which he assumed made it less English. Muslims and non-Muslims, he wrote, keep their distance and 'avoid eye contact'.[21] This was, if anything, evidence of integration. In the mid-nineteenth century, Ralph Waldo Emerson visited England and found us so well-mannered as to be rude: the English, he said, won't offer you a hand, won't meet you in the eye and won't even look you in the face unless introduced by a third party. 'In short, every one of these islanders is an island himself, safe, tranquil, incommunicable.'[22] George Orwell wrote, in 1941, that one of the defining qualities of English life is its 'privateness'. We are a nation 'of stamp-collectors, pigeon-fanciers, amateur carpenters, coupon-snippers, darts-players, crossword-puzzle fans'. Our definition of liberty was not economic, he insisted, but 'the liberty to have a home of your own, to do what you like in your spare time ... The most hateful of all names in an English ear is Nosey Parker.'[23]

All these years later and the English are still recognizably English, the Russians still Russian – possibly more Russian since the boot of communism was lifted from their necks. National culture has largely endured; in the West, however, Christian culture has not. I think this is tragic, partly because I am a Christian but also because it is foundational to Western identity and responsible for much that is best about us. Without it, we'll be less like ourselves, and the gap of faith will not remain empty but be filled, as it was in the past, with extreme ideologies. The way through this contains lessons for anyone interested in defending any tradition, religious or otherwise. For a start, one has to come to terms with failure. There is no point pretending that because the West used to be Christian it still must be, that the faith has just gone a bit quiet of late and will return of its own accord. The historical record shows that traditions ebb and flow, but if one is not careful they can peter out to nothing.

Only when a tradition acknowledges how out of touch it is with the prevailing culture will it find the right language to reinspire it. Massimo Recalcati, for example, writes that there was a time when praying was like breathing: 'it was a collective ritual that articulated our daily life. I cannot remember when I learnt to pray. It is as if I have always known how.' But the ritual of prayer is no longer transmitted by our society. In a post-Christian landscape, what was once regarded as 'objective' – something society took for granted – has become a wholly 'subjective' experience, and rather niche, too. Try praying in a railway carriage and see how many passengers move to another seat. When a way of living becomes subjective, the person who believes in it has to make a special effort to keep it going and to transmit it: religious 'parents are obliged to make a conscious decision,' argues Recalcati, to teach their kids to pray because they can't rely on them soaking it up from the surrounding culture. This is not necessarily a bad thing. It is entirely possible that one of the reasons why praying died out was because it was performed without much thought, a matter of following the herd – and when the herd changes direction, most of us are apt to follow. Prayer as a subjective experience requires greater commitment. The fact that the Muslim has to make extra effort to find somewhere quiet to pray, or the Jewish family to request time off for Passover from an employer who doesn't know what the word means, implies a greater degree of personal investment and conviction. And if someone is living faithful to a minority tradition, they *should* stand out from the crowd. Christians refer to evangelization through acts, of doing good things so that people stop and ask 'what inspired you to do that?' – the answer being 'my religion'. This could apply to any system of thought. The left has talked itself into thinking that practically all social transformation comes through political action – that individual effort is almost pointless unless you tackle 'systemic' problems, which is best achieved by capturing the state and remaking society from the top down. But there are plenty of ways to improve everyday life through individual action. Worried about wealth inequality? There's nothing to prevent you from giving your money and time to someone else, and previous generations of socialists – locked out of the state apparatus – did just that. They were militant volunteers. They founded libraries, unions, mutual societies, even ideal communities. The greatest investment often came from those who had the least.

Conservatives who want to prove their own commitment to the 'common good' will have to part with their pennies, too. They need, urgently, to reassess the relationship between free-market capitalism and tradition: is the goal to maximize profit or to preserve a healthy way of life? A choice must be made. If making money is your way of life, then I envy your bank balance but I fear for your soul. We'll know that the common good project has really broken with liberalism, and that it has won converts in the halls of power, when the Republican

Party, maybe, backs federal health insurance for all or the Conservative Party, say, supports a publicly-managed social care service. If we are going to put the state to good use, it should be to act as a protector against those impersonal forces that destroy anything of value, and if the new economic orthodoxy is to spend with abandon, why not splash the cash on things conservatives profess to love? Schools, theatres, elegant housing and the preservation of green spaces. The left, meanwhile, has to reconcile itself to the awkward fact that the poor like – and need – strong traditions. Making the world fairer does not necessitate wiping away its history. On the contrary, the struggles of human beings to build a better life are a treasury of knowledge from which to draw, and provide moral support to contemporary argument. William Morris and John Ruskin would probably have loved the Green New Deal. Environmentalism has somehow been cast as anti-worker: on the contrary, the promise of clean air, leisure, spiritual renewal and harmony with nature is exactly what an older generation of socialists dreamt of, conceptualising it not as a novelty but a return to the Eden that capitalism corrupted.

Finally, there is liberalism itself. Can a tradition that destroys tradition have a future? If it does, writes Larry Siedentop in *Inventing the Individual* – the last word on this subject – it lies in the past: 'If we in the West do not understand the moral depth of our own tradition, how can we hope to shape the conversation of mankind?' Modernity, he argues, has fallen for two heresies. One is to reduce liberalism to economic self-interest, which renders it utilitarian and unconcerned for justice. The other is to reduce it to individualism, undermining the principle of mutual reliance upon which citizenship rests. Liberalism must instead require the individual to see themselves in others and others in themselves, and by implication return to the original meaning of 'liberalitas' – generosity. This principle is not only beautiful but necessary.[24] As Auden wrote after the Germans declared war on Poland, 'We must love one another or die.'

Notes

INTRODUCTION

1 Agnès Poirier, *Notre-Dame: The Soul of France* (London: Oneworld Publications, 2020), p. 21.

2 Chelsea Racelis, 'The reactions of the fire at Notre Dame are an example of white supremacy', 17 April 2019, Michigan Daily. https://www.michigandaily.com/section/mic/reactions-fire-notre-dame-are-examples-white-supremacy, last accessed 28 September 2020.

3 For the complete history and debate surrounding the cathedral, see Poirier, *Notre-Dame*.

4 Nicole Winfield and Colleen Barry, 'Tourist Mecca Notre Dame Also Revered As Place of Worship', 17 April 2020, Associated Press. https://apnews.com/article/f309ea14c9b346acb1d3b72c2564c56b, last accessed 28 September 2020.

5 Jose Luís Corral Fuentes, 'An 800-year history of Paris's Notre Dame Cathedral', *National Geographic*, 15 April 2019. https://www.national-geographic.com/history/magazine/2017/05-06/notre-dame-de-paris/, last accessed 28 September 2020.

6 Simon Schama, *Citizens: A Chronicle of the French Revolution* (London: Penguin, 2004), pp. 657–8.

7 Victor Hugo, *The Hunchback of Notre-Dame* (London: Penguin, 2004), p. 25.

8 Poirier, *Notre-Dame*, pp. 101–19.

9 The debate over the historical meaning of populism, both left and right, is explored in Donald T. Critchlow, *In Defense of Populism: Protest and American Democracy* (University of Pennsylvania Press, 2020).

10 Aisha Gani, 'Ukip mistakes Westminster Cathedral for mosque', *Guardian*, 27 November 2014. https://www.theguardian.com/politics/2014/nov/27/-sp-ukip-mistakes-westminster-cathedral-for-mosque, last accessed 28 September 2020.

11   David Watkin, *A History of Western Architecture* (London: Laurence King Publishing, 2005), p. 476.

CHAPTER 1 DEFINING TRADITION

1   Edward Shils, *Tradition* (Chicago: University of Chicago Press, 1981), pp. 12–13.
2   Josef Pieper, *Tradition: Concept and Claim* (South Bend, Indiana: St Augustine's Press, 2010), pp. 9–22, 36, 30.
3   Shils, *Tradition*, p. 14.
4   For discussion, see Eric Hobsbawm, 'Introduction: Inventing Traditions', in Eric Hobsbawm and Terence Ranger (eds), *The Invention of Tradition* (Cambridge: Cambridge University Press, 2012), pp. 1–4.
5   Roger Scruton, *The Meaning of Conservatism* (South Bend, Indiana: St Augustine's Press, 2002), pp. 30–35.
6   Roger Scruton, *Conservatism: An Introduction to the Great Tradition* (New York: All Points Books), p. 49.
7   For a concrete example, see Donald N. Levine, *Wax and Gold: Tradition and Innovation in Ethiopian Culture* (Chicago: University of Chicago Press, 1972), pp. 1–17.
8   Christopher Lasch, *The Culture of Narcissism* (New York: W. W. Norton & Company, 1991), p. 7.
9   Gerard Russell, *Heirs to Forgotten Kingdoms* (London: Simon & Schuster, 2014), pp. 50–52.
10   Ibid., pp. 47–8, 64–5, 71–6.
11   Rukmini Callimachi, 'Enslaving Young Girls, the Islamic State Builds a Vast System of Rape', *New York Times*, 14 August 2015, p. 1.
12   Dia Chakravarty, 'The plight of the Yazidis appears to drift in and out of the world's conscience', *Sunday Telegraph*, 9 February 2020. https://www.telegraph.co.uk/opinion/2020/02/09/plight-yazidis-appears-drift-worlds-conscience/, last accessed 28 September 2020.
13   Interview with author, 6 February 2020.
14   Ralph Vaughan Williams, *National Music and Other Essays* (Oxford: Oxford Paperbacks, 1963), pp. 1–10.
15   Ibid., pp. 2–4, 232.
16   Ibid., p. 68.
17   J. H. Elliot, *Imperial Spain 1469–1716* (London: Penguin, 2002), p. 73.

18   Graeme Wood, 'What Isis Really Wants', *The Atlantic*, March 2015. https://www.theatlantic.com/magazine/archive/2015/03/what-is-is-really-wants/384980/, last accessed 28 September 2020. For an alternative view, see Mehdi Hasan, 'How Islamic is Islamic State?', *New Statesman*, 10 March 2015. https://www.newstatesman.com/world-affairs/2015/03/mehdi-hasan-how-islamic-islamic-state, last accessed 28 September 2020.

19   Not without controversy, of course. For a discussion of Islam, modernity and misogyny, see Muhammad Qassim Zaman, *Islam in Pakistan: A History* (Oxford: Princeton University Press, 2019), pp. 54–94.

20   François-René, vicomte de Chateaubriand, *The Genius of Christianity; or the Spirit and Beauty of the Christian Religion* (Miami: HardPress Publishing, 2015), pp. 177–83.

21   For a discussion of Islamic, Jewish and Christian attitudes towards the 'word of God', see Neil MacGregor, *Living with the Gods* (London: Penguin, 2019), pp. 297–314.

22   Adam Taylor, 'The powerful propaganda being spread online by women in the Islamic State', *Washington Post*, 23 March 2015. https://www.washingtonpost.com/news/worldviews/wp/2015/03/23/the-powerful-propaganda-being-spread-online-by-women-in-the-islamic-state/, last accessed 28 September 2020.

23   Bernard Lewis, *Race and Slavery in the Middle East: An Historical Enquiry* (London: Oxford University Press, 1992), pp. 5–6.

24   Rukmini Callimachi, 'ISIS' System of Rape Relies on Birth Control', NYT, 13 March 2016, p. 1.

25   Tim Stanley, '"The situation is very vulnerable": Iran-backed militias ethnically cleansing northern Iraq', *Daily Telegraph*, 12 July 2019. https://www.telegraph.co.uk/news/2019/07/12/situation-vulnerable-christians-faces-extinction-multicultural/, last accessed 24 October 2020.

26   Paul Connerton, *How Societies Remember* (Cambridge: Cambridge University Press, 2003), pp. 41–2.

27   Joseph Ratzinger, *Milestones: Memoirs, 1927–77* (Ignatius Press: San Francisco, 1998), p. 16.

28   Connerton, *How Societies Remember*, pp. 1–3.

29   Joseph de Maistre, *Considerations on France* (Cambridge: Cambridge University Press, 2006), pp. 46–7.

30 This was observed by Chateaubriand, as well: Chateaubriand, *Genius of Christianity*, p. 82.

31 De Maistre, *Considerations*, pp. 30, 46.

32 'Christian persecution "at near genocide levels"', *BBC News*, 3 May 2019. https://www.bbc.co.uk/news/uk-48146305, last accessed 24 October 2020.

33 For the view that it's largely about trade, see Andrew Brown, 'The silence on Christian persecution is because of trade, not political correctness', *Guardian*, 3 May 2019. https://www.theguardian.com/commentisfree/2019/may/03/jeremy-hunt-christian-persecution-political-correctness, last accessed 25 October 2020.

34 Catherine Pepinster, 'Misplaced post-colonial guilt holds us back from protecting persecuted Christians', *Daily Telegraph*, 26 December 2020. https://www.telegraph.co.uk/news/2019/12/26/misplaced-post-colonial-guilt-holds-us-back-protecting-persecuted/, last accessed 25 October 2020.

CHAPTER 2 THE WEST'S WAR ON TRADITION

1 Steven Pinker, *Enlightenment Now* (London: Penguin, 2019), pp. 3–14.

2 For a compelling left-wing critique, see Fred Dallmayr, *Post-Liberalism: Recovering a Shared World* (Oxford: Oxford University Press, 2019).

3 Patrick J. Deneen, *Why Liberalism Failed* (New Haven: Yale University Press, 2019), p. 33.

4 Dallmayr, *Post-Liberalism*, p. 3.

5 Deneen, *Why Liberalism Failed*, pp. 3–6.

6 John Gray, *Enlightenment's Wake: Politics and Culture at the Close of the Modern Age* (Oxford: Routledge Classics, 2007), p. 217.

7 Rod Dreher, *The Benedict Option: A Strategy for Christians in a Post-Christian Nation* (New York: Sentinel, 2018), pp. 25–6.

8 Edward Paice, *Wrath of God: The Great Lisbon Earthquake of 1755* (London: Quercus, 2009), pp. 188–95; Niall Ferguson, *Doom: the Politics of Catastrophe* (New York: Allen Lane, 2021), p. 89.

9 See John Gray's dissection of Pinker's simplistic history of the Enlightenment: John Gray, 'Unenlightened Thinking', *New Statesman*, 22 February 2018. https://www.newstatesman.com/culture/books/2018/02/unenlightened-thinking-steven-pinker-s-embarrassing-new-book-feeble-sermon, last accessed 24 October 2020.

10   Gray, *Enlightenment's Wake*, pp. 218–19.

11   Pinker, *Enlightenment Now*, p. 8.

12   Gertrude Himmelfarb, *The Roads to Modernity: The British, French and American Enlightenments* (New York: Random House, 2008), pp. 106–7.

13   Helena Rosenblatt, *The Lost History of Liberalism: From Ancient Rome to the Twenty-First Century* (Oxford: Princeton University Press, 2018), pp. 4–15.

14   Ibid., pp. 108–15.

15   Theodor Adorno and Max Horkheimer, *Dialectics of Enlightenment* (London: Verso, 1997), p. 13; Gray, *Enlightenment's Wake*, pp. xiv–xv.

16   Francis Fukuyama, 'The End of History?' *The National Interest*, No. 16 (Summer 1989), pp. 3–18.

17   Dallmayr, *Post-Liberalism*, p. 7.

18   Caroline Delbert, 'Why Some People Think 2+2=5 … And Why They're Right', *Popular Mechanics*, 7 August 2020. https://www. popularmechanics.com/science/math/a33547137/why-some-people-think-2-plus-2-equals-5/, last accessed 25 October 2020.

19   Lasch, *Narcissism*, p. 5.

20   Michael Oakeshott, *Rationalism in Politics and Other Essays* (New York: Liberty Fund Inc., 1991), p. 17; Adorno and Horkheimer, *Dialectic of Enlightenment*, p. 4.

21   Adrian Pabst and John Milbank, *The Politics of Virtue: Post-Liberalism and the Human Future* (London: Rowman & Littlefield, 2016), pp. 1–2.

22   See Christopher Caldwell, *The Age of Entitlement: America Since the Sixties* (New York: Simon & Schuster, 2020).

23   Pinker, *Enlightenment Now*, p. 30.

24   Ibid., p. 351; this view was parodied by Adorno and Horkheimer, *Dialectic of Enlightenment*, p. 6.

25   Jim Kuhnheinn and Lisa Lerer, 'For Obama and Clinton, twisty paths to "yes" on gay marriage', Associated Press, 27 June 2015. https://apnews. com/article/63f51fcd69bb4ce18ed6b7306d1b3c89, last accessed 24 October 2020.

26   Douglas Murray, *The Madness of Crowds: Gender, Race and Identity* (London: Bloomsbury Continuum, 2019), p. 9.

27   See Rod Dreher, *Live Not by Lies: A Manual for Christian Dissidents* (London: Penguin Random House, 2020).

28 Ivan Krastev and Stephen Holmes, *The Light that Failed: A Reckoning* (London: Penguin, 2019), pp. 49–54.

29 Ibid., p. 9.

30 Ibid., pp. 35–40.

31 For the best analysis of the populist revolts of 2016, see Roger Eatwell and Matthew Goodwin, *National Populism: The Revolt Against Liberal Democracy* (London: Pelican Books, 2018).

32 And it should also be stressed that there are as many differences between populist movements as there are similarities: Tim Stanley, 'After Liberalism', *Spectator*, 24 March 2020. https://spectator.us/after-liberalism/, last accessed 25 October 2020.

33 David Goodhart, *The Road to Somewhere: The New Tribes Shaping British Politics* (London: Penguin, 2017), pp. 22–4.

34 Bret Stephens, 'Goodbye Principled Conservatism', NYT, 30 October 2020. https://www.nytimes.com/2020/10/30/opinion/donald-trump-conservatism.html, last accessed 30 October 2020.

35 Scruton, *Invitation*, p. 3.

36 Ibid., p. 55.

37 Tim Stanley, 'I don't think Trump's trade war will work, but I like the idea', *Daily Telegraph*, 6 March 2018. https://www.telegraph.co.uk/politics/2018/03/06/dont-think-trumps-trade-war-will-work-like-idea/, last accessed 24 October 2020.

CHAPTER 3 THE INVENTION OF TRADITION

1 Christopher Harding, *Japan Story: In Search of a Nation, 1850 to the Present* (London: Allen Lane, 2018), p. 21.

2 Jared Diamond, *Upheaval: How Nations Cope with Crisis and Change* (London: Allen Lane 2019), pp. 105–9.

3 Harding, *Japan Story*, pp. 15–16.

4 William F. Buckley Jr, 'Our Mission Statement', *National Review*, 19 November 1955. https://www.nationalreview.com/1955/11/our-mission-statement-william-f-buckley-jr/, last accessed 20 October 2020.

5 Greg Lukianoff and Jonathan Haidt, *The Coddling of the American Mind: How Good Intentions and Bad Ideas Are Setting Up a Generation for Failure* (London: Penguin, 2019), p. 199.

6 Allan Bloom, *Closing of the American Mind* (New York: Simon & Schuster, 2008).

7   Rick Perlstein, *The Invisible Bridge: The Fall of Nixon and the Rise of Reagan* (New York: Simon & Schuster, 2014), pp. 82–3.

8   William F. Buckley, *God and Man at Yale: The Superstitions of Academic Freedom* (New York: Simon & Schuster, 2012).

9   Eric Metaxas, *Bonhoeffer: Pastor, Martyr, Prophet, Spy* (Nashville: Thomas Nelson, 2010), p. 106.

10 Max Simon Nordau, *Degeneration* (Wroclaw: Jefferson, 2016), pp. 1–14.

11 Ibid., pp. 64–7.

12 Ibid., p. 5.

13 Ibid., p. 16.

14 Ibid., p. 17.

15 For the most radical period of cultural revolution, see Schama, *Citizens*, pp. 651–69.

16 De Maistre, *Considerations*.

17 Edmund Burke, *Reflections on the Revolution in France* (London: Penguin, 2004), pp. 160–61.

18 Ibid., p. 301.

19 Ibid., pp. 156, 175, 247.

20 Ibid., p. 248. De Maistre, *Considerations*, p. 31.

21 De Maistre, *Considerations*, p. xviii.

22 Burke, *Reflections*, pp. 194–5.

23 Ibid., pp. 119–20.

24 Jack Lively (ed.), *The Works of Joseph de Maistre* (Oxford: Oxford University Press, 1965), p. 144.

25 Ibid., pp. 131–3.

26 Lively, *Works*, pp. xxxiii, 143–6, 157.

27 Ibid., p. 166.

28 Scruton, *Invitation to Conservatism*, p. 87.

29 Russell Kirk, *The Conservative Mind* (Hawthorne, CA: BN Publishing, 2008), p. 113.

30 Diamond, *Upheaval*, pp. 120–21.

31 Harding, *Japan Story*, p. 80.

32 Ibid., pp. 58–9.

33 Diamond, *Upheaval*, pp. 119–25.

34 Harding, *Japan Story*, p. 32.

35 Diamond, *Upheaval*, p. 116.

36 Harding, *Japan Story*, p.62.

37 Ibid., p. 97.

38 Ibid., pp. 106–7.

39 Simon C. Darnell, Russell Field and Bruce Kidd, *The History and Politics of Sport-for-Development: Activists, Ideologues and Reformers* (London: Palgrave Macmillan, 2019), p. 48.

40 Inazo Nitobe, *Bushido: Samurai Ethics and the Soul of Japan* (Mineola, NY: Dover, 2004), p. 8.

41 Stephen Vlastos, 'Past/Present Culture and Modern Japanese History', in Stephen Vlastos (ed.), *Mirror of Modernity: Invented Traditions of Modern Japan* (Berkeley: University of California Press, 1998), pp. 1–18.

42 Harding, *Japan Story*, pp. 66–7.

43 David Cannadine, 'The Context, Performance and Meaning of Ritual: the British Monarchy and the "Invention of Tradition", c 1820–1977', in Eric Hobsbawm and Terence Ranger (eds), *The Invention of Tradition* (Cambridge: Cambridge University Press, 2012), pp. 101–64.

44 David Lowenthal, *The Past Is a Foreign Country* (Cambridge: Cambridge University Press, 1985), p. 97.

45 Robert Colls, *Identity of England* (London: Oxford University Press, 2002), p. 61.

46 Owen Chadwick, *The Spirit of the Oxford Movement* (Cambridge: Cambridge University Press, 1995), p. 2.

47 Fergus Butler-Hallie, *A Field Guide to the English Clergy* (London: Oneworld Publications, 2018), pp. 3–5.

48 Kirk, *Conservative Mind*, pp. 233–43.

49 Lowenthal, *Foreign Country*, p. 9.

50 For this episode and the 'new pseudo-medieval reverence for majesty' see Boyd Hilton, *A Mad, Bad, and Dangerous People? England 1783–1846* (Oxford: Oxford University Press, 2008), pp. 29–33.

51 For consumerism and empire as a commercial product, see Paul Ward, *Britishness Since 1870* (London: Routledge, 2004), p. 45.

52 Andrew Cobbing, 'Tea, Aesthetics and Power', in Tim Cross (ed.), *The Ideologies of Japanese Tea: Subjectivity, Transience and National Identity* (Folkestone: Global Oriental, 2009), pp. 1–3.

53 Julia Skinner, *Afternoon Tea: A History* (London: Rowman & Littlefield, 2019), pp. 11–44.

54 Emalee Beddoes, 'The Art of Tea: Late Victorian Visual Culture and the Normalization of an International National Icon', MPhil thesis submitted to the University of Birmingham, 2014. https://etheses.bham.ac.uk/id/eprint/4915/2/Beddoes14MPhil.pdf, last accessed 20 October 2020.

55 Hobsbawm and Ranger, *Invention of Tradition*, p. 8.

56 Cross, *Ideologies of Tea*, p. 3.

57 Susan C. Townsend, *Yanaihara Tadao and Japanese Colonial Policy: Redeeming Empire* (Richmond: Curzon, 2000), pp. 244–5.

CHAPTER 4 THE USES OF NOSTALGIA

1 'How Christmas evolved from raucous carnival to domestic holiday', *The Economist*, 22 December 2017. https://www.economist.com/the-economist-explains/2017/12/22/how-christmas-evolved-from-raucous-carnival-to-domestic-holiday?fsrc=scn/tw/te/bl/ed/, last accessed 18 October 2020.

2 Svetlana Boym, *The Future of Nostalgia* (New York: Basic Books, 2001), p. 16.

3 Susan J. Matt, *Homesickness: An American Journey* (New York: Oxford University Press, 2011), p. 9.

4 Matt, *Homesickness*, p. 26.

5 Boym, *Future of Nostalgia*, p. 5.

6 Matt, *Homesickness*, p. 4.

7 Ibid., p. 33.

8 Ibid., pp. 12–21.

9 Ibid., p. 6.

10 Ibid., pp. 27–8.

11 Ibid., p. 6.

12 David E. Sanger and Maggie Haberman, 'Foreign Policy, in Trump's View, Is About Deals', NYT, 27 March 2016, p. 1.

13 Chris McGreal, 'Deaths of despair: why America's medical industry explains working-class suicides', *Guardian*, 19 March 2020. https://www.theguardian.com/society/2020/mar/19/us-healthcare-industry-working-class-deaths, last accessed 24 October 2020.

14 Robert D. Putnam and Shaylyn Romney Garrett, *The Upswing: How America Came Together a Century Ago and How We Can Do It Again* (New York: Simon & Schuster, 2021), p. 28.

15 Svetlana Alexievich, *Chernobyl Prayer* (London: Penguin, 2016), p. 85.

16 'Transcript: Pete Buttigieg's DNC remarks', CNN, 21 August 2020. https://edition.cnn.com/2020/08/20/politics/pete-buttigieg-speech-transcript/index.html, last accessed 21 October 2020.

17 Laura Freeman, 'Village greens are the very essence of English life. We must fight to protect them', *Sunday Telegraph*, 30 May 2019. https://www.telegraph.co.uk/news/2019/05/30/village-greens-essence-english-life-must-fight-protect/ last accessed 28 October 2020.

18 'Subdued Proms concludes after Rule, Britannia! Row', *BBC News*, 13 September 2020. https://www.bbc.co.uk/news/entertainment-arts-54115935, last accessed 20 October 2020.

19 'Norwich Cathedral accused of "treating God like a tourist attraction" after installing helter skelter', *Daily Telegraph*, 8 August 2019. https://www.telegraph.co.uk/news/2019/08/08/norwich-cathedral-accused-treating-god-like-tourist-attraction/, last accessed 20 October 2020.

20 'Research Excellence Framework: Impact', Research England. https://re.ukri.org/research/ref-impact/, last accessed 20 October 2020.

21 'Platypuses aren't weird, they're victims of colonial bias', *Sunday Telegraph*, 27 June 2021, p. 9.

22 'Lord Nelson's "heroic status" to be reviewed by National Maritime Museum', *Daily Telegraph*, 10 October 2020. https://www.telegraph.co.uk/news/2020/10/10/lord-nelsons-heroic-status-reviewed-national-maritime-museum/, last accessed 21 October 2020.

23 Christine Rousselle, 'Canadian Indigenous leaders call for end of targeting of churches', *Catholic News Agency*, 7 July 2021. https://www.catholicnewsagency.com/news/248297/canadian-indigenous-leaders-call-for-end-of-targeting-of-churches, last accessed, 13 July 2021.

24 Victoria Ward, 'Lord Baden-Powell statue boarded up after council bows to demands of former Scouts', *Daily Telegraph*, 12 June 2020. https://www.telegraph.co.uk/news/2020/06/12/lord-baden-powell-statue-boarded-council-bows-demands-former/, last accessed 25 November 2020.

25 D. H., 'Fall Guys: Statues, Thinking like Lewis Carroll, Lectures', *Times Literary Supplement*, 19 June 2020. https://www.the-tls.co.uk/articles/fall-guys/, last accessed 20 October 2020.

26 'Vandalism and the red hands of William Gladstone', *East End Review*, 16 November 2014. http://www.eastendreview.co.uk/2014/11/16/vandalising-gladstone/, last accessed 20 October 2020.

27 James Bartholomew, 'The Left's ignorance of Stalin's tyranny against the kulaks should worry us all', *Sunday Telegraph*, 6 November 2019. https://www.telegraph.co.uk/politics/2019/11/06/lefts-ignorance-stalins-tyranny-against-kulaks-should-worry/, last accessed 18 October 2020.

28 Tim Ross, 'Boris Johnson interview: We can be the "heroes of Europe" by voting to Leave', *Sunday Telegraph*, 14 May 2016. https://www.telegraph.co.uk/news/2016/05/14/boris-johnson-interview-we-can-be-the-heroes-of-europe-by-voting/, last accessed 20 October 2020.

29 Martin Kettle, 'Churchill would have been a committed voter to remain in EU', *Guardian*, 9 May 2016. https://www.theguardian.com/politics/commentisfree/2016/may/09/churchill-would-have-voted-remain-eu-cameron-johnson, last accessed 20 October 2020.

30 'Ronald Reagan speech to Parliament', 8 June 2012, The History Place. https://www.historyplace.com/speeches/reagan-parliament.htm, last accessed 20 October 2020.

31 Richard Overy, 'Why the cruel myth of the "blitz spirit" is no model for how to fight coronavirus', *Guardian*, 19 March 2020. https://www.theguardian.com/commentisfree/2020/mar/19/myth-blitz-spirit-model-coronavirus, last accessed 18 October 2020.

32 Hannah Furness and Edward Malnick, 'Queen addresses the nation: "Those who come after us will say that the Britons of this generation were as strong as any"', *Daily Telegraph*, 4 April 2020. https://www.telegraph.co.uk/royal-family/2020/04/04/queen-addresses-nation-come-us-will-say-britons-generation-strong/, last accessed 20 October 2020.

33 For an introduction to Fiddler and tradition, see Elizabeth Dreyer, *Manifestations of Grace* (Collegeville, Minnesota: The Liturgical Press, 1990), pp. 33–8.

CHAPTER 5 HURRAH FOR THE OLD

1 Steven Brindle, *Whitby Abbey* (London: Geoff Neal Litho Ltd, 2016), pp. 18–36.

2 Mike Ashley, 'The Fear of Invasion', British Library, 15 May 2014. https://www.bl.uk/romantics-and-victorians/articles/the-fear-of-invasion, last accessed 19 October 2020.

3 Bram Stoker, *Dracula* (New York: Oxford University Press, 2011), p. 26.

4 John Osborne, *Plays 2* (London: Faber & Faber, 1998), p. 212.

5   Anthony Esolen, *Nostalgia: Going Home in a Homeless World* (Washington DC: Regnery, 2018), p. xxvii.

6   *Opening Night*, 1977.

7   Peter Kreeft, 'Critical Thinking for Christians', *Catholic Culture*, 2020. https://www.catholicculture.org/culture/library/view.cfm?recnum=9243, last accessed 19 October 2020.

8   T. S. Eliot, 'Little Gidding', in T. S. Eliot, *The Poems of T. S. Eliot*, Vol. I: *Collected and Uncollected Poems* (London: Faber & Faber, 2015), pp. 201–10.

CHAPTER 6   TRADITION AND IDENTITY

1   Ruchang Zhou, *Between Noble and Humble: Cao Xueqin and the Dream of the Red Chamber* (New York: Peter Lang, 2009), p. 51.

2   T. S. Eliot, *The Four Quartets* (Orlando: Harcourt Books, 2014), pp. 23–34.

3   Jonathan Haidt, *The Righteous Mind: Why Good People are Divided by Politics and Religion* (London: Penguin, 2013), pp. 3–31.

4   Mary Douglas, *Purity and Danger: An Analysis of Concepts of Pollution and Taboo* (London: Routledge, 1984), pp. 2, 116.

5   David Gollaher, *Circumcision: A History of the World's Most Controversial Surgery* (New York: Basic Books, 2000), pp. 1–2.

6   Gollaher, *Circumcision*, p. 48.

7   Charles P. Mountford, *Brown Men and Red Sand* (Sydney: Angus & Robertson, 1962), pp. 44–7.

8   Andreas Lommel, Extract from 'Unambal', Bradshaw Foundation, http://www.bradshawfoundation.com/unambal/circumcision_initiation.php, last accessed 19 October 2020.

9   Mark Stratton, 'Why some men in Papua New Guinea cut their skin to resemble crocodiles', *BBC News*, 26 August 2018, https://www.bbc.co.uk/news/stories-45297699, last accessed 19 October 2020.

10 Mountford, *Brown Men*, pp. 44–6.

11 Gollaher, *Circumcision*, p. 11.

12 Mountford, *Brown Men*, pp. 44–53.

13 Lynne Hume, 'Accessing the Eternal: Dreaming, "The Dreaming" and Ceremonial Performance', *Zygon*, Vol. 39, No. 1 (March 2004), pp. 237–56.

14 David M. Friedman, *A Mind of its Own: A Cultural History of the Penis* (New York: Simon & Schuster, 2008), pp. 52–3.

15 Jacobus de Voragine, *The Golden Legend: Readings on the Saints* (Princeton: Princeton University Press, 2012), pp. 74–6.

16 Tom Holland, *Dominion: The Making of the Western Mind* (London: Little, Brown, 2019), p. 35.

17 Ibid., pp. 37–9.

18 Peter Aggleton, '"Just a Snip"?: A Social History of Male Circumcision', *Reproductive Health Matters*, 17 May 2007, pp. 15–21.

19 Michel Houellebecq, *Submission* (London: Penguin, 2015), p. 91.

CHAPTER 7 TRADITION AND ORDER

1 James Gallagher, 'Fertility rate: "Jaw-dropping" global crash in children being born', *BBC News*, 14 July 2020. https://www.bbc.co.uk/news/health-53409521, last accessed 19 October 2020.

2 Pope Francis, 'Holy Mass for the Congolese Community', Vatican, 1 December 2019. http://www.vatican.va/content/francesco/en/homilies/2019/documents/papa-francesco_20191201_omelia-comunitacattolica-congolese.html, last accessed 19 October 2020.

3 Steven Mintz and Susan Kellogg, *Domestic Revolutions: A Social History Of American Family Life* (New York: The Free Press, 1988), p. 108.

4 Betty Friedan, *The Feminine Mystique* (London: Penguin, 2010), pp. 274–310.

5 David Brooks, 'The Nuclear Family Was a Mistake', *The Atlantic*, March 2020. https://www.theatlantic.com/magazine/archive/2020/03/the-nuclear-family-was-a-mistake/605536/, last accessed 19 October 2020.

6 Glenn T. Stanton, 'Why Sex And Gender Are Not Two Different Things', *The Federalist*, 15 October 2019. https://thefederalist.com/2019/10/15/why-sex-and-gender-are-not-two-different-things/, last accessed 30 November 2020.

7 Michelle Goldberg, 'Leave Drag Queen Story Hour Alone!', NYT, 7 June 2019, p. 3.

8 Kate Heard and Kathryn Jones, *George IV: Art and Spectacle* (London: Royal Collection Trust, 2019), pp. 180–81.

9 Jeffrey Gettleman, 'The Peculiar Position of India's Third Gender', NYT, 17 February 2018, p. 4.

10 Sophie Hunter, 'Hijras and the Legacy of British Colonial Rule in India', LSE, 17 June 2019. https://blogs.lse.ac.uk/gender/2019/06/17/

hijras-and-the-legacy-of-british-colonial-rule-in-india/. Last accessed 19 October 2020.

11   Dion J. Pierre, 'Demands for Segregated Housing at Williams College Are Not News', *National Review*, 8 May 2019. https://www.nationalreview.com/2019/05/american-colleges-segregated-housing-graduation-ceremonies/, last accessed 5 July 2021.

12   Emma Graham-Harrison, 'Women-only carriages around the world: do they work?', *Guardian*, 26 August 2015. https://www.theguardian.com/world/2015/aug/26/women-only-train-carriages-around-the-world-jeremy-corbyn, last accessed 19 October 2020.

13   Nick Duffy, 'UK's first-ever Pride train staffed by all-LGBT+ crew makes its kaleidoscopic maiden journey', PinkNews, 25 August 2020. https://www.pinknews.co.uk/2020/08/25/pride-train-lgbt-crew-avanti-west-coast-london-manchester-julia-hartley-brewer/, last accessed 20 October 2020.

14   Ben Steverman, 'Millennials are Causing the US Divorce Rate to Plummet', Bloomberg, 25 September 2018. https://www.bloomberg.com/news/articles/2018-09-25/millennials-are-causing-the-u-s-divorce-rate-to-plummet, last accessed19 October 2020; Laura Donnelly, 'Millennials Shunning Alcohol as Getting Drunk is No Longer Cool', *Daily Telegraph*, 10 October 2018. https://www.telegraph.co.uk/news/2018/10/10/doubling-number-teetotal-millennials/, last accessed 19 October 2020; Kate Julian, 'We Are Young People Having So Little Sex?', *The Atlantic*, December 2018. https://www.theatlantic.com/magazine/archive/2018/12/the-sex-recession/573949/, last accessed 19 October 2020.

15   Murray, *Madness of Crowds*, pp. 77–80.

16   For the conservative response to WAP, see Charles Holmes, 'The Conservative Crusade Against Wet-Ass Pussy', *Rolling Stone*, 11 August 2020. https://www.rollingstone.com/music/music-news/wet-ass-pussy-ben-shapiro-conservative-backlash-1042491/, last accessed 19 October 2020.

17   Dale Ahlquist, *The Complete Thinking: The Marvelous Mind of G. K. Chesterton* (San Francisco: Ignatius Press, 2012), p. 81.

18   Cardinal John Henry Newman, *An Essay on the Development of Christian Doctrine* (New York: Cosimo Classics, 2009).

19   Rodney Stark, *The Rise of Christianity* (San Francisco: HarperCollins, 1997), pp. 73–94; Holland, *Dominion*, pp. 92–3, 125.

20   Holland, *Dominion*, p. 81.

21 Karen Cheatham, 'Let Anyone Accept This Who Can: Medieval Christian Virginity, Chastity and Celibacy in the Latin West', in Carl Olson (ed.), *Celibacy and Religious Traditions* (New York: Oxford University Press, 2008), p. 93.

22 Holland, *Dominion*, p. 207.

23 Ulrich L. Lehner, *The Catholic Enlightenment: The Forgotten History of a Global Movement* (New York: Oxford University Press, 2016), pp. 1–11.

24 Ibid., pp. 74–6.

25 Ibid., pp. 80–5.

26 Ibid., pp. 90–1.

27 Ibid., p. 95.

28 And note that Chateaubriand argues that the world is generally unhappy when overburdened with souls. Chateaubriand, *Genius of Christianity*, pp. 81–2.

29 Lehner, *Catholic Enlightenment*, pp. 92–3.

30 Ibid., p. 102.

31 Ibid., p. 99.

32 Ibid., pp. 176–8.

33 James Bowman, *Honor: A History* (New York: Encounter Books 2006), p. 8.

34 Ruth Sutherland, 'Tackling the Root Causes of Suicide', NHS, 1 August 2018. https://www.england.nhs.uk/blog/tackling-the-root-causes-of-suicide/, last accessed 19 October 2020.

35 Massimo Recalcati, *The Telemachus Complex: Parents and Children After the Decline of the Father* (Cambridge: Polity, 2019), pp. 1–8.

36 Alex Shepherd, 'Sucking Up to the Boss Baby', *New Republic*, 8 December 2017. https://newrepublic.com/article/146182/sucking-boss-baby, last accessed 20 October 2020.

37 Jordan B. Peterson, *Maps of Meaning: The Architecture of Belief* (New York: Routledge, 1999).

38 Jordan Peterson: 'Women Want/Need Real Men Not Boys', YouTube, 10 February 2018. https://www.youtube.com/watch?v=zbjTQmZRNss, last accessed 19 October 2020.

39 Jason Wilson, 'What do incels, fascists and terrorists have in common? Violent misogyny', *Guardian*, 4 May 2018. https://www.theguardian.com/commentisfree/2018/may/04/what-do-incels-fascists-and-terrorists-have-in-common-violent-misogyny, last accessed 24 October 2020.

CHAPTER 8 TRADITION AND FREEDOM

1   Matthew B. Crawford, *Why We Drive: On Freedom, Risk and Taking Back Control* (London: Bodley Head, 2020), p. 5.

2   Walter Bagehot, *The English Constitution* (London: Henry S. King and Co., 1872), pp. 33, 257, 8.

3   Ryszard Kapuściński,, *The Emperor: Downfall of an Autocrat* (London: Penguin, 2006), pp. 43–4.

4   Mark Easton, 'Coronation 1953: Magic Moment the TV Cameras Missed', *BBC News*, 4 June 2013. https://www.bbc.co.uk/news/uk-22764987, last accessed 19 October 2020.

5   Lowenthal, *Past Is a Foreign Country*, p. 97.

6   Pieper, *Concept and Claim*, p. 5.

7   Reuters, 'Ethiopians Celebrate a Mass for Exhumed Haile Selassie', NYT, 1 March 1992, p. 12.

8   1 Sam. 8: 7–8.

9   Benedict XVI, 'General Audience', Vatican, 1 June 2011. http://www.vatican.va/content/benedict-xvi/en/audiences/2011/documents/hf_ben-xvi_aud_20110601.html, last accessed 19 October 2020.

10 1 Sam. 8:11–13.

11 1 Kings 11.

12 Barry Bearak, 'Riots Break Out as Nepal Gets 3rd King in 4 Days', NYT, 5 June 2001, p. 1.

13 Thomas Hobbes, *Leviathan* (Oxford: Oxford World's Classics, 2008), pp. xxxiv–xxxvi; Horst Bredekamp, 'Thomas Hobbes' Visual Strategies', in Patricia Springborg (ed.), *The Cambridge Companion to Hobbes' Leviathan* (Cambridge: Cambridge University Press, 2007), pp. 30–33.

14 Scruton, *Invitation to Conservatism*, p. 70.

15 De Maistre, *Considerations*, pp. 41–3.

16 Ibid., pp. 66–70.

17 Lively, *Works*, p. 140.

18 Ann Hughes, 'The Execution of Charles I', *BBC History*, 17 February 2011. http://www.bbc.co.uk/history/british/civil_war_revolution/charlesi_execution_01.shtml, last accessed 19 October 2020.

19 Leander de Lisle, *White King: Charles I, Traitor, Murderer, Martyr* (London: Chatto & Windus, 2017), pp. 254–66.

20 De Maistre, *Considerations*, p. 110.

21 Connerton, *How Societies Remember*, pp. 7–9.

22   Peter King, *Keeping Things Close: Essays on the Conservative Disposition* (London: Arktos, 2015), p. 3

23   Simone Weil, *The Need for Roots* (Oxford: Routledge Classics, 2002), p. ix.

24   Simone Weil, *An Anthology* (London: Penguin, 2005), pp. 116–21; Stratford Caldecott, *Beauty in the Word: Rethinking the Foundations of Education* (Tacoma: Angelico Press, 2012), pp. 34–5.

25   Chateaubriand, *Genius of Christianity*, p. 84.

26   Weil, *Anthology*, pp. 116–17.

27   King, *Keeping Things Close*, pp. 15–17.

28   'Ipsos Mori Veracity Index', Ipsos Mori, November 2020. https://www.ipsos.com/sites/default/files/ct/news/documents/2020-11/veracity-index-2020_v2_public.pdf, last accessed 29 November 2020.

29   Pauline Bock, 'Manu or Mr President? Macron's double standards show his lack of cool', *Guardian*, 20 June 2018. https://www.theguardian.com/commentisfree/2018/jun/20/president-macron-double-standards-france, last accessed 19 October 2020.

30   Christopher Hope, 'Do as I say ... Neil Ferguson's public comments on lockdown – the very rules he flouted', *Daily Telegraph*, 6 May 2020. https://www.telegraph.co.uk/news/2020/05/06/do-say-prof-neil-fergusons-public-comments-lockdown-rules/, last accessed 19 October 2020.

31   An official is respected, says de Maistre, only in so far as they are respectable. The more titles a man has, the more absurd his uniform, the more likely he is to be a source of ridicule. De Maistre, *Considerations*, p. 59.

32   Christopher Booker, *Group Think: A Study in Self-Delusion* (London: Bloomsbury Continuum, 2020), p. 13.

33   G. K. Chesterton, *On Lying in Bed and Other Essays* (Calgary, Alberta: Bayeux Arts, 2000), p. 87.

34   Conduct, says Burke, is the only language that never lies. Burke, *Reflections*, p. 200.

35   Burke, *Reflections*, p. 105.

36   De Maistre, *Considerations*, p. 67.

37   Scruton, *Invitation to Conservatism*, pp. 33–4.

38   Ron Chernow, *Alexander Hamilton* (London: Head of Zeus, 2016), pp. 695–718.

39   Kirk, *Conservative Mind*, pp. 62–98.

40 Michiko Kakutani, 'What the Founding Fathers Had That We Haven't', *NYT*, 27 June 2006. https://www.nytimes.com/2006/06/27/books/27kaku. html, last accessed 19 October 2020.

41 Letter, John Adams to Mercy Warren, April 1776, University of Chicago. https://press-pubs.uchicago.edu/founders/documents/v1ch18s9.html, last accessed 19 October 2020.

CHAPTER 9 TRADITION AND EQUALITY

1 John Burtka, 'Under Trump, a Very Different Agenda for Conservatives Emerges', *Washington Post*, 22 June 2019. https://www.washingtonpost. com/opinions/2019/07/22/under-trump-very-different-agenda-con- servatives-emerges/, last accessed 20 October 2020.

2 Catherine Rampell, 'Trump is the True Socialist', *Washington Post*, 25 July 2019. https://www.washingtonpost.com/opinions/ trump-is-the-true-socialist/2019/07/25/4f45410c-af1a-11e9-8e77- 03b30bc29f64_story.html, last accessed 20 October 2020.

3 Daniel Avery, 'These 50+ Brands Are Celebrating Pride by Giving Back to the LGBT Community', *Newsweek*, 3 June 2019. https://www. newsweek.com/these-30-brands-are-celebrating-pride-giving-back- lgbt-community-1441707, last accessed 19 October 2020.

4 Margaret Thatcher interviewed by Douglas Keay, 23 September 1987, Margaret Thatcher Foundation. https://www.margaretthatcher.org/ document/106689, last accessed 20 October 2020.

5 Scruton, *Invitation to Conservatism*, p. 109.

6 Eliza Filby, 'Margaret Thatcher: her unswerving faith shaped by her father', *Daily Telegraph*, 14 April 2013. https://www.telegraph.co.uk/news/ politics/margaret-thatcher/9992424/Margaret-Thatcher-her-unswerving- faith-shaped-by-her-father.html, last accessed 21 October 2020.

7 Charles Moore, *Margaret Thatcher: The Authorized Biography*. Vol. Three: *Herself Alone* (London: Penguin, 2009), p. 297.

8 Daniel Bell, *The Cultural Contradictions of Capitalism* (New York: Basic Books, 1998), pp. xvi–xx.

9 For the transformation of the American Dream, see Sarah Churchwell, *Behold, America: The Entangled History of 'America First' and 'the American Dream'* (London: Bloomsbury, 2018), pp. 143–52.

10 John Cloud, 'Why Ann Coulter Matters', *Time*, 9 June 2006. http:// content.time.com/time/nation/article/0,8599,1202595,00.html, last accessed 20 October 2020.

11 Bell, *Contradictions*, pp. 16–17.

12 Ibid., pp. xxii–xxiv.

13 Ibid., pp. 17, 63–7.

14 Andrew Kaczynski, 'Trump, comparing sex to Vietnam, said in 1998 he should receive the Congressional Medal of Honor', CNN, 14 October 2016. https://money.cnn.com/2016/10/14/media/trump-stern-vietnam-stds/index.html, last accessed 20 October 2020.

15 Max J. Rosenthal, 'The Trump Files: When Donald Destroyed Historic Art to Build Trump Tower', Mother Jones, 10 September 2020. https://www.motherjones.com/2020-elections/2020/09/trump-files-when-donald-destroyed-priceless-art-build-trump-tower/, last accessed 19 October 2020.

16 Rabbi Sacks, 'The Home We Build Together', Jonathan Sacks, 20 December 2018. https://rabbisacks.org/rabbi-sacks-home-build-together/, last accessed 20 October 2020.

17 Luc Gilleman, *John Osborne: Vituperative Artist: A Reading of His Life and Work* (London: Routledge, 2002), p. 207.

18 James Bloodworth, 'Labour is becoming a historical re-enactment society', *International Business Times*, 11 July 2016. https://www.ibtimes.co.uk/jeremy-corbyns-labour-tribute-act-socialism-trade-unions-back-nostalgic-leader-1570061, last accessed 20 October 2020.

19 Friedrich Engels, *The Condition of the Working Class in England* (London: Penguin, 1987), pp. 250, 255.

20 John Tomaney, 'After Coal: Meanings of the Durham Miners' Gala', *Frontiers in Sociology*, 15 May 2020. https://www.frontiersin.org/articles/10.3389/fsoc.2020.00032/full, last accessed 20 October 2020.

21 Emphasis added. E. P. Thompson, *Customs in Common* (London: Penguin, 1991), p. 9.

22 Tomaney, 'After Coal'.

23 E. P. Thompson, *The Making of the English Working Class* (London: Penguin, 2013), pp. 464–9.

24 Tomaney, 'After Coal'.

25 Alistair Bonnett, *Left in the Past: Radicalism and the Politics of Nostalgia* (London: Bloomsbury Continuum, 2010), pp. 24–5.

26 Thomas Carlyle, *Selected Writings* (London: Penguin, 2015), p. 248.

27 Colls, *Identity of England*, p. 61.

28 PD Anthony, John Ruskin's Labour: A Study of Ruskin's Social Theory (Cambridge: Cambridge University Press, 1983), 9. 143.

29 Eugene McCarraher, 'We Communists of the Old School' in Adrian Pabst (ed.), *The Crisis of Global Capitalism: Pope Benedict XVI's Social Encyclical and the Future of the Political Economy* (Cambridge: James Clarke & Co., 2012), pp. 89–120.

30 G. K. Chesterton, *In Defence of Sanity* (San Francisco: Ignatius Press, 2011), pp. 260–9.

31 Francis O'Gorman, *The Cambridge Companion to John Ruskin* (Cambridge: Cambridge University Press, 2015), pp. 249–62.

32 John Ruskin, *Unto This Last* (New York: Cosimo Classics, 2006), p. 76.

33 Pope Francis, 'Laudato Si', Vatican, 24 May 2015. http://www.vatican.va/content/francesco/en/encyclicals/documents/papa-francesco_20150524_enciclica-laudato-si.html, last accessed 20 October 2020.

34 John Ruskin, *Unto This Last and Other Writings* (London: Penguin, 2007), p. 226.

35 John Bellamy Foster, *The Return of Nature: Socialism and Ecology* (New York: NYU Press, 2020), pp. 80–2.

36 Jim Bissett, *Agrarian Socialism in America: Mark, Jefferson and Jesus in the Oklahoma Countryside, 1904–1920* (Norman, Oklahoma: University of Oklahoma Press, 1999), pp. 3–8, 94–7.

37 Bob Holman, *Keir Hardie: Labour's Greatest Hero?* (Oxford: Lion Books, 2010), pp. 198–200.

38 Lasch, *Narcissism*, p. xvii.

39 Roger Scruton, *England: An Elegy* (London: Chatto & Windus, 2000), p. 256.

40 Sohrab Ahmari, 'The New American Right', *First Things*, October 2009. https://www.firstthings.com/article/2019/10/the-new-american-right, last accessed 20 October 2020.

41 Carlyle, *Selected Writings*, pp. 85–6.

CHAPTER 10 TRADITION AND FAITH

1 Françoise Dunand, *Roger Lichtenberg, Mummies and Death in Egypt* (Ithaca: Cornell University Press, 2006), p. 56.

2 Prakash A. Raj, *Kathmandu and the Kingdom of Nepal* (Kathmandu: Nabeen Publications, 1990), p. 17.

3   Jacqueline I. Stone, *Ritual Thoughts at the Last Moment: Buddhism and Deathbed Practices in Early Medieval Japan* (Honolulu: University of Hawaii Press, 2016), 232.

4   Barry Bearak, 'Dead Join the Living in a Family Celebration', NYT, 5 September 2010, p. 7.

5   Amanda Bennett, 'When Death Doesn't Mean Goodbye', *National Geographic*, March 2016. https://www.nationalgeographic.com/magazine/2016/04/death-dying-grief-funeral-ceremony-corpse/, last accessed 19 October 2020.

6   Chateaubriand, *Genius of Christianity*, p. 506.

7   Paul Hamilton, *The Oxford Handbook of European Romanticism* (Oxford: Oxford University Press, 2016), p. 65.

8   Chateaubriand, *Genius of Christianity*, pp. 480–1.

9   Jean-Marie Roulin, 'François-René de Chateaubriand: Migrations and Revolution', in Paul Hamilton (ed.), *The Oxford Handbook of European Romanticism* (Oxford: Oxford University Press, 2016), p. 55.

10 François Auguste de Chateaubriand, *Atala*, Project Gutenberg, 13 December 2016. https://www.gutenberg.org/files/44427/44427-h/44427-h.htm, last accessed 19 October 2020.

11 'Death is Nothing At All', by Henry Scott Holland.

12 Michel Foucault, *The Birth of the Clinic* (Oxford: Routledge Classics, 2003), pp. 36–40.

13 Chateaubriand, *Genius of Christianity*, p. 510.

14 W. H. Auden, *Prose*: Vol. VI, *1969–1973* (Princeton: Princeton University Press, 2015), p. 702.

15 Victor Sebestyen, *Lenin: The Dictator* (London: Weidenfeld & Nicolson, 2018), pp. 503–10.

16 Richard John Neuhaus, *The Naked Public Square: Religion and Democracy in America* (Grand Rapids: William B. Eerdmans Publishing Company, 1984), p. 86.

17 Alan Jacobs, *Year of Our Lord 1943: Christian Humanism in an Age of Crisis* (New York: Oxford University Press, 2018), pp. 5–36.

18 Ibid., p. 63.

19 Humphrey Carter, *W. H. Auden: A Biography* (Boston: Houghton Mifflin, 1981), p. 282.

20 Jacobs, 1943, pp. 5–6.

21 Melanie Williams, *Collected Essays in Law, Lives and Literature* (London: UCL Press, 2005), p. 14.

22 K. A. Lantz, *The Dostoevsky Encyclopaedia* (Westport, Connecticut: Greenwood Press, 2004), p. 54.

23 'Christopher Hitchens 2010 "Does atheism poison everything" vs David Berlinski', YouTube, 5 September 2014. https://www.youtube.com/watch?v=6PbYoQw8M48, last accessed 20 October 2020.

24 This point is explored in Alasdair MacIntyre, *Marxism and Christianity* (London: Duckworth, 1995), pp. xiii–xiv.

25 Caldecott, *Beauty*, p. 142.

CONCLUSION

1 Various, 'Against the Dead Consensus', *First Things*, 21 March 2019. https://www.firstthings.com/web-exclusives/2019/03/against-the-dead-consensus, last accessed 20 October 2020.

2 Andrew Higgins, 'Church Spreads Putin's Anti-Western Gospel', NYT, 14 September 2016, p. 1.

3 Maria Kiselyova, 'Russia Inaugurates Cathedral Without Mosaics of Putin, Stalin', Reuters, 14 June 2020. https://www.reuters.com/article/us-russia-military-church-idUSKBN23L0K7, last accessed 20 October 2020.

4 Solomon Volkov, *St Petersburg: A Cultural History* (New York: Free Press Paperbacks, 1995), pp. 1–56.

5 Chris Miller, *We Shall Be Masters: Russian Pivots to East Asia from Peter the Great to Putin* (Harvard: Harvard University Press, 2021), pp. 3–5.

6 Stephen Kirby Carter, *The Political and Social Thought of F. M. Dostoevsky* (Oxford: Routledge, 2015), pp. 98–100.

7 Neil Cornwell, *The Routledge Companion to Russian Literature* (London: Routledge, 2001), p. 55. For further consideration of Russian Orthodox identity, see Christian Gottlieb, 'Russian Philosophy and Orthodoxy', in Augustine Casiday (ed.), *The Orthodox Christian World* (Oxford: Routledge, 2017), pp. 492–503.

8 Raisa Ostapenko, 'The significance of the Russian Soul in understanding contemporary geopolitics', 8 June 2015. http://cambridgeglobalist.org/?p=993, last accessed 18 October 2020.

9 Laura Engelstein, *Slavophile Empire* (Ithaca: Cornell University Press, 2009), p. 193.

10   Lynn Ellen Patyk, *Written in Blood: Revolutionary Terrorism and Russian Literary Culture, 1861–1881* (Madison: University of Wisconsin Press, 2017), pp. 213–14.

11   Catherine Merridale, 'The Romanov Tercentenary: Nostalgia Versus History on the Eve of the Great War', *The Historian*, Winter 2013/14, pp. 6–11.

12   'Religious Belief and National Belonging in Central and Eastern Europe', Pew Forum, 10 May 2017. https://www.pewforum.org/2017/05/10/religious-belief-and-national-belonging-in-central-and-eastern-europe/, last accessed 20 October 2020.

13   Grace Davie, *Religion in Britain Since 1945: Believing with Belonging* (London: Wiley, 1994).

14   Alison Comyn, 'Priest Defends Comment at First Holy Communion', *The Argus*, 26 May 2018. https://www.independent.ie/regionals/argus/news/priest-defends-comment-at-first-holy-communion-36930260.html, last accessed 20 October 2020.

15   Gregory A. Smith, 'Just one-third of U.S. Catholics agree with their church that Eucharist is body, blood of Christ', Pew, 5 August 2019. https://www.pewresearch.org/fact-tank/2019/08/05/transubstantiation-eucharist-u-s-catholics/, last accessed 20 October 2020.

16   Gorbachev began his career as General Secretary with a sincere attempt to revive Leninism. See William Taubman, *Gorbachev: His Life and Times* (New York: Simon & Schuster, 2017), p. 215.

17   J. S. Rafaeli, 'These Are the Radical Roots of British Gay Pride', *Vice*, 4 July 2019. https://www.vice.com/en/article/wjvawn/uk-gay-pride-history-gay-liberation-front, last accessed 20 October 2020.

18   Kirsty Walker, 'Hunters Defy the Ban with Record Turnout', *Daily Mail*, 26 December 2006. https://www.dailymail.co.uk/news/article-424837/Hunters-defy-ban-record-turnout.html, last accessed 20 October 2020.

19   Immigration has not only returned religion to London but Londoners are now more likely to self-define as religious compared to the rest of the country, by 62–53 per cent. According to a 2020 study, 'Christian Londoners help their neighbours more than their non-religious counterparts, are more likely to volunteer for a charitable initiative, and are more likely to make charitable donations.' Harriet Sherwood, 'London more religious than rest of Britain, report finds', *Guardian*, 24

June 2020. https://www.theguardian.com/world/2020/jun/24/london-more-religious-than-rest-britain-report-finds, last accessed October 19, 2020.

20   Kevin Kelly, *What Technology Wants* (New York: Penguin, 2010), pp. 217–25.

21   Tim Stanley, 'How Republicans became the anti-Islam party', *Spectator*, 1 November 2019. https://www.spectator.co.uk/article/how-republic-ans-became-the-anti-islam-party, last accessed 20 October 2020.

22   Ralph Waldo Emerson, *The Later Lectures of Ralph Waldo Emerson, 1843–1871*, Vol. 1: *1834–1854* (Athens: University of Georgia Press, 2001), p. 200.

23   George Orwell, *The Lion and the Unicorn* (London: Secker & Warburg, 1941), p. 15.

24   Larry Siedentop, *Inventing the Individual: The Origins of Western Liberalism* (London: Penguin, 2015), p. 363.

Acknowledgements

When I was a lecturer, at the beginning of every term I'd tell my students, 'You may very well be right and don't assume I'm never wrong.' In the course of writing this book, I've delved into areas I previously knew nothing about, read authors I'd never heard of, and strayed into debates where I probably don't belong – and my goal isn't to 'lay down the law' but spark a discussion, to encourage others to challenge and correct me, and bring their own interpretations to the subject. I eagerly await refutation.

In the meantime, I must thank my publisher, Robin Baird-Smith, who has been kind and blunt in exactly the right proportions. I've never worked with better. The following, through conversations or emails, helped inspire and direct me (sometimes without realising it): Simon and Diana Heffer, Thomas Holland, Giles Fraser, Benedict Kiely, Douglas Murray, Alban Nunn, Rupert Russell, James Siemens and Ed Tomlinson. I am indebted to Nick Waghorn, who guided me through Burke and De Maistre, and to Daniel Joyce and David Oldroyd-Bolt who read the text from cover to cover. Blame them for any errors.

Thanks to the wonderful staff at Bloomsbury, including Jamie Birkett and Julia Mitchell, and to all my *Telegraph* editors who granted me time off to work on the project. Thanks to Mum, especially for looking after my puppy. And a big thanks to Chris Morris, without whose friendship and counsel nothing would be possible.

Index

Note: page numbers followed by * or † refer to the notes at the bottom of the page, those followed by 'n' refer to the endnotes, and those in italic refer to figures.